A
Blissful
Feast

A
Blissful
Feast

CULINARY ADVENTURES IN ITALY'S
PIEDMONT, MAREMMA, AND LE MARCHE

TERESA LUST

PEGASUS BOOKS
NEW YORK LONDON

A BLISSFUL FEAST

Pegasus Books, Ltd.
148 West 37th Street, 13th Floor
New York, NY 10018

Copyright © 2020 by Teresa Lust

First Pegasus Books paperback edition June 2021
First Pegasus Books cloth edition March 2020

Interior design by Maria Fernandez

Library of Congress Cataloging-in-Publication Data is available.

ISBN: 978-1-64313-767-4

10 9 8 7 6 5 4 3 2 1

Printed in the United States of America
Distributed by Simon & Schuster
www.pegasusbooks.com

For Bert, Margot, and Joseph

CONTENTS

INDEX OF RECIPES

LE MARCHE

INTRODUCTION

When I set out to write about my culinary adventures in Italy, I knew I would start in the Piedmont region in the northwest, home of my mother's ancestors. From there I would move on to the dishes, ingredients, and cooks I encountered during my travels throughout the country, though I hadn't yet decided where those travels would take me. While I didn't have a full itinerary in mind, and I wasn't quite sure what I was looking for, I knew even then that my grandmother's cooking prompted the journey. Her recipes sent me on my way.

My maternal grandparents came to America in the early years of the last century and landed in the Yakima Valley of Washington State. As with many children and grandchildren of Italian immigrants, food is what tied my family to our heritage. It is what set us apart. My mom learned to cook from my grandmother Teresa, so we ate polenta and risotto for dinner in the 1970s, a time when the only other people I knew who ate these foods were either related to me or of Italian descent as well. We had dainty anise cookies and hand-shaped ravioli at Christmas. My mother put up quarts of Roma tomatoes each September for sauce, and pints of a tomato-based, sweet-and-sour vegetable medley she called generically "antipasto," which she served as an hors d'oeuvre. There was always a 5-liter tin of olive oil in the pantry and a whole salame in the refrigerator, along with a wedge of Parmesan cheese.

My grandparents' refrigerator was a museum of curiosities, its shelves filled with bowls and jars of cured or marinated things—hard-boiled eggs and pickled beets, brined pig's feet and smelly cheeses. If we were lucky when we visited, there might be a plate of leftover *semolina dolce*. These subtly sweet, lemon-infused fritters are made with a porridge-like custard that sets up firm when cool. The mixture is cut into diamonds or squares, dipped in beaten egg, dredged in fine breadcrumbs, and then fried in a skillet. A beloved comfort food, my mother made semolina dolce, too, upon request at birthdays and homecomings, or after orthodontist appointments. These golden diamonds are tender and yielding once cooked, and can be pleasantly gummed by mouths too achy to chew.

On occasion we might find a bowl of sliced beef tongue on my grandmother's refrigerator shelf. My mother prepared this dish as well (my paternal grandparents raised cattle on their farm just outside town, so we ate most all the lesser parts of the steer). I took a lurid delight in bringing tongue sandwiches to school, knowing no one would want to swap me for a peanut butter and jam. Though my three sisters didn't each share my enthusiasm for tongue sandwiches, we all appreciated boiled beef tongue for its entertainment value. Our mom would put a tongue on to simmer in a large stockpot on the back burner of the range. I remember rounding up the neighbors and trotting them into the kitchen, where we had pulled a stepstool up to the stove. "See the hideous cow's tongue!" we called out like carnival barkers. "Not for the faint of heart!" My elder sister pulled back the lid with a flourish, and one by one we let each kid peer into the pot, where the 15-inch tongue lolled about, folded back on itself in the bubbling broth, looking like nothing else but what it was.

Once tender, my mother cut a shallow slit along the tongue's centerline and peeled back the skin with its gruesome taste buds, as if shimmying it out of a girdle. She trimmed away the gristle, then sliced the remaining flavorsome flesh into thin rounds, which she marinated in lemon, olive oil, garlic, and plenty of finely chopped parsley. After my grandmother passed away, my mom carried on the tradition of bringing parsleyed beef tongue to the buffet table at holiday gatherings, and any leftovers went into those school-lunch sandwiches.

When I took my first cooking job after college, as an intern-cum-skullery maid at the historic Ark Restaurant and Bakery on the Long Beach Peninsula in Washington, I reminisced about my mom's beef tongue to chef Jimella Lucas. She put it on the antipasto platter at the Northwest Garlic Festival that summer, sliced paper-thin with a meat slicer to pretty it up. She called it something vague, like *affettate di manzo*, "beef slices," so diners wouldn't be put off by the thought of it, and people raved.

My focus shifted to French-inspired and American farm-to-table cuisine over the next several years, in my subsequent cooking and baking positions in restaurants in California, New Hampshire, and Vermont. I learned to keep my knives sharp so I could efficiently fillet a halibut or bone a duck, I learned to sauté tournedos and grill entrecote on the line, to make a light *beurre blanc* and an even lighter *genoise*, and I saved my Italian family dishes for my own kitchen.

Then I started traveling to Italy, where I enjoyed meals at the tables of cousins, aunts, and uncles in the countryside near Torino. One new dish or ingredient or flavor combination after the next, yet all of them punctuated by a touch of the familiar. Waiting on the table one evening was a majolica bowl containing *antipasto alla piemontese*, my mother's antipasto. Another night we ate *lingua in salsa verde*, my family's beef tongue in parsley, and at a midday meal one Sunday I partook in the Piedmont's grand *fritto misto*, a bounteous feast of savory and sweet fried delicacies. We had veal and turkey cutlets pounded thin, silver-dollar-sized rounds of zucchini and eggplant, sliced porcini mushrooms—all of them lightly breaded and fried until golden. A separate platter held fruits and pastries that had received the same treatment—wedges of apple and pear, ladyfingers and amaretti cookies, and diamond-shaped morsels that I recognized immediately. My mother's semolina dolce.

It was as if a part of me had been dining at those tables all along. I wanted to explore this connection to my mother's cooking, wanted to trace the origins of the dishes my grandmother used to make, wanted to expand my repertoire. I quickly realized that in order to delve into my grandparents' native cuisine, I would have to learn some Italian. So I started auditing college courses, and during the off-season, when the restaurant where I cooked in Vermont would close, and my husband, Bert, was out on his geography field studies in the mountains somewhere, I headed to Italy to take language classes. I searched for small schools in places little visited by tourists, so I would have no choice but to use Italian, and if the websites from these schools had intriguing things to say about the local cuisine, so much the better. That is how I came upon the Maremma in southern Tuscany, and Le Marche in central Italy, where I encountered culinary traditions with an allure of their own. I could have kept going—to Emilia-Romagna, to Abruzzo, Puglia, Basilicata,

Campania, or Sicily. Doubtless I would have found what I was searching for in these places too. But I had to stop somewhere, and the Piedmont, the Maremma, and Le Marche kept calling me back, kept offering me their culinary stories. Before I knew it, I had plenty to write about, and I'd become fluent in Italian in the process.

A Blissful Feast interweaves my personal journey with snippets of cultural and natural history, portraits of the people who served as my guides, and recipes for local specialties. The language itself adds another thread to the tapestry, for the fanciful names, the culinary terms, and the whimsical if only partially translatable phrases bring added significance to every dish.

Underpinning each chapter is the story of my journey from chef to cook. This is an ironic and unexpected transformation, since your average culinary memoir tends to head in the opposite direction, but in my case perhaps it was inevitable. After the restaurant where I was working shut its doors for good, my husband and I decided to start a family. We had a daughter, followed a few years later by a son, and the Italians were an obvious source of inspiration at mealtime, for they have been masters of home cooking for generations. Through the course of it all I discovered that learning to cook like an Italian does not come from memorizing recipes, but from making a meal out of what's on hand and in season, and from cultivating an intimate relationship between food, family, and friends. A thousand thanks to all the cooks in my life who helped impart these lessons, and long live the pleasures of the Italian table.

A
Blissful
Feast

PART I
THE PIEDMONT

1

THE GNOCCHI LESSON

Somehow the pictures of the gnocchi lesson were lost. No one knows what happened to them. This was in the days before iPhones, before digital cameras even, back when you took rolls of film to a camera store and waited five to seven business days for the pictures to be developed. My elder sister Nancy, who took the photos with her Nikon FG, could have sworn there were seven rolls of film, but the shop clerk assured us there were only six. So while we had plenty of photos chronicling our trip—shots of the Mole Antonelliana piercing the skyline of Torino, of the bronze statue of the war hero Garibaldi in the center of the city, of the spiral staircase inside the Basilica of Superga, of the chandelier in the Stupinigi hunting lodge—we did not have a single picture of the morning we made gnocchi. No matter. I'm just a snapshot taker, but Nancy, ever the family photographer, has a cinematic sense of composition and a whimsical flair for unexpected camera angles. I've no doubt she captured the gnocchi lesson with artistry.

Nancy and I had accompanied our mother on a pilgrimage to Rocca Canavese, twenty miles northwest of Torino in Italy's Piedmont region. Rocca Canavese is not on everyone's list of must-see destinations in Italy. It has no shrines or Eucharistic miracles. With its sixteen hundred inhabitants, it's too small to host many of the amenities you'd want in a properly charming Italian village—there is no pizzeria, no wine bar, no gelato shop. It does have a piazza, a bocce court, a medieval church, some ruins of a Roman fortress from antiquity. For a while it even had a genuine expatriate—*l'inglesina*, a little old British widow, if I remember right. But those are not what drew us there. Instead we came because

Rocca Canavese is the birthplace of my maternal grandparents and home to the families they left behind when they moved to America at the turn of the last century.

My mom wanted us to know our origins, wanted to introduce us to her relatives, which included an entourage of aunts, uncles, and cousins, young and old, who met us at the train station in Torino. After a full permutation of handshakes, hugs, and kissed cheeks, we rode by cavalcade out of the city to my grandparents' ancestral village in the foothills of the Alps. My mother's cousin, whom everyone called Zia Giuseppina whether she was their aunt or not, and her husband, Felice, whom they called Zio, were waiting for us on the balcony of their 17th-century farmhouse on the flats leading into town. Giuseppina wore her graying hair in an upswept twist and had a crisp apron over her wool skirt, and after another round of greetings and embraces she ushered us into the house where she had prepared a full state dinner.

The meal lasted three hours. At the end of the evening, after we'd hauled our luggage into Giuseppina's guestrooms and readied ourselves for bed, my mother called my sister and me to her room. She had propped herself upright with pillows in bed and pulled the covers across her lap. In one hand she had a small spiral notebook and in the other she held a pen. She motioned for us to have a seat beside her; she needed help remembering the succession of courses Giuseppina had served. She wanted to record the meals we enjoyed during our visit, wanted to regale her siblings back in Washington State with stories of eating our way through The Family, as there were many banquets still to come, many aunts and cousins waiting a turn to welcome us to their table.

Working together, we managed a full accounting, or nearly so: There were breadsticks and assorted rolls waiting on the table when we sat down, along with two unlabeled half-magnums of red wine. First up were platters and bowls of assorted antipasti: Thin slices of prosciutto, mortadella, and home-cured fennel salame. Piquant marinated red peppers the size of a walnut, stuffed with tuna and anchovies. Hard-boiled eggs with parsley sauce. Halved plum tomatoes dolloped with hand-whisked, herbed mayonnaise. A bowl of *vitello crudo*—minced raw veal, akin to steak tartare—seasoned with lemon, salt, and garlic. (Nancy and I exchanged glances, wondering how we would stomach a polite spoonful of this, even as we watched all the children at the table heap it greedily onto their plates. It had a delicate flavor and a velvety texture, much to our surprise.)

Then came the dish that sparked the cooking lesson: handmade *gnocchi*, ethereal potato nuggets with an aromatic meat and tomato sauce. *Fantastico.* Our bowls were cleared away, and, after a brief pause, Giuseppina spooned out servings of *involtini di vitello,* veal cutlets pounded thin, rolled around a filling of breadcrumbs and herbs, then simmered in white wine. Accompanying these little veal packets was a dish of braised escarole and onions. The fruit and cheese course followed, with a wooden bowl of russet apples and golden pears making the rounds, along with creamy, sweet Gorgonzola, aged Parmigiano-Reggiano, and a straw-colored mountain cheese whose name we didn't know. For dessert we had tiramisu—espresso-soaked ladyfingers layered with sweetened mascarpone custard and grated chocolate. Heady grappa in dainty-stemmed glasses and tiny porcelain cups of espresso brought the meal to a close.

My mother had grown up with a few of these Piedmont specialties; she'd learned to make them from my grandmother Teresa. Many, though, were new to her. With her menu journal as a prompt, she intended to duplicate them for my father once she returned home to Washington. She set a good precedent. I'd been cooking professionally ever since college, working in intimate, artisanal places of the farm-to-table variety. I realized a diary of meals could be an invaluable restaurant tool and I started keeping a journal of my own.

Increasingly, though, my focus was shifting and I found myself drawn to the cooking of the home. Inviting people to my table to share in a meal I'd poured my heart into gave me immense satisfaction. I didn't yet have children, but my husband and I had begun to contemplate the idea, and I looked forward to cooking for them, too. Small wonder, then, that Italian cuisine resonated so deeply with me. For at its core Italian cooking is home cooking. Italian mothers, aunts, and grandmothers have been preparing the bulk of the meals across generations, and even the men who have dominated Italy's restaurants and trattorie are serving dishes mamma used to make. No one better than an Italian home cook understands the ability of food to define a culture and a place, to draw family, friends, even strangers together, to communicate when words are not enough.

As I lay in bed that night, my mind spinning through the many courses, the unexpected flavors, the pacing and unfolding, the laughter and conversation at Giuseppina's meal, I promised myself that this visit to Italy would not be my last. I wanted to journey there again and again, to forge bonds with my Italian relatives, to experience firsthand the country's varied cuisine, to incorporate an Italian sensibility at my own table. And if I ever had a chance to spend time in a kitchen with an Italian home cook, I wouldn't pass it up.

An opportunity presented itself two days later in the form of the gnocchi lesson. At the time, my mother, sister, and I had only a few travelers' phrases in Italian between us, plus some rusty high school Spanish and a year of college French. The English-speaking cousin who had interpreted for us all weekend had returned to work, leaving us to communicate with Giuseppina and Felice through charades, pidgin Italian, and a pocket dictionary. After a tour of the vegetable garden and a walk through the neighborhood, Giuseppina decided a cooking lesson was the obvious way to fill the rest of the morning. The gnocchi we'd raved about at the inaugural meal? She would teach us to make them.

Gnocchi are little potato dumplings, generally served as a pasta course with a meat- or tomato-based sauce, or perhaps just with melted butter and cheese. The name means "little lump" or "knot"—the kind of thing you might get on your shin when you slip on the stairs, or on your head when you bump into a low stairwell ceiling. While you can find gnocchi throughout Italy, they are a specialty of the Piedmont and other northern regions. Their origins date back to flour-and-breadcrumb dumplings of the Middle Ages. After the potato (*Solanum tuberosum*) made its way to Italy from South America in the 16th century, it took a couple hundred years for it to gain acceptance in the kitchen. It belonged to the disreputable nightshade family, whose Old World members include the poisonous mandrake and belladonna of witches' brews and jilted lovers' potions. At one time or another herbalists and physicians blamed it for everything from leprosy to syphilis. At the very least they found it excessively flatulent, unfit for those of a refined digestion, though satisfactory for mountain peasants with their coarse mettle and ironclad bellies. But a few grain shortages and famines over the years helped folks reconsider. As they say, there is no sauce better than hunger. While nobody ever figured out a way to turn potatoes into flour that yielded decent bread, someone did discover they could be made into tender, cloudlike gnocchi. By the mid–19th century, gnocchi made from potatoes had become the standard. They cost less to make, since potatoes were often cheaper than flour, and people came to prefer them to the flour-and-breadcrumb variety.

Giuseppina started the lesson by selecting four fist-sized potatoes from a bin in the pantry. She chose wrinkled old russets, with buds just beginning to sprout from the eyes. She lifted up a little round red-skinned potato, shook her head, and tossed it back into the bin. Although I didn't understand her then, she was trying to tell us that old potatoes are better than new ones for gnocchi, and thick-skinned baking potatoes are better than thin-skinned, waxy boilers because they have less moisture and a more floury texture. She put the potatoes, still in their jackets, into a pot of water on the stovetop, let them boil gently until tender when pierced with a knife, twenty minutes or so, then drained them in a colander. As soon as they were cool enough to handle she peeled the skins and pressed the potatoes through a ricer onto a shallow tray, which she placed in a warm spot on top of the woodstove to let the potatoes finish drying out. I've since seen other cooks employ similar measures—steaming the potatoes instead of boiling them, for instance, or putting the riced potatoes into a slow oven for a bit, otherwise the gnocchi can end up soggy. In my own kitchen, I've found that roasting the potatoes on a rack in the oven at 400°F until tender keeps them dry and fluffy. Once baked, I split them in half to let the remaining steam escape.

Giuseppina transferred the riced potatoes to a flour-dusted pastry board on the kitchen table, then sprinkled another handful of flour over the top. She worked the flour into the potatoes with a pastry scraper and created a mound with a well in the middle. Into this crater she broke an egg, stirred it up with a fork, and continued blending the mixture with the help of her scraper until it came together. She added another sprinkle of flour and finished by kneading the dough a few times, until it formed a smooth, soft loaf. She didn't measure a thing, but the standard proportions are about two pounds potatoes, two cups flour, and a medium egg for six people.

Giuseppina scraped her work surface clean, dusted it with more flour, and cut the loaf into slices, which she rolled into long ropes as thick as a finger. She cut the ropes into half-inch pieces and sprinkled them with semolina flour to keep them from sticking. She brought out a small, ridged wooden paddle, aptly called a *rigagnocchi*, which I knew from one of my cookbooks to mean "gnocchi ridge-maker." Holding the paddle in one hand, she picked up a piece of dough in the other and placed it on the grooved side of the board. With a single sweeping motion she used her thumb to push the lump down and along the ridges so that it curled up on itself and flicked softly onto the pastry board. The finished gnocchi had tiny grooves on one side from the paddle, and a dimple on the other from her fingerprint. She showed us how to accomplish the same thing with the tines of a fork, although the ridges left behind weren't as well defined and the resulting gnocchi weren't quite as pretty. Some cooks dismiss this step as too time-consuming, but others insist on it, especially when company comes, because it creates more surface area for catching the sauce and renders the gnocchi thinner through the middle so they cook more evenly.

She put us to work with forks in hand. Our first attempts were overly smashed or lopsided or otherwise imperfect, but we soon got the hang of it. It didn't take us long to shape them, though I wondered if Giuseppina might have done the job faster without us. While we worked she asked my mother for updates on all the other American relatives and was glad to hear that everyone was doing *bene, bene, benissimo.* Nancy put down her fork periodically, cleaned her hands, and picked up her camera. She walked around the room snapping pictures, stood on a chair for a better vantage point, knelt down to frame the gnocchi from a low-angle point of view across the table. She had my mother and Giuseppina pose for her, clasping flour-covered hands and raising their forks. She set up the timer to take a group portrait of the four of us surveying our handiwork. My mom would have been almost sixty then, Giuseppina a decade older. I noticed they shared the same angular jaw, same high forehead. I inherited my mother's olive complexion and dark hair, and people often say I look the "most Italian" of her four daughters. But with their northern Italian origins, many of my mother's relatives are fair complected, and I saw something of Nancy in Giuseppina's smile.

Giuseppina arranged our gnocchi in a single layer on semolina-dusted baking sheets and covered them with a linen towel. That afternoon at the midday meal, after the assorted antipasti and before the braised chicken, she dropped the gnocchi into a large pot of boiling, salted water, working in batches to keep them from crowding. Once they floated to the surface she let them bob about for ten to fifteen seconds then removed them with a slotted spoon to two warm baking dishes. Onto the first dish she ladled the leftover meat sauce from the previous night, and she layered the gnocchi in the second dish with melted butter and handfuls of fontina cheese. Fontina is an alpine cow's milk cheese made in the nearby Aosta Valley. Nutty and woodsy, it is the Piedmont's premier cooking cheese for the luscious way it melts when heated. Gnocchi prepared in this style, Giuseppina explained, are called *gnocchi alla bava*, which I later learned means "drooling" gnocchi, in reference to the strands of melted cheese that appear when you lift a spoonful of the steaming dumplings from the platter. Served this way, Giuseppina said, even Felice would eat them. With the help of my dictionary I understood Felice had had his fill of potatoes during the war, when there was little to sauce them with but the starchy water they'd been boiled in. But potato gnocchi alla bava—that was food for the gods. Giuseppina gave each dish of gnocchi a gentle stir to coat them evenly and brought them to the table.

Nancy didn't take any pictures of the finished gnocchi, sauced and glistening in their serving dishes. This was back when it was considered impolite to bring a camera to the table, back before people thought to take pictures of their meal before they ate it. But I wish she had. Just as I wish we hadn't misplaced the gnocchi-lesson photos. Of all those six (or seven) rolls of film, those were the images I most wanted to see. Giuseppina's arthritic, flour-covered hands, our forks with dough stuck between the tines, trays of gnocchi covering the kitchen table, the four of us working side by side. Still, when I pull out my menu journal and read through the entry for that day, the memory remains, as vivid as the ridges from a wooden gnocchi paddle.

GNOCCHI ALLA BAVA

GNOCCHI WITH MELTED BUTTER AND FONTINA

Serves 4 to 6

FOR THE GNOCCHI:
- 2 pounds russet potatoes
- 2 cups all-purpose flour, plus more for dusting
- 1 medium egg
- semolina flour, for dusting

FOR SERVING:
- 4 ounces fontina cheese, grated
- 4 ounces (1 stick) butter, melted
- salt and freshly ground pepper, to taste

Preheat oven to 400°F. Pierce the potatoes with a fork or skewer a few times to help the moisture escape as they cook. Bake for 45 to 60 minutes, until a fork slips in without resistance, then remove from the oven and split them in half to let the steam continue escaping. Peel the potatoes as soon as they are cool enough to handle and put them through a ricer. Transfer the riced potatoes to a pastry board dusted with a tablespoon of all-purpose flour, then sprinkle the rest of the flour over the top. Work the flour into the potatoes with a pastry scraper and create a mound with a well in the middle. Break the egg into the center, stir it with a fork, and continue blending the mixture with the help of the scraper until it comes together. Finish by kneading the dough a few times, dusting it with additional flour if needed, until it forms a smooth, soft loaf.

Cut the loaf into slices and roll out on a flour-dusted work surface to form ropes as thick as a finger. Cut the ropes into half-inch pieces and sprinkle with semolina flour to keep them from sticking. Roll each piece down a gnocchi paddle or the back of a fork, leaving ridges on one side and a dimple from your finger on the other.

Just before serving, bring a large pot of water to a boil over high heat. Add a heaping tablespoon of salt, and when the foaming subsides, begin adding the gnocchi, working in batches to keep them from crowding. Stir a couple times to dislodge any gnocchi that have stuck to the bottom of the pot, and boil gently until tender, about 10 to 15 seconds after they float to the surface.

Remove gnocchi with a slotted spoon to a baking dish, drizzle with melted butter, and sprinkle with grated cheese. Continue layering until all the gnocchi are cooked. Season with salt and pepper to taste and give the gnocchi a final stir to coat them evenly. Serve hot.

Note on salting the pot: Most Italian cooks add coarse sea salt to the pot before blanching vegetables or cooking things like pasta or gnocchi. I once assumed this coarse salt had some mystical or otherwise transformative property essential to the cooking process, but I found out otherwise. Cooks in Italy use coarse salt because that's what Mamma used, and Mamma used it because it was cheap. Coarse sea salt isn't cheap in the United States, so I rely on kosher salt instead. Fine sea salt also works well. Just don't use iodized salt, which imparts a bitter flavor to boiled foods. Giuseppina told me the pot of water needs salt *in abbondanza*. She added a handful to the pot and I do, too. This comes out to about a heaping tablespoon of salt for 4 quarts of water, which renders many American cooks aghast, accustomed as they are to meting out salt by the pinch or sprinkle. With an abundant dose, the salt can penetrate the pasta (or gnocchi), seasoning it from within. Salt applied after cooking can't accomplish this feat, and results in dishes that taste salty rather than flavorful. So cast aside your fears and salt the pot of water in abbondanza!

2

THE BREAD OF KINGS

During that first visit, my mother, sister, and I spent the better part of an afternoon wandering idly through the historic center of Torino. We window-shopped at the designer stores along Via Roma, listened to street musicians, and observed a tattoo artist at work in Via Garibaldi. We walked through the Royal Gardens of the Palazzo Reale in the rain, and we saw the produce vendors dismantle their towering displays at the end of the day in the open market in Porta Palazzo, said to be the largest outdoor market in Europe.

We also passed through Piazza Savoia in the city's old Roman Quarter, where a granite obelisk rises up seventy feet in the center of the square. If we'd been able to read the Italian on the interpretive placard we would have learned that the monument, built in 1853, commemorates the passage a few years earlier of the Siccardi Laws that abolished the jurisdiction of ecclesiastical courts over civil affairs. Named for Count Giuseppe Siccardi, the minister of justice who presented the legislation, the laws effectively wrested power from the Church and placed it in the hands of the State. This radical move did not sit at all well with the Pope, but it helped put the Piedmont at the fore of the nationalist movement that would bring about the unification of Italy a few years later.

At the base of the monument is the inscription *La legge è uguale per tutti*, which effectively translates as "Everyone is equal under the law." Although we didn't realize it at the time, a wooden box had been buried underneath the obelisk when it was erected—a time capsule of sorts—with a collection of items to serve as a testament to the city's civility. Among the contents was a copy of the laws, an issue of the local newspaper, a few coins, a bag of the region's prized Arborio rice, a bottle of its noble Barbera wine, and a packet of *grissini*.

Grissini are Italian breadsticks, and Torino is their native city. They stand a world apart from the factory-minted, packaged breadsticks familiar to countless diners in the United States, the kind you can occasionally still find tucked between the salt and pepper shakers and the Chianti-flask candleholder in red-and-white checked tablecloth restaurants. Chalky and stale, those breadsticks have a commissary flavor that gives them about as much appeal as a saltine cracker, though they suffice for nibbling absently while waiting for the waiter to take your order.

True grissini, *i veri grissini torinesi*, are made by hand. Crisp and delicate, long as an arm, thin as a finger, knobby and gnarled like arthritic old bones, they have a yeasty, slightly nutty flavor with a hint of toasty sweetness from their golden crust. They are served at royal banquets and family meals both special and quotidian, snapped in half, then placed in a tumbling stack like kindling directly on the table or else wrapped primly in a linen napkin.

They appeared at every family meal during our trip, and the day we went to meet our cousin Catterina we had an opportunity to try our hands at making them.

Catterina and her husband own a *panetteria*, or bakery, in Rocca Canavese's main piazza. They had been unable to attend the dinner in honor of our arrival, but Catterina recognized my mother immediately when we entered the shop. She rushed from behind the cash register and greeted us with a stream of Italian spoken so quickly as to be incomprehensible to our unpracticed ears, along with a chiropractic hug and a kiss on each cheek that needed no translation. She would have been barely forty then, her hair, cut blunt above the shoulders, was still its natural light brown shade. Her baker's cap had slipped to one side with all the embracing.

She ushered us behind the counter to see the racks and bins brimming with an assortment of specialty breads: *Pane normale, integrale,* and *ciabatta*. Plain bread, whole wheat, and a flat, airy loaf shaped like an old slipper, along with a couple types of pizza by the slice. One by one she held up an array of rolls of whimsical form and name: *rosette, tartarughe, manine, palla di neve, carciofi, coppiette, biove.* I had her write down the words in my notebook so I could look them up later. Roses, turtles, little hands, snowballs, artichokes, double crescents, and soft, billowy rounds. Catterina beamed as she said each name and giggled infectiously as we tried to repeat her words. Listening to the musical sounds coming from her mouth was in great part what made me resolve to learn Italian.

Catterina escorted us across a narrow alley to see the *laboratorio*, where the actual baking took place. And a laboratory it was, with a hulking nine-door baker's oven and a battery of oversized stainless-steel contraptions that collectively mixed, kneaded, portioned, or proofed the various doughs. Her husband, Augusto, wore baker's whites, though their color more accurately resembled unbleached flour. Same for his shoes, which were the customary soft white bedroom slippers I've seen on bakers in both France and Italy.

Augusto was making grissini. He stood behind an age-worn machine, a groaning, whirring metal box that drew a long sheet of risen dough across a conveyor belt and into its mouth. Once inside, the dough was portioned and cut into slender batons that emerged on the other side. Working in time to the creaking gears of his machine, he stretched the strips into four-foot lengths, pulling them apart from the ends while simultaneously administering a light, twirling flick of the wrist as if giving a jump rope half a turn. He stopped the machine for another round of greetings, then started it back up again, only slower this time, so we could try our hands at shaping a few grissini. Our breadsticks arced and squiggled. When they weren't thick and lumpy on the ends, they were swollen in the middle. That perfect flick of the wrist only came with practice.

Augusto loaded the baking sheet into the oven, our misshapen grissini awkwardly noticeable amid the uniformity and precision of all the rest. When the breadsticks emerged from the oven I noticed he set ours aside. They would appear on the table that afternoon for our midday meal; good enough for the family to eat, but not acceptable for paying customers.

Although they have long been the iconic bread of Torino, you can find artisanal grissini (singular: *grissino*) throughout the Piedmont, and like any signature food they are a point of pride in their native land. Likewise, their origins are the stuff of legends. By most accounts they trace to a sickly 17th-century prince from the House of Savoy. Vittorio Amedeo II, a frail child with a weak digestion, was only nine years old when his father died of fever in 1675. His mother—Madame Royale, as she took to being called—assumed control as regent of the Savoy Duchy, which included what is now the Piedmont of Italy and part of France. She summoned her private physician, Don Teobaldo Pecchio, to examine her son, concerned he might never gain the stamina required of a proper duke. The doctor diagnosed poor nutrition as the culprit and consulted with the court baker, one Antonio Brunero, who developed a thin, crusty bread expressly for the heir apparent. He started with a traditional loaf from the region, called a *ghersa* in Piedmontese dialect. Long and slender, it shared a common lineage with the French baguette. Brunero made it progressively longer and thinner until it was no wider than his thumb, as long as his outstretched arms, and essentially all crust. He added the diminutive "*ino*" to its name, *ghersino*, which became grissino in Italian.

In those days common thinking maintained that the crust of the bread contained all the nutrients, while the soft interior crumb, though tasty, was void of nutritional value and hard to digest. My mother's own theory might have descended tangentially from this notion. "Eat your crusts," she used to say, "they'll make your hair curly." This would fill me with angst, as I had unruly curls already and wanted nothing more than to have long, straight hair, parted down the middle like Laurie Partridge or Marcia Brady, so I slipped my crusts to our Brittany spaniel whenever I could.

Signor Brunero's salubrious bread apparently worked wonders, because young Vittorio Amedeo made a full recovery. His mother might actually have preferred a more marginal outcome—a cure effective enough to have the poor boy feeling better, but not so complete as to give him the energy and acuity to govern on his own, for she very much enjoyed running things herself.

She tried to marry Vittorio Amedeo off to his cousin, Infanta Isabel Luisa of Portugal, an arrangement that would have landed him permanently in Lisbon and left Madame Royale to tend to the Piedmont, but he would have none of it. He obstinately took to his sickbed with a feigned malady not even grissini could cure, until finally the nuptials were called off. He asserted his claim to the duchy and his mother reluctantly stepped aside. He ended up marrying the docile Anna d'Orleans, niece of Louis XIV of

France. Madame Royale approved of the union, as the demure girl had no interest in state affairs. Anna likewise turned a blind eye to affairs of the extramarital sort, which pleased Vittorio Amedeo as well.

Vittorio Amedeo II went on to become the first Savoy king—of Sicily, and then Sardinia—which was logistically quite a stretch from clear up north in Torino, but those were the only kingdoms available at the time and he had to start somewhere. His Machiavellian determination to expand his domain and rid it of foreign influences provided the germ for an independent country of Italy and earned him the nickname *la volpe Savoiarda*, the "Savoy Fox." A century and a half later, in 1861, his descendant Vittorio Emanuele II was crowned the first king of the newly united Italy. Which, the baker-historians of the Piedmont like to say, means there would be no nation of Italy today were it not for the invention of grissini.

Grissini remained on the royal table of subsequent Savoy monarchs, eventually becoming known as *il Re dei pani, il pane dei Rei*, the king of breads, the bread of kings. As for the Savoy Fox, his ghost is said to haunt the corridors of Venaria Reale, his favorite hunting lodge west of Torino. He wears a black cloak and carries a grissino burning at one end as a candlestick.

No legend as tidy as this could possibly have come about without sweeping a few contradictory facts under the rug. Some researchers date the origins of grissini back several centuries earlier. Bread in the Piedmont was sold then not by weight as it is today, but by the loaf, and during grain shortages or times of inflation bakers made smaller loaves to keep prices from rising. When the Black Plague arrived in the Piedmont on the heels of a series of famines, droughts, and other calamities during the 14th century, an economic crisis ensued that had bakers turning out smaller and smaller loaves. The long, thin ghersa grew steadily thinner and longer until it became a breadstick. Writing in the 16th century, the doctor and botanist Costanzo Felici mentioned bread "made of soft dough, which when fermented is drawn out into long shapes." Similarly, the Florentine Abbot Vincenzo Ruccellai noted in his diary a novelty he encountered while passing through the Piedmont on his way to Paris in 1643: bread, *"lungo quanto un braccio e sottile sottile"*—long as an arm, and very, very thin.

The duke's grissini would have been daintier than these earlier versions, made of fine white flour, which the doctors wrongly thought to be more healthful than milled whole grain. Slender breadsticks graced the tables at the Savoy court, to the delight of visiting nobles and dignitaries, and soon became popular among the aristocracy across the Piedmont, who alone could have afforded white flour in the first place.

Napoleon discovered grissini as he pushed through Torino on his campaign to conquer Italy. Hoping what he called *les petits batons de Turin* might soothe his chronic ulcer, he brought Torinesi bakers back to Paris to make breadsticks for him there. Try as they might, the bakers could not replicate grissini once they arrived in France. In Torino it's said that Parisian air and the River Seine could not substitute for the fresh mountain air of the Alps and the waters of the Po, but no one knows the true explanation. So Napoleon established a stagecoach service between Torino and his palace and had his breadsticks delivered.

Years later, I spoke enough Italian to ask Augusto about his recipe. Like most professional formulas, it was measured by weight rather than volume and it relied on kilos, coming as it did from a baker whose countrymen have used the metric system since the days of Napoleon. Back in my own kitchen I found it easy enough to reduce his multi-kilo measures to quantities more practical for home baking. Translating the metric weights into cups and tablespoons proved a different story, but I managed to do it. I didn't want the lack of a kitchen scale to keep anyone from making grissini, although I had to round up or down a few times to make things come out evenly. Still, when I make grissini at home I measure by weight. It's quicker, more accurate, and doesn't leave all those measuring spoons and cups to clean up.

Pour 100 grams (½ cup) tepid water into a large stainless bowl and add half a teaspoon granulated yeast and a teaspoon malt extract. Malt extract is a syrup made from partially sprouted grain, usually barley. Italian bakers often use a small amount of it in their breads to nourish the yeast. You can find malt extract at most health food stores or brewer's supply houses, though a teaspoon of honey makes a good substitute. Stir well until the malt syrup is dissolved and add 100 grams (1 cup) flour. Mix until smooth, then cover the bowl with a piece of plastic wrap or a larger, upturned bowl, and set aside at cool room temperature overnight.

The next day this starter dough, known as a *biga*, will be bubbly and more than double in size. Italian bakers often use a biga, because the secondary yeasts and good bacteria that develop during the long, slow initial rise impart a rich aroma and flavor to their breads, as well as improved texture and keeping qualities. Stir in another 400 grams (3 cups) flour, 180 grams (¾ cup) room temperature water, a teaspoon of salt, and 50 grams (a scant ¼ cup) best-quality lard, also at room temperature.

Lard is rendered pork fat. The two types most prized for cooking are leaf lard, which is the snow-white fat that surrounds a pig's kidneys, and fatback, which comes from the strip along the back under the skin. Connoisseurs consider leaf lard to be milder and thus superior in quality, but fatback is easier to find. Both lend a singular flavor, slightly nut-like but never meaty, to breads and a tender flakiness to pastries. Called *strutto* in Italian, this lard is not the solid block found in your average supermarket. That lard is a hydrogenated blend of fat from any old part of the pig, to which preservatives and stabilizers have been added to boost its shelf life. Processed lard gives baked goods a greasy component that I find disagreeable. Strutto, meanwhile, is a traditional cooking fat in much of the Piedmont, especially the northern stretches where olive groves do not flourish because of the cold, and olive oil was so scarce and precious as to be used primarily for drizzling over tender lettuces and anointing babies at the baptismal font.

The Savoy court bakers fortified the duke's grissini with lard, and authentic recipes still include it for its savory note. If your diet includes pork products it is worth the effort to seek it out, because grissini made with freshly rendered lard truly are inimitable. Good butchers sometimes stock house-rendered lard, or you can buy kidney leaf or fatback and render it yourself. Or you can substitute olive oil, as many Italian bakers do, claiming it makes their grissini lighter, not to mention vegetarian. Other bakers use half olive oil and half butter to create breadsticks with a tender, soft crumb for their customers whose teeth are not as strong as they once were.

Stir the dough with a wooden spoon until it comes together, then turn it out onto a lightly floured surface and knead until smooth and supple, about ten minutes. Return the dough to a bowl and cover once again with an upturned bowl or piece of plastic wrap. After an hour, turn the dough out onto a cutting board sprinkled with coarse semolina flour, then shape it into a rectangle about fourteen inches long and four inches wide. Semolina is a type of durum wheat flour with a lovely yellow color and a number of uses, from pasta and porridge to couscous and puddings. Bakers often dust their cake pans and cookie sheets with coarsely ground semolina to prevent sticking and it serves the same purpose with grissini.

Brush the tops and sides of the dough lightly with olive oil, cover with plastic wrap, and let rise another two hours or so, until the dough has doubled in volume. Cut the risen dough in half lengthwise, then crosswise into strips no wider than a finger. Pour about a cup of semolina into a pile on the counter in front of you, then, working with one piece of dough at a time, roll each strip in the semolina to coat evenly. Lift the strip, pinching each end gently, then pull your hands apart, keeping them parallel to the table and stretching the grissino to fit the length of your baking sheet. If a breadstick turns out to be too long, cut it to size and bake the resulting snippet separately—the odds and ends become tough when combined and re-stretched. Place the grissini on a baking sheet, spaced about an inch apart, and bake at 400°F for twelve to fifteen minutes, until crisp and nicely browned.

Augusto used a sturdy wire-mesh baking sheet that allowed heat to circulate around the grissini, creating a light, crisp texture. On my initial attempt to make grissini at home, I had the brilliant idea of duplicating his mesh sheet with an old expandable window screen from a discarded stack in the cellar. I hosed off the cobwebs, adjusted the screen to fit the oven, and lined it with grissini. I congratulated myself on my ingenuity as I peered through the oven window and watched the grissini bake. Then the screen reached a critical kindling point and a cloud of black smoke began seeping through the oven vents along with a noxious odor of burning glue that soon had me doubled over in a fit of coughing. My geriatric cat left her warm cushion by the radiator and rushed to the door, begging to be let out.

I grabbed my oven mitts and removed the smoldering screen to a snowbank outside, where it sputtered and melted beyond repair. For a moment I considered trying to salvage the grissini. Perfectly browned and lovely to behold, they certainly looked untainted. But the thought that I might inadvertently have infused them with carcinogens outweighed their beauty. I sighed and dumped them in the wastebasket. On my second attempt I used a plain old cookie sheet with fine results. Better still were subsequent batches, placed on a sheet of parchment paper and transferred to a preheated pizza stone, which is how I bake them to this day.

While I can't make four-foot grissini in my home oven, the only real shortcoming I've noticed is that my breadsticks don't seem to keep quite as well as the true breadsticks of Torino. Augusto's grissini maintain their crisp texture for at least a week, while mine grow slightly tough after a day or two. Perhaps it's my oven, or maybe those mesh screens make a difference after all. Or else I should blame the water or the air. It's more an academic observation than a problem really. When I make grissini for dinner, we almost always eat the entire batch in a sitting. They rarely have time to cool off, let alone last until the next day, so I don't let myself feel too disappointed. After all, Napoleon's bakers couldn't make breadsticks, either, and they were only across the Alps at the Tuileries. Centuries later and an ocean away, my grissini might not be the bread of kings, but they have a splendor of their own.

GRISSINI TORINESI STIRATI A MANO

HAND-STRETCHED BREADSTICKS OF TORINO

(Makes about 3 dozen)

FOR THE BIGA:

- ½ teaspoon granulated yeast
- ½ teaspoon malt extract (can substitute honey)
- 120 g (½ cup) tepid water
- 120 g (¾ cup) all-purpose flour

Combine yeast, malt extract (or honey), and water in a large stainless steel or glass mixing bowl and stir to dissolve. Add flour and stir until smooth. Cover with an upturned bowl or large plate, or a piece of plastic wrap and set aside at cool room temperature overnight.

FOR THE DOUGH:

- all of the biga from the previous day
- 375 g (3 cups) flour
- 180 g (¾ cup) room temperature water
- 1 teaspoon salt
- 50 g (¼ cup) best-quality lard, room temperature (can substitute olive oil or 2 tablespoons each olive oil and room temperature butter)
- about 1 cup coarse semolina flour, for dredging
- olive oil, for coating dough

The next day, the biga should be bubbly and more than doubled in size. Add the flour, water, salt, and lard, and stir until the dough comes together. Turn out the dough onto a lightly floured surface and knead until smooth and supple, about 10 minutes. Return the dough to a bowl and cover once again with an upturned bowl or piece of plastic wrap. Let rise at cool room temperature for 1 hour.

Sprinkle a large cutting board generously with semolina flour. Turn the dough out onto the board and shape into a rectangle, about 14 inches long and 4 inches wide. Brush the top and sides of the dough lightly with olive oil, cover with plastic wrap, and let rise about 2 hours—dough should about double in volume.

Preheat the oven to 400°F.

Cut the risen dough in half lengthwise, then crosswise into strips no wider than a finger, about half an inch. Pour about a cup of semolina into a pile on the counter in front of you, then, working with one piece of dough at a time, roll each strip in the semolina to coat evenly. Lift the strip, pinching each end gently, then pull your hands apart, keeping them parallel to the table and stretching the grissino to fit the length of your baking sheet. If a breadstick turns out to be too long, cut it to size and bake the resulting snippet separately—the odds and ends become tough when combined and re-stretched.

Place the grissini on a baking sheet, spaced about an inch apart, and bake for 12 to 15 minutes, until crisp and nicely browned. Work in batches if necessary, stretching the grissini just before loading them into the oven. The grissini are best if eaten the day they are made.

3

HEIRLOOM PIZZELLE

I have my uncle Joey to thank for restoring the ties to our relatives in Rocca Canavese. The eldest of my mother's four siblings, he picked up a thread during the 1960s that had frayed to the breaking point as the strains and successive blows of history, distance, and time took their toll. There had been the war years when the mail and passenger ships could not get through, the obligations of work and home as my grandparents built a life in Washington State, the passing one by one of the family members left behind in Italy. Still, the homeland exerted its allure on my uncle. He wanted to tread in the footsteps of his immigrant parents, wanted to meet the relatives living parallel lives in Italy, and feel the specters of his forebears amid the cobbled alleys and Roman ruins.

His wife, Mary, deserves plenty of credit, too. Not only was she my uncle Joey's unflappable travel companion, undaunted by officious customs agents and prepubescent pickpockets and a perplexing array of flush mechanisms in public restrooms, she took it upon herself to learn the language. While my uncle and aunt relied on an interpreter when they made their first visit to Rocca Canavese, on their subsequent trips Mary could converse with the relatives in Italian. She could also send them Christmas cards and wedding announcements, and write them multi-page letters to keep in touch. She set up pen-pal exchanges between the cousins of my generation and translated our letters back and forth.

When I started studying Italian after my first visit to Rocca Canavese, Mary passed along a stack of her textbooks and dictionaries, along with a deck of flashcards, some old tourist brochures, and a couple CDs to build my vocabulary and sharpen my comprehension. I pored through these materials, hoping to chip away at the language barrier that had kept so much out of my reach during that initial trip. As I read Mary's notes and lists of conjugated verbs or listened to her Living Language CDs on the way to work, it didn't seem so outlandish to think that I, too, could learn a foreign language as an adult. My steps were slow and stumbling, but I realize now that Mary gave me the resilience to persevere.

She also gave me her pizzelle iron. Or rather I came into possession of it, and this too, was thanks to my uncle Joey. She used the iron each Christmas to make an heirloom Italian cookie that is a holiday staple in my extended Italian-American family.

Pizzelle are thin golden wafers typically flavored with anise, sometimes vanilla, lemon, or almond, then baked in a waffle-like griddle designed expressly for the purpose. You can now find packaged pizzelle throughout the year in most any grocery store, but the dozen or so cookies lined up inside each cellophane-wrapped box taste dusty and stale, not unappealing so much as uninviting, as if the toll of industrial manufacture has weighed too heavily—although teething babies seem to find them well suited for gumming. Yet when pizzelle are made at home they are a different cookie altogether; beautiful to the eye, exquisite in texture and flavor, and imbued with culture and tradition, as if possessed of some sort of vital leaven that elevates them from unremarkable to exceptional. This is perhaps an odd metaphor to use with a cookie that gets squashed flat between two iron plates, but the fact remains.

The name *pizzelle* is a diminutive of pizza, a word that conjures up images of a baked disk of bread dough glistening with tomato sauce and melted mozzarella, although it originally referred to the shape of a thing: flat and round. Pizzelle, then, are "little flat rounds." A specialty of the remote Abruzzo region of central Italy, the spelling varies from village to village, as does the name. Pizzelle, piazelle, pizelle. *Neole, cancellate, ferratelle.* This last refers to the iron, or ferrous metal, from which the presses were once made. (Think back to chemistry class: Fe, from the Latin *ferrum* is the symbol for iron on the periodic table.)

Early irons had long handles to keep the baker from burning her fingers as she cooked her pizzelle on the hearth or over a stovetop flame, patiently creating crisp, golden rounds by holding each side over the fire for the time it took to say a Hail Mary. Irons evolved and the grids were embossed, generally with a basket-weave pattern on one side and a decorative design to mark a special occasion on the other—flowers or a cross for Easter, perhaps a snowflake or star for Christmas. There was often a spot to emblazon the family initials or crest, and these fanciful implements became precious heirlooms, passed down from mother to daughter, included in trousseaus, bequeathed in wills.

My grandmother Teresa had one of these long-handled contraptions, though she did not inherit it, did not pack it along with a recipe in her steamer trunk in 1914 when she left her family near Torino at the age of fifteen and crossed the ocean to become a governess in America on the eve of the First World War. She encountered pizzelle for the first time not in Italy, but in the United States, as they were not a specialty of her native Piedmont region. In Italy, you must understand, cooking has traditionally been highly regional, with few dishes attaining national popularity until fairly recently. Pizza, for example—that famous big, flat round—was virtually unknown in northern Italy until after World War II when Neapolitans migrated to the industrialized north in search of jobs and brought their favorite street food with them. (According to family lore, my grandfather first encountered pizza on the ship when he left Torino for the United States as a boy. An American passenger asked him where one might find pizza. My grandfather, who hadn't yet learned much English and had no idea what pizza was, assumed the gentleman must have been looking for the toilet, so he gave the man directions to the bathroom. My mom says Grandpa Joe never got over his embarrassment, and bristled at the mention of pizza forever after.)

Likewise, pizzelle were an unfamiliar commodity in Italian regions outside the Abruzzo, but the Abruzzese who settled in America introduced the cookie to their new neighbors and its popularity spread throughout Italian-American communities. My grandmother came into possession of her recipe and stovetop iron from one of her women friends in the immigrant community of Cle Elum, the bustling mining town in the Cascade Mountains of Washington State where she set up housekeeping as a young bride after the war.

Teresa called the cookies "*ficelle*"—with the "ce" pronounced Italian-style, like the "ch" in church: "fi-chell-ay." As far as I can tell this is not a name used in the Abruzzo. It is a French word, pronounced "fi-sell." Now, this is no great surprise. For the residents of Rocca Canavese at the western foot of the Alps, Standard Italian was a second language at the time, taught in grades one through eight to those lucky enough to remain in school that long. My grandmother's native tongue, the language on which she was weaned, so to speak, was Piemontese, the dialect spoken by denizens of the Piedmont region of northern Italy since at least the 12th century. Piemontese was the language of my grandmother's formative years, but she and my grandfather used it only seldom in their adopted homeland. It came in handy, for instance, when discussing Christmas presents in front of their five children, who had been born and raised in America and were taught only English as a point of patriotic pride. Occasionally, phrases in Piemontese bubbled forth unbidden when my grandmother spoke impulsively. Words in Piemontese were what she resorted to when her English failed her (I've been told it is a particularly colorful language for swearing), and doubtless it was in Piemontese that Saint Peter addressed her when he granted her admittance at the gate.

Piemontese is peppered with French words. In fact, linguists trace it more directly to French than to Standard Italian, a reflection of Piedmont's close cultural ties to France and the House of Savoy. When the Savoy family went on to head the newly forged Kingdom of Italy in 1861, French was the lingua franca of the Italian royal court, and His Majesty Victor Emmanuel II spoke it with his cabinet ministers. But he spoke Piemontese to his wife and children. He gave orders to his horse and his soldiers on the battlefield in Piemontese, and he used Piemontese when he whispered sweet nothings into the ears of his many mistresses. Born and raised in Torino, he spoke only rudimentary, thickly accented Italian. Then again, fewer than ten percent of his subjects across Italy could speak Italian, either, corresponding roughly to the number who could read and write. The rest spoke a host of dialects, all descending from Vulgar Latin, the common spoken form of Latin used by the ancient Romans. With the collapse of the Roman Empire and the subsequent parade of invaders, cultures became fragmented and isolated, giving rise to a kaleidoscope of mutually unintelligible languages throughout the peninsula. Milanese, Piemontese, Friulian, Pugliese, Neapolitan—some say there is a dialect for every city, every village in the country. So, just like its culinary traditions, language in Italy has a deep-rooted regional character.

Not until the 1950s, with the economic boom and educational reforms that followed the war, did Standard Italian begin to spread throughout the country. These dialects are now dying out, spoken only by the elder generations. Today's youth can usually understand their grandparents who speak to them in dialect, but they generally respond in Italian.

I only wish I could understand why my grandmother called her cookies "ficelle." Curiously, the word means "string" in French. Parisian bakeries turn out crisp, crusty loaves, skinnier even than baguettes, which are called ficelles. *Grandmères* make *boeuf à la ficelle* by tying a string to a joint of beef, lowering it into a cauldron of aromatic broth, and simmering until meltingly tender. In the days of communal hearths, the string allowed each cook to recognize her cut of meat. But pizzelle are flat like pancakes, and if I remember my high school geometry, a string is one dimension shy of a pancake. The only other dish I know that is even remotely related is *ficelles picardes*. A specialty of the Picardy region of France, these are savory crepes spread with sautéed mushrooms, a paper-thin slice of ham, and Gruyère cheese. They are rolled up, covered with cream and more cheese, and baked in the oven. Sublime, but no more a string than my grandmother's cookies.

Regardless, the answer seems destined to remain a mystery, making it yet another of those family questions that went unasked until it was too late—questions like: Where was Grandpa's sister buried, the one who died in infancy of teething? And what about Grandpa's uncle, who left Italy to seek his fortune in the tin mines of Bolivia? Whatever happened to that branch of the family tree?

My mom inherited my grandmother's old stovetop iron at some point, though she'd cast it aside in favor of a convenient electric one by the time she was making pizzelle with my three sisters and me. It now hangs, rusty and forgotten, gummed up with dust and kitchen oil, from a hook in the pegboard above my father's workbench. I keep telling myself I really should clean it up, see what kind of cookie it turns out. All it would take is some double-ought steel wool and a little elbow grease. At home in New Hampshire, I make pizzelle with the iron I received as a wedding gift. After years of service it is in its prime, with a well-seasoned patina that faithfully keeps the cookies from sticking. As for my aunt Mary's pizzelle maker, I keep it at my parents' house, even though my mom has a couple irons of her own. My husband and I pack up our children to spend Christmas in Yakima each year, and the holidays don't seem complete without pizzelle made from Mary's iron.

Its harvest gold exterior suggests its age as circa 1970. Its aluminum plates are black and luminescent, all but oozing the vestigial cooking oil of pizzelle batches past. The heating elements have grown temperamental and sluggish with time, so each set of cookies takes progressively longer to attain the requisite golden hue, and I occasionally have to stop work completely, let the iron catch its breath for a few minutes before proceeding. I should just throw it out, but I resist.

I actually think of it as my uncle Joey's iron, because for years the two of us made pizzelle together at Christmas. The first time was the December after Mary passed away. (She had a lingering heart condition after a bout with rheumatic fever during her youth. Although the doctors said she wouldn't live a full life, she had a husband and a family, she traveled the world and made it to seventy-four, which seems pretty full to me.) I'd been back at my parents' house for a few days and was helping my mother with her pre-holiday checklist. When I brought up her pizzelle iron from the storeroom closet in the basement, she suggested I give Joey a call. He and Mary had a long tradition making pizzelle together, she said; I should ask him to join me. So I phoned him and extended the invitation, unsure whether my offer would be a comfort or a reminder of his recent loss.

Turns out he was looking for an excuse to get out. He'd just had his driving privileges restored after having a hip replacement, but he wasn't quite ready to return to work yet at the family engineering firm where he was semiretired, so we made plans for the following afternoon. He called back that evening. "Do you have all the ingredients? I can pick up some eggs."

"Oh, you don't need to do that," I said. "I've already looked. We've got plenty."

"Just thought I'd make sure. Bye."

Five minutes later the phone rang again. "What about anise? Have you got enough anise extract?"

I stretched the phone cord across the kitchen to the spice cupboard and started to rummage inside. My mother's spice cabinet is better stocked than an apothecary's dispensary, but it wouldn't hurt to double check. Behind three bottles of vanilla, a tin of poppy seeds, several half-packets of Knox Gelatine, a custard cup containing a broken strand of beads, was a bottle with no label. I unscrewed the cap and took a whiff, the scent was unmistakable.

"Mom's got a full bottle of anise," I said.

"I found a bottle up here, too. I'll bring it down, just in case."

"Good idea. See you tomorrow."

"Bye."

Thirty seconds later, and again the phone: "What about the recipe?"

I assured him the recipe was the original, written in my grandmother's very hand. And in answer to his follow-up call, yes, my mom had a pizzelle iron, but sure, he was welcome to bring Mary's iron along, too.

The next afternoon there was a knock at the back door and Joey appeared in the kitchen, a bottle of anise extract and a pizzelle iron in hand. It was uncustomarily quiet in my parents' house, with my mother off at some holiday luncheon and my father still at the office. My husband had gone skiing, we didn't have children yet, and there was an inexplicable lull in the parade of siblings, grandchildren, cousins, and neighbors who traipsed freely through the place in the course of a day. I bid him come in, took his coat, and pulled a chair up to the kitchen counter so he could sit and rest his hip. He got himself situated, then reached into his breast pocket and extracted a stained, brittle piece of paper.

"I brought Mary's recipe," he said. "In case you couldn't find yours."

I placed the sheet of paper on the counter beside the recipe from my mother's file, compared my aunt's perfect Palmer penmanship to my grandmother's unsteady hand. Yes, the recipes were one and the same. In that quaint manner of old family recipes, the ingredients were few and measured in easy proportions. In equally typical fashion, there were no directions. The recipe was little more than a grocery list intended merely to jog the memory, the procedure so basic as to need no explanation, so familiar that further elaboration would have been a waste of ink: One cup sugar, one cup oil, one cup eggs, three teaspoons anise extract, three cups flour. My aunt's recipe included a cryptic addendum: Not too hard.

Was this a directive or just a piece of commentary? Don't beat the batter too hard or the resulting cookies will be tough? Or was she reminding herself pizzelle weren't too hard to make? No matter. Both interpretations

were apropos. Making them isn't difficult, although it does take some
time. You could say a couple rosaries' worth of Hail Marys before you
used up all the batter, which is perhaps what prompted the market for
commercially packaged pizzelle in the first place.

I plugged in Mary's iron, pulled the ingredients and utensils from
their respective cupboards and drawers, and started preparing the batter.
I dumped the sugar into a large mixing bowl and whisked in the oil. In
Italian recipes, unspecified cooking oil, *olio*, means olive oil, which gives
a welcome background flavor and delicate texture to pizzelle. But until
recently olive oil was a luxury here in the United States, difficult if not
impossible to find outside cities with large Italian communities, and my
grandmother made do with whatever vegetable oil she had on hand. I'm
sure she just used Wesson.

I cracked the eggs into a one-cup measure—five of them, minus
the bit of overflow that slipped over the lip of the cup onto the counter.
I've always liked this feature of my grandmother's recipe. It evokes the
days when eggs came from a coop instead of a carton, and they came in
all sizes, not just large grade AA, twenty-four ounces to the dozen. I
whisked in the eggs and then the anise extract with its distinctive aroma.

Anise extract is distilled from the seeds of the anise plant, *Pimpi-
nella anisum*, a native of the eastern Mediterranean. An annual herb, it
has broad umbels and feathery leaves resembling Queen Anne's lace, to
which it is related. The seeds and the resulting extract have a haunting,
licorice-like flavor, and both have long been favored in Italian cooking.
The ancient Romans believed anise to be a potent aid to digestion,
and they ended their lavish banquets with dainty anise cakes in hopes
of ameliorating the offenses they had wrought against their gullets in
the preceding umpteen courses. Italians often still serve a glass of anise
liqueur at the end of heavy meals, and many of their traditional desserts
and pastries are laced with anise to settle the overtaxed stomach.

I sifted the flour over the bowl, stirred it into the batter, and as we
waited for the iron to heat I said, "Can I make you a cup of tea?"

Joey considered this for a moment. His eyes took on a mischievous
glimmer, "Have you got anything stronger?"

"Well, let's have a look," I said, warming to the idea immediately.
I crossed the kitchen and opened my parents' liquor cabinet, rubbing

my hands together expectantly. I pulled out a dusty, unopened bottle of port—a ten-year-old tawny of brilliant body and amber hue, said the label. Nothing too precious, but certainly serviceable. I poured us each a glass, we made a silent toast, and with the first sip I discovered the illicit thrill of raiding the parental liquor cabinet does not completely fade after adolescence.

The light on the pizzelle iron blinked. It was time to make cookies. Which meant, I assumed, that Joey would sit and watch while I did all the work. But he found a spoon and plopped a dollop of batter on each side of the iron and closed the lid. Half a minute later he opened the iron a hair's breadth and peeked inside. The cookies were set, but still as pale as heavy cream, so he left them to sizzle and sputter a while longer. The sweet scent of browned sugar and licorice wafted up from the griddle when he lifted the lid a second time. He grabbed a fork, holding it with thick, stiff fingers as he gingerly pried the golden cookies from the griddle and laid them on the cooling rack. He removed his glasses, cleaned them with his handkerchief so as to better inspect his handiwork. The batter had oozed slightly beyond the raised margin of each cookie—a minor cosmetic imperfection, hardly worth mentioning. But Joey furrowed his brow. He was an engineer, after all. Precision had been his life's work, and he expected no less from his cookies. "You got a knife?" he said as he spooned more batter into the iron. "Maybe you could clean those edges up while they're still soft."

I found a paring knife to trim the edges of each cookie, and a division of labor was established: He manned the iron while I wielded the knife and we sipped our port through three dozen pizzelle. One of my sisters dropped by after work, then another, and then the third with her children and a dog in tow. My mother came home, and soon the house had returned to its normal din. The pizzelle were disappearing as fast as we could make them, another round of port had been poured, and a tradition was born.

From then on my uncle Joey and I had a standing date at Christmas for pizzelle-making and port. Over the years we would try assorted measuring scoops and spoons, ever hoping to find one that doled out just the right amount of batter, and more than once he arrived with some fancy new nonstick iron he'd picked up on his travels, but we always returned to our original equipment and routine—except the winter he had to cancel a train trip across Russia and a cruise through the Panama Canal in order to make enough time to die. He was eighty by then, and had recently been diagnosed with metastatic cancer. The prognosis was for a couple months at best, and we both knew it would be his last Christmas.

I picked him up at his house because he couldn't drive, and we drank Earl Grey tea because port interfered with his meds. The usual circus of sisters and cousins and dogs dropped in, and before we knew it most of our pizzelle had been eaten. When my mother saw the paltry stack that remained she started to smolder. How could she hope to have any left for dessert at Christmas dinner? I promised her I'd make another batch the following day.

When our baking session ended I helped Joey into his coat and started to pack up his pizzelle iron.

"I could leave that here, if you want," he said, "since you'll be making more tomorrow."

"You don't mind?" I said. "I like the pattern on yours." I held the door for him. "Are you doing anything tomorrow? Want to come back again?"

"Sure," he said. He had a doctor's appointment in the morning, but the afternoon was open. "I'd like that," he nodded, and he squeezed my hand as I escorted him to the car. "It'd be nice to make them one more time."

So we made them twice that year, and now I make them twice every year: first in New Hampshire for friends and neighbors, and then in Washington to share with family. My daughter and son are now old enough to work the iron, and they have both become connoisseurs of the trimmings. In time I'll make sure to pass along the pizzelle recipe. That way they'll have an heirloom to treasure, even if I never get that stovetop iron scoured clean. Perhaps I'll never know what my grandmother's dialect term for the cookies meant, but I'll always know what they mean to me.

※

PIZZELLE

(Makes about 2 dozen)

- 1 cup sugar
- 1 cup olive oil (or grapeseed oil or salad oil)
- 1 cup eggs (about 5 large eggs)
- 3 teaspoons anise extract
- 3 cups all-purpose flour

Whisk together sugar, olive oil, eggs, and anise extract in a large bowl. Sift the flour over the batter and stir with a wooden spoon or heavy spatula until smooth.

Preheat pizzelle iron and brush with oil if needed to keep batter from sticking. Once the iron is hot, drop a tablespoon of batter into the center of each circle on the iron, close the lid, and cook about 2 minutes, until pizzelle are golden brown.

(You might have to experiment to determine the precise amount of batter and cooking time. Some irons have a light to indicate when the cookies are done, but I've found this to be only marginally accurate.)

Remove pizzelle to a cutting board, trim the edges if needed, and place on a cooling rack. Repeat until you've used up all the batter. Sipping a glass of port or a cup of tea helps to pass the time while waiting for the pizzelle to cook.

4

UNA BUONA FORCHETTA

During our final pizzelle-making session I discovered my uncle Joey was a great one for advice on things to see and do while visiting our Italian relatives. I told him I was making plans for my first extended sojourn in the Piedmont, and he started plying me with recommendations, starting with Torino. He and Mary had made numerous trips there over the years. They often stayed a few days at the Hotel Roma near the Porta Nuova train station in Torino's historic center before heading out to the countryside to see The Family in Rocca Canavese. The hotel serves grand breakfasts, including a singularly flaky brioche, which Joey informed me was the ideal prelude to a day spent walking about the city.

My uncle and aunt would spend hours ambling through Torino's baroque piazzas and arcaded streets adorned with Corinthian pillars and iron grillwork and glass ceilings. The city center has almost eleven miles of these covered walkways, commissioned over the centuries by various Savoy princes, who wished to enjoy their daily *passeggiata* even in inclement weather, sheltered from the rain and wind.

They might tour the museums, perhaps take in an exhibit at the Museo Egizio. Established in 1824 by King Carlo Felice, the museum's extensive collection of Egyptian artifacts is the largest outside Cairo, many of the treasures acquired—some would say looted—after Napoleon's campaigns in Egypt. Or they would visit the Galleria Sabauda, home to works by Italian and Flemish masters, or the charming Marionette museum, or the Automobile museum, or the Museum of Alpine History.

They liked to ride the glass elevator up some 275 feet to the top of the Mole Antonelliana to enjoy the panoramic view of the city and the surrounding snow-covered Alps. With its spire dominating the skyline, the Mole is Torino's iconic tower. Architect Alessandro Antonelli originally conceived the building as a Jewish temple, but he ran out of money and died before the project saw completion. The Mole stood empty for years, but now houses the National Museum of Cinema. My uncle and aunt would take another elevator to the top of Fiat's Lingotto Factory to see the rooftop test track. The automobile manufacturer opened the factory in 1923, and featured a unique assembly line that spiraled up five floors through the building, with raw materials entering on the ground floor and finished cars emerging on the roof for a test-drive. (The test track famously appeared in the movie *The Italian Job*, the 1969 version, with Michael Caine in a MINI Cooper.) Too bad Fiat shuttered the plant in the early eighties—watching those drivers, now that had been a thrill.

Afterward Joey and Mary might stop at Caffè al Bicerin for its namesake coffee drink, a steamy concoction of dark espresso, hot chocolate, and foamed milk, which the café has been serving since 1763. *Bicerin* is a Piedmont dialect term for "drinking glass," and glass, rather than porcelain, is the requisite material for the mug; all the better to appreciate the drink's three distinct layers. Alexandre Dumas sang its praises, as did Nietzsche and Puccini. If not a bicerin, Joey and Mary would sample chocolates from Giordano or Peyrano or Pfatisch, which are among the best chocolate shops in the city. In the early 19th century, a Torinese chocolatier patented a steam contraption that mixed ground cocoa beans with sugar, a laborious practice previously done by hand. His invention gave rise to the first chocolate bars, and confectioners from across Switzerland, Belgium, and France were soon coming to Torino to learn the chocolate maker's trade.

Before returning to their hotel Joey and Mary would tuck into Gelateria da Silvano, where the hazelnut gelato was particularly sublime. For dinner, they ate the city's classic dishes—*vitello tonnato,* an improbable yet delectable combination of cold sliced veal with a creamy tuna sauce; *tajarin,* thin, hand-cut pasta strands; *brasato di barolo,* beef braised in Barolo wine; or the grand *bollito misto*—a variety of meats, including perhaps capon and beef and sausage, simmered in broth and served with an assortment of piquant sauces. They took these meals at some of Torino's most storied restaurants. Tre Galline, Porto di Savona, or Del Cambio, where a bronze plaque still marks the favorite table of Italy's first prime minister, Count Camillo Cavour. He supped on veal sweet-breads and cockscombs while masterminding the unification of Italy in the late 19th century.

My uncle Joey was what Italians like to call *una buona forchetta*. Though little more than a bird in stature, my aunt Mary was *una buona forchetta*, too. A good fork. This is one of those expressions that loses much in translation. Minds leap to conclusions, and even if you land close to the mark, English doesn't quite have the words to get it right. Dictionaries often say it means "a hearty eater," but that implies a lack of discernment, conjures images of someone who downs burgers and fries or cheese puffs solely to stuff his gullet, but a buona forchetta has a much more discriminating palate. I've also seen the term defined as "a gourmand," which, when used correctly (though it seldom is), means someone who eats and drinks too much. Yet that is a sin a buona forchetta rarely commits. Gourmet, connoisseur, epicure—none of those are quite right, either, connoting an effete fussi-ness a buona forchetta does not possess. All these words fail to underscore the genuine appreciation of good food, be it simple or complicated, rustic or refined, that is the hallmark of a true buona forchetta. Every mamma, every cook, loves to have a buona forchetta at the table. Not to encourage gluttony, not to put on airs, but because it is so satisfying to see one's efforts in the kitchen bring such pleasure.

Which might explain why, much as Joey and Mary enjoyed their restaurant meals in Torino, they looked forward even more to the meals they ate *in famiglia*, at the homes of our Italian relatives, seated elbow to elbow at long dining tables covered with hand-crocheted linens, bottles of wine and platters of food stretching from one end to the other. My aunt Mary would often bring recipes back with her to the States and prepare them for our own extended-family meals.

Joey went on to reminisce about the meals he'd enjoyed there, in par-ticular the times he'd spent at Zia Giuseppina's table. With great detail he told me all about her ambrosial agnolotti, the delicate layers of her lasagne, and her *fritto misto,* crisp and light, never greasy. She'd stewed a chicken for him once, in a rich tomato sauce with strips of sweet red and yellow peppers. And then there was her rabbit. Joey had nearly come to tears recounting Giuseppina's rabbit, which he'd savored more than once, served on an earthenware platter at family banquets. He removed his glasses and made as though to wipe a smudge from one lens. The rosemary-imbued sauce, the tender flesh of the thigh as it gave way to the knife. It was one of the most delicious things he'd ever tasted. What he would give to be bound for Torino once more. He'd ask Giuseppina to cook a rabbit for him, he would, and he advised me to do the same. "Make sure to have a piece for me," he said. I took his words to heart, and set off for Rocca Canavese the following autumn with Giuseppina's rabbit on my list of culinary rites of passage.

Giuseppina blushed when I passed my uncle's words of praise on to her shortly after my arrival. She was in her mid-seventies then, her thick hair had turned a soft pearl-gray that complemented her delicate features. At five-foot-two or so, she had grown slightly stooped over the years, but her eyes still had a youthful brightness. We were seated at her kitchen table drinking espresso from her moka pot and I had just asked her for a cooking lesson. I had to muster the nerve, because I knew what the first step would be. She took my hands in hers. She would be happy to give me a lesson. She would have Felice slaughter a rabbit that afternoon, and we would cook it the following day. It needed to spend the night soaking in a water bath to ensure its tenderness.

Could I not watch Felice kill the rabbit?

"Ma no, cara mia," she said, and shook her head, wanting to know why I would ever want to see such an ugly sight.

Because I wanted to learn how it was done.

She thought I couldn't possibly be serious.

Yes, I said. I was serious. It interested me.

But, no.

But, yes.

Giuseppina was not interested in the slightest. Any slaughtering that needed to be done she gladly relinquished to Felice. He had strong hands and had raised rabbits since he was a boy. He could accomplish the task with minimal unpleasantry. She informed me with no small degree of pride that all the housewives in the neighborhood brought Felice their rabbits and chickens to dispatch for the table.

All the more reason I should have a lesson from him, I said. He was a recognized master. Well into retirement after a career at Fiat in Torino, Felice busied himself not only with rabbits, but a flock of chickens, an enormous garden, a few rows of fruit trees. He had a sturdy, compact frame and the weathered complexion of a farmer. He wore horn-rimmed glasses and his ash-white hair was closely cropped around an ample bald spot.

After he woke from his siesta I accompanied him to his hutches, which he had built in what had once been the horse stall underneath the living quarters of his family's 17th-century home. The afternoon sun flooded the room as we opened the door, but the only other source of light was what filtered dimly through a small, screened window. This seemed to me a rather heartless arrangement until Felice explained that rabbits, being underground dwellers, prefer darkness to light. Their name in Italian, *coniglio*, stems from the Latin *cuniculus*, which once referred to the rabbit's earthen tunnels, but came to mean the animal itself.

Felice pointed out his two matronly does, his chunky piebald buck, and about ten offspring of varying ages and sizes. He opened a cage and hoisted out a particularly robust one by the ears, then grabbed onto its feet, stretching it out to its full length. He let it dangle upside down as he reached to a nearby bench where lay the requisite implements of the abattoir. After selecting a small wooden baton, he gave a solid rap to the nape of the animal's head and it instantly fell limp. Felice exchanged the club for a thin-bladed knife to slit the rabbit's throat, and as scarlet blood drained onto the bare earth it gave a few reflexive twitches, then ceased moving. All the while the rabbit's brethren nibbled Swiss chard stems and dozed with eyes half-closed, oblivious to the fate of their hutch-mate.

But the cat sure came running. She sidled up to Felice, gave a coquettish rub against his ankles and purred expectantly. Felice reached for two metal S-hooks that had leather lashes attached, tied one to each hind foot, then suspended the rabbit from two nails on the wall, belly out and feet splayed. After a few strokes with his knife on a whetstone he slit through the fur from stern to stem, then cut across laterally to each "knee" and "elbow" joint. He slipped off the skin effortlessly, like peeling back a glove, and with a quick slice to each forefoot the hide fell to the ground. The next incision went down through the belly cavity, and Felice extracted the entrails just as Giuseppina appeared in the doorway.

She handed me a metal bowl to collect the liver and heart for the meat sauce she had simmering upstairs on the stovetop. Felice cut the rabbit's feet away at the S-hook and tossed an unidentifiable morsel to the cat, who dropped her demure act and charged for it greedily. As I watched her slink off to enjoy her tidbit under the rose hedge I noticed the bowl had grown warm in my hands from the rabbit's residual body heat. Within five minutes Felice had cleaned up all traces of the deed, and our dinner lay nestled in its bowl of water in the sink for the night.

The next morning Giuseppina gave me pause with the news that our rabbit had been six months old and it weighed over six pounds. She all but apologized for cooking it up so young—it needed to get much bigger before it reached its true potential. Yet according to my cookbooks those were alarming numbers. The optimal rabbit for the table is eight to ten weeks of age, and weighs two-and-a-half pounds, three pounds tops. With advancing age and size a rabbit grows tough and dry proportionally. One look at our hefty Methuselah and I wondered what sort of magic Giuseppina worked with that water bath to make it tender. I asked her about my cookbooks' rule of thumb, and said you'd never find a rabbit like hers in an American market.

That, broke in Felice, was because people have grown too lazy to raise good rabbits any more. He looked up from the paper he'd been reading at the kitchen table. When you feed a rabbit a prisoner's diet of nothing more than water and processed grain pellets, you can expect its flavor to reflect its rations accordingly. And his rabbits? For them he grew corn and mustard greens in his garden. In spring he dug them dandelions and clover. Giuseppina fed them cabbage leaves and carrot peelings and apple cores from the kitchen. Felice grew more animated, spoke more rapidly as he outlined their diet. There was a time, he continued, when everyone raised animals this way, but now people just toss the poor wretches two scoops of pellets and wash their hands of them until tomorrow, arrivederci, ciao. With that Felice brushed his hands together dismissively as if ridding them of dust, and I realized that not just in America, home of bland tomatoes and insipid poultry, has technology exacted its toll on flavor.

His argument did not surprise me. Farmers have long known that an animal's diet influences the quality of its meat. The famous prosciutto of Parma has a uniquely nutty taste and velvety texture because the pigs from which it is made enjoy a diet that includes whey from the making of Parmigiano cheese. Bretons in France prize their *agneau prés sales*, or salt-meadow sheep. They pasture their flocks along the seashore, where the ocean mist permeates the grass with salt, and the lambs acquire an uncommon piquancy, pre-salted from the inside out. Likewise the people of Provence appreciate the distinctive flavor of their local wild rabbits, which feed on the thyme and rosemary that grow on the hillsides. The award for the most discerning French palate should perhaps go to Louis XVIII, who supposedly could tell the origins and diet of any wild hare in his kingdom, merely by the scent of it frying in the pan. I don't feel obliged to believe this claim. If his majesty declared with a whiff that here was a hare that had once munched watercress in the Perigord, who would dare contradict him?

As Felice spoke I watched Giuseppina pat the rabbit dry, joint it at the fore and hind legs with poultry shears, and cut the saddle cross-wise into two-inch lengths. She set half the pieces aside for the next day's meal, which drove home the immense size of the creature: most recipes tell you a rabbit serves three to four people, and Giuseppina got double the yield out of hers.

She set a heavy sauté pan over a lively flame, coated the bottom of the pan with olive oil and a spoonful of butter, then browned the pieces on both sides, along with two peeled whole cloves of garlic. She removed the rabbit pieces to a plate, added another spoonful of olive oil to the pan, and sautéed a small diced onion and a large sprig each of chopped rosemary and parsley until soft. She added salt and pepper, then a healthy pour of white wine, scraping up the browned bits from the bottom of the pan with a wooden spoon. She nestled the rabbit pieces back into the simmering pot and let signor coniglio simmer lazily, covered, turning the pieces once or twice here, adding a splash of water there, until the meat became tender to the pierce of a knife, about an hour and a half. A less gargantuan rabbit, I made mental note, would want only an hour. Toward the end of the cooking she removed the lid to let the pan juices thicken slightly.

At one o'clock Felice came inside from a morning spent harvesting corn. A few minutes later their unmarried son Giorgio returned from his appointments in the city, and we sat down to the midday meal. It seemed our rabbit was cause for celebration, for although it was a weekday, we ate with all the sumptuous festivity of a Sunday dinner. We started with paper-thin slices of prosciutto di Parma and Giuseppina's sweet peppers preserved with olive oil, wine vinegar, and tuna. Next came *agnolotti con sugo di carne*, a delicate veal and spinach stuffed pasta specialty of the Piedmont, which Giuseppina sauced lightly with the meat sauce she had prepared the previous afternoon. I couldn't refuse a second spoonful, nor did I decline when Felice poured me a second glass of wine.

Then Giuseppina brought the rabbit to the table. She had transferred it steaming and glistening to an earthenware platter, perhaps the very dish of my uncle's reminiscences. She served me up a double helping, a foreleg and a slice from the saddle. Then she nudged a garlic clove out of the way with her ladle and spooned the pan juices over the meat. Giorgio passed me a bowl of butter-glazed turnips from Felice's garden.

A savory aroma of herbs and wine had infused the rabbit and I inhaled deeply as I raised knife and fork. Any notions I'd had about tough old rabbits evaporated as my knife slid in cleanly, and the meat slipped effortlessly from the bone. The flavor was decidedly more pronounced than chicken, but milder than wild game, and without the stringiness that often accompanies it. I lacked the superlatives even in English to do it justice, so I said only, *"Delizioso!"* The three of them nodded and Giuseppina beamed, and I understood full well how her coniglio had brought tears to Joey's eyes. I said as much, and Giuseppina sighed. That Joey, she said, now there was a buona forchetta.

※

CONIGLIO AL VINO BIANCO
E ROSMARINO

BRAISED RABBIT WITH WHITE WINE AND ROSEMARY

(Serves 4)

- 1 rabbit, about 3 pounds, cut into serving pieces
- 2 tablespoons kosher salt
- 1 tablespoon red wine vinegar
- water, enough to cover rabbit
- 2 tablespoons olive oil, plus additional, if needed
- 2 tablespoons butter
- 1 small onion, diced
- 1 large sprig fresh rosemary, chopped
- 1 large sprig fresh parsley, chopped
- salt and freshly ground pepper
- 1 cup white wine
- about 1 cup meat broth or water, as needed

The day before serving, place rabbit pieces in stainless bowl, sprinkle with salt, drizzle with vinegar, and add enough water to cover. Refrigerate overnight.

The next day, remove rabbit pieces from water and pat dry. Heat 2 tablespoons olive oil and butter in a heavy sauté pan or Dutch oven over medium-high heat. Place rabbit pieces in pan and sear on both sides until nicely browned, about 10 minutes total. Remove meat to a plate, add more olive oil if needed, and sauté onion, rosemary, and parsley until soft, about 5 minutes. Season with salt and pepper, then deglaze pan with white wine, scraping up the browned bits from the bottom of the pan with a wooden spoon. Return the rabbit pieces to the pan and adjust the heat to maintain a gentle simmer. Let cook, covered, for about 1 hour, until meat is tender when pierced with a knife. Check the progress occasionally, adding broth or water if the braising liquid is cooking away. Remove the lid for the last 10 minutes of braising to allow the pan juices to thicken slightly. Transfer to a heated platter and serve.

5

AN AMERICAN RABBITRY

Once we'd had our fill of rabbit, Giuseppina brought out a bowl of purple figs and russet pears. She made coffee and served it around. After the meal, Felice retired to his room for a nap. Giorgio headed back to work and Giuseppina let me help her do the dishes. It was a significant gesture, a sign that after several weeks I had finally succeeded in passing from houseguest to family.

As I dried cups and saucers and handed them to Giuseppina to be put away she said she'd been thinking. She had an idea. She told me the rabbits she raised with Felice enjoyed local renown. She took great pleasure in making gifts of them to friends who had since moved into Torino and could no longer raise rabbits of their own. She happened to have another rabbit coming right along. Felice could butcher it for me on the morning of my departure, and if she wrapped it well, I could pack it in my suitcase on the plane. I could cook it at home the next night for dinner, wouldn't that be nice?

Tempting as it sounded, I had to decline. It might not survive the six-hour layover in Amsterdam, I explained. Besides, one of the customs agents might seize it, and I couldn't bear the thought of some stranger enjoying her rabbit for dinner. She gave a reluctant nod. Especially not a customs agent, she said. *Peccato*. What a shame.

So when it came time to return to New Hampshire I slipped only six bottles of Barolo, a bottle of grappa, three liters of olive oil, half a kilo of dried porcini mushrooms, a bag of coffee beans, and a jar each of chestnut honey, marinated artichokes, preserved peppers, and fig jam into my bags. (Ah, those were the days, back before baggage fees and weight limits.) Instead of a butchered rabbit I went away with Giuseppina's recipe, a vivid taste memory, and a firm resolve to find a source for rabbits near home.

I quickly learned you can't just pick one up from your butcher; there simply isn't a market for them. There was a time during World War II—when victory gardens were all the rage and meat was rationed—when the government encouraged the consumption of rabbit as a patriotic act. Rabbits could be raised at minimal expense in backyard hutches, which meant more beef to feed the troops overseas. But after the war Americans dismantled their hutches and went back to eating steaks and burgers without a second thought.

A chef where I once worked tried putting stuffed loin of rabbit on the menu, but it languished there unordered, so he had to pull it off. "Americans!" he said in exasperation. They have a problem with rabbit, and the problem is this: No matter how you slice it, no matter how you sauté or fricassee it, a rabbit will always be a bunny. Braise a rabbit and carve it at the table? Few Americans can even consider the idea without conjuring up images of Thumper or Peter Cottontail. With its docile eyes, its satiny ears, you would need a cold, cold heart indeed to consider a rabbit in comestible terms.

Anthropomorphism, that's what makes us balk. All those cute celebrity bunnies have caused us to humanize the delicious rabbit, rendering it inedible. If we could only stop ascribing our uniquely human characteristics and motivations to an animal that occupies a much lower branch on the phylogenetic tree, we'd all be eating rabbit twice a week. Though as explanations go, it turns out the cuddle factor barely scrapes the surface. An aversion to rabbit on the menu has deep and far-flung roots.

For some diners, the reason stretches back to the pages of Leviticus. There the Lord tells Moses that the hare, though it chews the cud, does not have hooves and is therefore unclean for the Israelites. Actually, hares should be doubly banned, since not only do they lack hooves, they aren't really ruminants, lacking the multiple stomachs required for chewing cud.

That the Lord confused his own handiwork should make taxonomists take heart, for they have had their share of trouble classifying rabbits. For the longest time they lumped them in with rodents in light of their oversized, ever-growing front teeth. This did little for the rabbit's status in culinary circles, whose members have generally eschewed eating rat or their sundry kin (though the ancient Romans considered dormouse a delicacy, and Magellan's crew paid a half a ducat apiece for mice when they ran out of provisions after rounding the tip of South America). Then zoologists discovered that rabbits, hares, and the guinea pig–like pika distinguish themselves not only by their front incisors but by the location of their scrotum in front of the penis rather than behind it, and the group was granted a classification order of its very own: the Lagomorpha. Apparently female Lagomorphs rate only as honorary members of the order, lacking as they do the pertinent anatomical distinction.

Together the rabbit and hare make up the family Leporidae. As for the difference between the two, there has been ample confusion about that as well. Hares are born well-furred with eyes open, while rabbits are born naked and with eyes shut, except the swamp rabbit of the southeastern United States, which enters the world with fur. The jackrabbit, too, first appears with fur, but only because it is really a hare. Platina, the 15th-century Vatican librarian and cookbook author, wrote that hares are of two types: the larger, which live above ground, and the smaller, called rabbits, which live primarily underground in warrens. This seems as valid a distinction as any, certainly better than my own premise—that rabbits live in cages and hares live in the wild—and no worse than what the zoologists managed to come up with.

The European rabbit (*Oryctolagus cuniculus*) from which domesticated rabbits descended is native to the Iberian Peninsula. The Romans introduced it throughout the continent; they kept rabbits in walled gardens and thought them a delicacy. Because the Catholic Church did not consider unborn rabbits to be meat, they were a food that could be eaten during Lent, and monks came to raise rabbits for the table. Tending a rabbit warren turned out to be a very productive enterprise, as rabbits can have six litters a year, with up to a dozen young per litter. But their propensity to breed, well, like rabbits, is what turned them from a delicacy to a scourge, for throughout the centuries they managed to escape their confines, occasionally with devastating results, tunneling up the earth underneath the ground, and stripping the vegetation above it. During the Middle Ages, French nobles imported rabbits for the hunt, containing them in private game preserves. The rabbits dug their way free and spread to such an extent that King Louis XVI ultimately granted permission for even peasants to hunt them. And once peasants could hunt and eat rabbits, it was only a matter of time before the nobility turned up their noses at rabbit meat. They would not deign to eat the vermin wreaking havoc across the royal grounds.

The 17th-century restaurant critic Grimod de la Reynière begged genteel hosts to bar it from the table if they had the slightest concern for their reputations. In Italy rabbit was long considered too rustic for refined palates, though it was not without its champions. The 19th-century Florentine cookbook author Pellegrino Artusi could not understand why his fellow countrymen refused to set aside their prejudices against it. Similarly, the Italian civil servant, physician, and gastronome Alberto Denti di Pirajno considered the gentry's disdain for rabbit an aberration in the collective Italian sense of taste; in his 1950 collection of recipes, *Il gastronomo educato,* he wrote that rabbit meat has two distinct flavors, depending on how the animal is slaughtered: Rabbits killed by a blow to the back of the neck have a wild, gamy flavor, while those dispatched by slitting the throat taste like chicken.

Paupers, meanwhile, could not afford to be so particular. With their empty stomachs in mind they took full advantage of the rabbit's remarkable fertility. With a steady supply of rabbit braising in the pot or turning on the spit, they had a lean, flavorful, and economical source of protein ready to hand. Today their recipes have become classics throughout Europe. *Lapin à la moutarde. Hasenpheffer. Paella con conejo. Coniglio al cacciatore.*

That commercial rabbit breeders in the United States have failed to tap this procreative potential is not for lack of trying. They would have rabbit burger in every freezer and rabbit nuggets at the drive-thru if they could. Unfortunately *O. cuniculus* obstinately refuses to thrive under the sweatshop conditions that have worked so well with its accommodating barnyard mate, the chicken. Instead it needs spacious quarters, fresh air, and attentive care to maintain its vigor in captivity. Which adds an ironic corollary to my original hypothesis: Indeed, Americans do not eat rabbits today because they seem to us too human. But only by raising them humanely can we eat them at all.

And that's really why you won't find rabbit at your average supermarket. My organic food co-op occasionally carries frozen rabbit from an upscale purveyor who ships it from hundreds of miles away, but they sell it at a prohibitive price. So I started asking around, checked at the feed store and a couple farmers' markets, but to no avail. Finally, I called my county extension agent, who sent me a brochure listing a host of New Hampshire farmers who sold everything from eggs and cheese to maple syrup, emus, llamas, and cashmere goats. I found a listing for someone who raised rabbits a few towns from me and I gave the number a call.

"Rabbits? Why yes, I've got rabbits," said a woman's husky voice. "Cute little things, no bigger'n a kitten. And tame. I've been raising them inside. They'll eat right outta your hand."

"I see. Well . . . I'm not actually looking for a pet," I said. "I'm trying to find rabbits for cooking."

"Oh, for cooking! Heavens yes! I've got those out back," she said. "You sure called at the right time. I've got an order for the whole lot of 'em next week." Her words reminded me of a conversation I'd had with a nine-year-old girl whose grandmother cleaned a restaurant where I once cooked in rural Vermont. Mandy would sit and chat with me in the kitchen while her grandmother vacuumed the dining rooms before dinner service. One day she mentioned that her pet rabbit had just had babies. "You want one?" she asked. "They're real cute. They taste good, too." I was struck by the girl's ability to simultaneously consider a rabbit both pet and food. Now, here on the other end of the phone, was a woman who regarded the rabbit as dual-purpose as well. It was a rather practical convention.

The woman explained that the local volunteer fire department was hosting its annual wild-game supper the following weekend. It was their biggest fundraiser of the year. They would have venison and partridge, maybe pheasant, even moose. They'd put in an order for as many rabbits as she had on hand. She hadn't given them an exact number, but she figured they wouldn't miss one or two. How many would I like?

"Two," I told her. I realized I'd forgotten one key detail. "Um . . . will they still be, you know, alive?"

"Landsakes, no. We'll get them slaughtered and dressed Thursday morning and they'll be all ready for you Thursday afternoon."

I thanked her and said how delighted I was to have discovered her, how I'd canvassed the area for a source for rabbits and all but given up my search. We both found it a pity that more Americans didn't eat rabbit; they didn't know what they were missing. Even if you managed to find it at a supermarket, she informed me, it was nearly always frozen, cut into pieces, and packaged in some cardboard box. Who knew how long it had been sitting there? Even worse, who knew what you were really getting?

Her comments called to mind an open meat market I once visited in the Testaccio neighborhood of Rome. I watched butchers lay out cuts of lamb and veal and kid on marble tables. Plucked chickens hung by their feet on racks for display, along with rows of rabbits that dangled with their fluffy white cottontails still attached to prove they were not cats. Surely butchers wouldn't foist cat off on unsuspecting buyers here in America, I thought. Probably not. American cities don't have Rome's supply of strays.

The woman gave me directions to her house, and a week later I found myself twenty miles from home, turning onto a rutted gravel driveway that spliced a stand of birch and maple woods. The driveway brought me to a weathered yellow trailer that rested on a sunken foundation. Nestled around the trailer were assorted heaps of bricks, spent tires, empty barrels, coils of barbed wire fencing. In the front lawn a rusty Dodge pickup without wheels was perched on cinder blocks, a white pine sapling springing up from its open front hood. A muscle-bound, mottled-brown dog tore up to my car, braced itself on stiff legs, and met me with a rumbling growl and strip of fur bristling down the length of its back.

"Don't worry, he's friendly," a voice called from the front door. A woman in her forties wearing denim overalls and a sleeveless blouse stepped out onto the porch and beckoned me toward her. "He's all bark, that one." She motioned me forward and brushed a strand of dishwater blond hair behind her ear. "You here for the rabbits? C'mon up."

I opened my door a tentative inch and the dog began to bark feverishly. Drawing in my breath I mustered a meek, "Down, boy," which immediately had him growling again, though he reluctantly retreated and let me make my way to the house.

The woman introduced herself as Mrs. Jarvis. We exchanged greetings, and she ushered me inside. "Your rabbits are all ready," she said. "'Scuse me just a sec, I got 'em back here in the fridge for you." She disappeared into the kitchen, calling over her shoulder, "Pardon the mess."

My eyes scanned the room. With the exception of a path to the sofa I could not find a bare inch of space in the whole place. There were stacks of magazines and books from floor to ceiling, boxes of empty cans and bottles, bundles of newspapers, baskets of laundry. On the countertops and tables lay heaps of stuffed animals, balls of yarn, tea cups, broken radios. Piles of letters and a set of cast iron skillets occupied the seats of the dining room chairs.

"Meant to get the place cleaned up," she said from the kitchen, "but I haven't had a minute to myself all day. Been up since dawn butchering—had twenty of 'em to do, and I don't like it one bit, but it's got to be done." I could hear the refrigerator door open and shut, a rattling of utensils. "Then I got my mother and my mother-in-law to nurse," she continued. "They both had strokes."

As if my eyes had needed the prompt against the background clutter, I suddenly pulled into focus two white-haired women slumped motionless in wheelchairs in the back corners of the room. I nodded to each of them and smiled timidly, unsure if they were even aware of my presence. I felt beads of perspiration on the back of my neck and a wave of panic swept over me. What was I doing there? With their sanitary plastic packaging, those gourmet rabbits from New York suddenly seemed like the better choice, no matter the price.

Just then Mrs. Jarvis reentered the room carrying two ziplock bags. She had my rabbits in hand, pink-fleshed, haunches curled up in the fetal position, no cottontail attached. I opened my wallet, pulled out a few bills and paid her. She said she'd have a new batch ready in six weeks, I should give her a call. She also had eggs, and fryers at the end of the summer, not to mention quail. She had geese, too, but they were just pets. Did I want to see them? She kept them just a few steps out back.

I hesitated. After seeing the house, perhaps it was better not to know the conditions under which her animals lived. But I followed her out the door, past a collapsing shed, past more tires and scrap plywood and railroad ties to a henhouse. Although constructed of the faded lumber and chicken wire I had expected, I could not have been more surprised at the sight of it. It was immaculate. Spacious and airy, its only odor was the pine scent of the fresh sawdust that covered the ground. A fat gray goose paraded across the yard to Mrs. Jarvis and she tickled its neck. A Leghorn rooster with sleek white plumage and a brilliant red cockscomb strutted up to the gate while his harem of six laying hens and a brood of chicks tussled over a bucket full of lettuce leaves and carrot peelings. Mrs. Jarvis pulled back a sheet that protected a separate, massive hutch from the sun. Inside were half a dozen rabbits, bright-eyed, alert, and plump, all of them. One of the does looked our way, twitched her nose, then sidled up to the edge of the enclosure to sip crystal-clear water from the spout of a glass feeder. Another nibbled lazily on some strawberry tops. They were healthy, robust animals, well-cared for by any measure.

Mrs. Jarvis walked me back to my car. Her dog lay snoring underneath the porch. It summoned the energy only to open its eyes and give a half-hearted thump of its tail as I walked by. Somehow the trailer with its clutter inside and out now seemed not so much dirty to me as overburdened with possessions. The anxiety that had seized me dissipated, disappeared altogether. In an age when the notion of sound animal husbandry is meaningless to most Americans, I had found a shining example of it, albeit in an unlikely spot. I reached to shake Mrs. Jarvis's hand as I said goodbye and told her she would be hearing from me again soon. I stepped into the car and placed my parcel on the seat beside me. Felice and Giuseppina would have approved. No doubt about it, I was headed home with rabbits fit even for their table.

CONIGLIO IN PEPERONATA

BRAISED RABBIT WITH RED AND YELLOW BELL PEPPERS

(Serves 4 to 6)

This is my version of a dish I sampled at a dinner party while in Rocca Canavese. Piedmontese cooks often prepare chicken in peperonata as well.

- 1 rabbit, about 3 pounds, cut into serving pieces
- 2 tablespoons kosher salt, plus additional, to taste
- 1 tablespoon red wine vinegar
- water, enough to cover rabbit
- 2 tablespoons olive oil, plus additional 3 tablespoons for sautéing peppers
- 1 tablespoon butter
- 1 cup white wine
- 2 red bell peppers and 1 yellow pepper, trimmed and cut into half-inch squares
- ½ onion, diced
- 1 clove garlic, peeled and left whole
- 1 sprig fresh rosemary, finely chopped
- salt and freshly ground pepper, to taste
- 1½ cups canned crushed tomatoes
- ½ cup water, if needed

The day before serving, place rabbit pieces in a stainless bowl, sprinkle with salt, drizzle with vinegar, and add enough water to cover. Refrigerate overnight.

The next day, remove rabbit pieces from water, pat dry, and season lightly with salt. Heat 2 tablespoons olive oil and butter in a heavy sauté pan or

Dutch oven over medium-high heat. Place rabbit pieces in pan and sear on both sides until nicely browned, about 10 minutes total.

Deglaze the pan with wine, lower the heat to maintain a gentle simmer, cover, and let cook gently, about 30 minutes, adding spoonfuls of water if the cooking liquid is evaporating too quickly. (Remove from the heat if you finish this step before the peppers are done cooking.)

MEANWHILE, PREPARE THE PEPERONATA:

In a separate skillet, heat 3 tablespoons olive oil over high heat. Add the bell peppers, onion, whole clove of garlic, rosemary, salt, and freshly ground pepper, and stir to coat vegetables in oil. Reduce heat to low and let simmer until peppers are softened, about 10 minutes, stirring occasionally. Add the crushed tomatoes, stir to combine, cover, and let simmer about 20 more minutes.

Add the rabbit pieces along with the pan juices to the simmering pepper mixture, tucking the rabbit into the sauce. Stir, cover, and continue to simmer, 20 more minutes, or until the rabbit is tender when pierced with a knife. Transfer to a warm platter and serve.

6

EAT YOUR TURNIPS

The buttered turnips that Zia Giuseppina served alongside her braised rabbit made for a fabulous dish in their own right—ever so sweet, their edges lightly caramelized from long, slow simmering. Still, a meal of rabbit and turnips! That is a hard sell for most Americans. Indeed, if rabbit is an underappreciated meat, the virtues of the turnip are equally unsung. Mere mention of the turnip makes most adults wrinkle their noses. Few children have even heard of it because so many parents won't have it in the house. It has long been dismissed as a poor man's food, fit for ploughmen and sharecroppers, suitable for their oxen and swine, but not good enough for diners with a refined palate.

Maybe a bad family pedigree is to blame. The turnip, *Brassica rapa*, belongs to the Mustard family, along with other similarly snubbed vegetables like cabbages and Brussels sprouts, cauliflower and broccoli. Although the origins of these domesticated crops have eluded scholars, most believe they are native to Asia or Europe. The whole lot has been categorically dismissed as ill-suited for those with a delicate digestion. The 17th-century English herbalist Nicholas Culpeper deemed them as windy a food as could be eaten, unless you ate bagpipes or bellows. (Broccoli might once have aspired to a loftier place in the vegetal hierarchy, served from copper saucepans with hollandaise sauce, but it got its comeuppance when President George H. W. Bush banned it from the White House table.) The brassicas are high in fiber and complex carbohydrates, and some people do find them easier to digest than others, though the distinction has nothing to do with social class. Rather, it tends to be a matter of familiarity. Once a body becomes accustomed to Brassica plants it usually digests them readily.

Adding further insult, the turnips and other brassicas contain sulfur compounds that break down when boiled and release hydrogen sulfide into the air, the same gas that gives rotten eggs their characteristic odor. The older the turnip and the longer you cook it, the smellier it becomes. I think it is this last point that has ruined so many people's appetite for the vegetable. During their youth they were traumatized by a surfeit of smelly old turnips, boiled mercilessly, English boardinghouse style, and they've never managed to recover.

Young turnips given a light touch are another story. My grandmother grew turnips in her garden and I ate them willingly as a child. My mother sliced them up raw and added them to crudité platters when she and my father entertained. Stark white, crisp, and mild with a pleasant peppery note, I used to sneak them from the tray before the guests arrived. My mother also slipped turnips into her beef stew, where they soaked up the flavors of the simmering meat and added an earthy essence of their own. Or she tossed them with olive oil and rosemary and roasted them in a hot oven with potatoes, carrots, onions—any root vegetable she could find in the pantry—to make one of our family's favorite winter side dishes. Years later I cooked in a restaurant in Vermont where we served sautéed turnips glazed with maple syrup alongside roast duck breast, giving a New England imprint to the classic French *canard aux navets*. One night a customer ordered the dish, but asked could he please substitute potatoes or rice—anything, for that matter—for the turnips? I must have been feeling rather churlish that evening, because I refused and sent the plate out with its rightful turnips. The server reported back a few minutes later with compliments. I made a convert out of that diner. To his astonishment, but not mine, he found he actually enjoyed eating his turnips.

Plutarch tells a story, perhaps untrue, of the celebrated Roman military hero Manius Curius Dentatus, who was approached by a delegation of Samnites between one of his many battles. The Samnites arrived at his home bearing gifts of gold and silver, hoping to buy Dentatus's loyalty against the Romans. They found him cooking turnips in the embers on his hearth, and when he refused their offers they knew it was pointless to press him. A man satisfied with a meal of turnips had no need of their riches. The late–Baroque era painter Jacopo Amigoni depicted the scene in a canvas that now hangs in the Museum Bredius in The Hague. The story is said to illustrate the general's frugal and incorruptible nature. What if instead it underscores the true value of the turnip? Why else would a man as great as Dentatus prize it above a chest of precious metals?

At Giuseppina's table I discovered a trove of recipes and folklore surrounding the vegetable that made me appreciate it even more. Turnips, she said with a knowing nod, were more than just tasty; they were nutritious and therapeutic as well. When she boiled them, she saved the water for soup—it was full of vitamins to make you strong. (She's right. Turnips are a good source of vitamin C and trace minerals, which leach into the cooking water and create a rich, nutritious broth.) To treat a cold, she instructed, peel and thinly slice a raw turnip, then layer the slices in a bowl, sprinkling sugar between the layers. Leave the bowl for at least eight hours and collect the syrup that has formed. Take two spoonsful, morning, noon, and night, and the cold will go away. It never fails, she assured me.

I'd never heard that before. I told her I'd give it a try next time I had a sore throat or runny nose, though I knew I would rely on my usual Advil Cold and Sinus tablets instead.

Felice grew those turnips in his garden. They were an old variety, he said, cultivated throughout the Piedmont and the Po River Plain. He motioned to a wire basket full of turnips on the drainboard by the kitchen sink. They awaited cleaning, with bright green tops still attached and moist soil clinging to the taproots. They were smooth and round, but flat like river rocks, maybe three inches in diameter and an inch high. Each turnip was white as porcelain at its base with a rosy-purple veneer on top—the part that had grown above ground. Felice had a twenty-foot row of them still in the garden. Before the first frost in a few weeks he would lift them from the ground and store them for the winter in the cantina.

I told Felice I had never had much luck with turnips in my vegetable garden at home. A cool weather crop, turnips need seventy days or so to mature. Most gardeners sow them in March for harvest in May. But New Hampshire springs are just too short. We can have snow on the ground into April and I often can't work the soil for planting until the first week in May. Summer arrives just as the seedlings are starting to flourish, but before the bulbs enlarge. When the heat sets in, the plants turn their energy to producing seeds, and whatever spindly taproot has had a chance to develop becomes pithy and bitter.

Although Piedmont winters are not nearly as harsh as those of northern New England, the region is cold by Italian standards and it gets its fair share of snow. Felice was well versed in the peculiarities of coaxing produce out of the ground under challenging conditions. He embarked on a series of questions in crop management. How was my soil? Did I enrich it well? What about water? Did the garden get at least an inch of rain a week? And did I thin the seedlings? Crowding only makes them bolt and go to seed.

Yes, yes, and yes. Every fall I shoveled in a thick layer of composted manure from the dairy farmer up the road. I depended on Mother Nature for the water, but we usually got a couple good, soaking rains a week; during dry spells I dragged out the garden hose. And I tried to space the plants about four inches apart.

His diagnostic interview complete, Felice sat quietly for a moment, pondering his prescription, then gave me a rather unconventional lesson in turnip horticulture for the cold-climate gardener. I should skip spring turnips altogether and plant an autumn crop, he advised. That way I would miss the summer heat, and the plants would thrive in the cooler fall weather. I should sow the seed during the first week in August, but only on days with an R.

Excuse me? Days with an R?

Yes. *Martedì*, for example, or *mercoledì*, but not *sabato* or *domenica*.

This was an unexpected piece of advice. I'd heard of planting turnips and other underground crops during the waning moon. Old-time gardeners claim the dimming light makes plants draw their energy downward, encouraging the development of robust, flavorful roots. And I knew to eat oysters in months with an R. The adage dates to the days before refrigeration when you could get sick from eating a spoiled oyster during the warm stretch from May to August. During my first kitchen job, when my duties included shucking upward of two hundred oysters a day, I learned the advice still holds, though for a different reason. Warmer ocean temperatures in late spring and summer make the hermaphroditic oyster spawn. Such fervent lovemaking renders it physically spent. Instead of plump and toothsome with a fresh, briny taste, it becomes flaccid and insipid. It cooks up okay, a dusting of breadcrumbs and a dip in hot oil for an oyster fry will mask the loss of flavor, but it is quite lackluster served raw on the half-shell.

But planting on days of the week with an R? It seemed to me some sort of hybrid theory or lesser-known corollary. Why? What did the day of the week have to do with anything?

Felice had no idea.

And which language should I use? Back in America should I speak Italian or English to determine the day? He did not know the answer to that question either. To be safe, we decided I should sow my seeds on a Friday, *venerdì*, since it was the only day in the week with an R in both languages. He went to his garden shed and came back with a handful of seeds, which he sealed in a small manila envelope and labeled *rapa piemontese* in his shaky italic script.

I brought his seeds home with me and the next summer I planted them in my garden with such success I've followed his instructions ever since. When my seed catalogs come I order *rapa di Milano coletto* or Milan Purple Top seeds each year. Milan isn't part of the Piedmont, but it's just across the Po River Plain, and the heirloom turnips have the same flat root and coloring as the ones Felice grew. I don't know whether the Rs have anything to do with it or not, but the first week of August is a good window for planting in my area. And Felice's rule is much easier to remember than the only similar one I could find in my research, from an article in the British periodical Hardwicke's *Science-Gossip* of 1874, "Turnips will thrive wonderfully when sown as many days after the festival of Neptune as the moon was old when the first snow fell the previous winter." Turns out the author cribbed from Pliny, who added the sower should preferably be stripped. This instruction doesn't seem terribly feasible for the modern-day gardener. Pliny also suggested offering up a prayer: "I sow this for myself, and for my neighbors," which is as nice a sentiment as any.

Most years I get a beautiful crop of sweet young turnips by early October. When the weather doesn't cooperate—too much rain or an early frost, as happens some seasons, I still enjoy an ample supply of lush turnip greens, which some nutritionists claim are the best part of the plant anyway. A good source of calcium and vitamin C, even my kids will eat them, braised with bacon and onions. I'm teaching them early to appreciate the virtues of the turnip.

RAPE STUFATE AL TIMO

STEWED TURNIPS WITH THYME

(Serves 4 to 6)

- 2 pounds small to medium-sized turnips
- 3 tablespoons butter
- 2 large sprigs fresh thyme
- salt and freshly ground pepper
- pinch sugar
- ½ cup chicken broth

Peel the turnips, slice in half lengthwise, then place cut-side down and slice thinly. Heat the butter in a large sauté pan over medium-high heat. Add the turnips and thyme sprigs and sauté about 5 minutes, until lightly browned. Season with salt, pepper, and a pinch of sugar, then add chicken broth. Cover pan, adjust heat to maintain a gentle simmer, and cook until turnips are tender, about 20 to 30 minutes, stirring occasionally. Remove lid for the last few minutes of cooking to allow liquid to reduce slightly. Discard the thyme stems (most of the leaves will have fallen off during cooking) and serve.

7

TWO REMEDIES FOR COLD

On a subsequent visit to Rocca Canavese I encountered Giuseppina's turnip syrup firsthand. Actually it was my cousin Catterina's turnip syrup, and it was but one weapon among many in her arsenal of home remedies against the common cold. I was staying with Catterina and her family, helping out in their bakery. It was autumn again, a foggy, damp stretch in November. A week had passed since my arrival, and like clockwork I had come down with a stubborn cold. My head ached and my chest had seized tight with congestion. Colds and international travel often went hand in hand with me in those days before children—either my body couldn't withstand the barrage of commingling germs found in the cramped quarters of a plane, or, jet-lagged and fatigued, I buckled before the first stray microbe that came along once the plane had landed. (Ever since becoming a mother with two viral vectors bringing a steady stream of pathogens into the house, I have built up my resistance.)

Catterina heard me break into a fit of coughing at the breakfast table. *Dio mio!* she said. I sounded like an old smoker with emphysema. She took off for the cantina. All she needed was a turnip, she called out over her shoulder; she'd have me feeling better in no time. I heard rustling in the other room, the opening and closing of cabinets, and a few minutes later she returned with the turnip. She sliced it up, layered it with sugar in a bowl, and left it on the kitchen counter for the day. That evening she served me *pasta in brodo*, tiny squares of egg pasta floating in a rich poultry broth and garnished with a shower of grated Parmigiano. An Italian interpretation of chicken noodle soup, I suppose—eat this, you'll feel better. It is an international cold remedy *per eccellenza*.

After dinner, Catterina called me over to inspect the turnip bowl. The syrup was ready, she pronounced, straining a clear, dense liquid into a second bowl. I bent over the counter and gave it a whiff. Earthy and sweet smelling, it seemed harmless enough. She held up a spoonful, and I leaned toward her, mouth agape like an infant awaiting her porridge. Just then, in walked Catterina's sixteen-year-old son Giovanni, looking for a schoolbook he had left on the sideboard. His eyes took in the scene unfolding before him, scanned back and forth between the two of us and the bowl of turnips. His pupils dilated, fixed on Catterina's hand poised in midair with the spoon. "Don't do it!" he yelled, his voice panged with urgency, as if she'd been holding a handgun instead. It was the very thing he had said to me—same words, same desperate tone, same look of dread—on a previous visit. He had returned from his after-school job one evening and found us alone in the kitchen: me, seated on a stool with a tablecloth tied around my neck, and Catterina standing behind me, a lock of my hair in one hand and a pair of scissors in the other.

He had been right about the haircut. It took two trips to the stylist to even me back out once I'd returned to the States. But I had already resigned myself to taking my medicine as prescribed. It seemed pointless to resist. Catterina had made up her mind to cure me, come what may.

Giovanni shook his head in disgust. The only thing worse than having a cold, he said, was taking turnip syrup to get rid of it. Did I know how it worked? He would tell me. It worked because it tastes so foul the body heals itself so it won't have to endure another spoonful.

The hows and whys are not important, said Catterina, as long as it works.

She raised her spoon again, I opened my mouth like a good girl, and she administered the dose. The syrup was cloying and viscous, coating my tongue and throat as I swallowed, though as medicines went, I'd tasted worse. I was about to say as much when I broke into another fit of coughing. Giovanni gave me an I-told-you-so look, gathered his book, and headed back upstairs to his studies.

Oh dear, said Catterina, rubbing her hands together. Perhaps I needed a little something else to ease my cough. She grabbed a bottle of red wine from a cupboard and a saucepot from beside the stovetop. She would make me a little *vin brulé* and send me straight to bed.

Vin brulé? What was that?

It is hot spiced wine, Piedmontese-style. The name means "burnt wine" in dialect, referring to the traditional method of igniting the wine with a long match to burn off most of the alcohol before serving. Its history traces to the monasteries of the Middle Ages, when monks performed the often overlapping duties of vintner and apothecary. They infused their wines with various herbs and spices depending on the affliction to be treated, and devised vin brulé as a warm tonic for treating colds and the flu. The drink also proved an excellent antidote against the chill and draft of winter, warming the body from within.

Italy experienced a *miracolo economico* after the Second World War, which raised the standard of living considerably in cities across the north—Venice, Milan, Torino, Bologna. But prosperity took its time reaching the remote villages of the Piedmont. Until well into the 1960s, Catterina recounted, few people could afford fuel to heat their homes and firewood was scarce. So on winter evenings, especially Saturdays, families would congregate with their neighbors in someone's barn. They would build a fire, each family contributing a log or two, and they kept warm around it into the night, telling stories and singing songs, roasting chestnuts and drinking vin brulé.

I watched as Catterina put sugar into the saucepot, one spoonful per person. She rummaged in her spice cabinet for a moment, added two sticks of cinnamon and six whole cloves, then put in a couple fresh bay leaves from a tree just off the terrace. She upended the bottle of wine and measured it by eye, glug, glug, glug. One glass per person, she said, plus one for the pot. She gave the saucepot a stir, then set it over a medium flame, swirling it gently to help the sugar dissolve. The scent of cinnamon and cloves wafted upward as steam began to rise from the pan. Before the wine reached a boil Catterina turned off the heat. She ignited a long match and carefully lit the surface of the wine, which burst into a rollicking blue flame. When the fire subsided she made me lean over the pot and inhale the vapors. Beneficial for clearing congestion from the chest and sinuses, she said. And it smells good, too.

Catterina ladled us each a steaming cup and we settled into the sofa beside the kitchen table, sipping vin brulé. The mug in my hands gave up its heat to my fingers. The hot wine soothed my throat. With each sip it eased the body ache brought on by the cold and warmed me to the core. Most of the alcohol had burned off when the wine was ignited, but what little remained left me relaxed and blissful, a little light-headed. Or maybe it was just my fever.

As we drank we exchanged family lore—our grandmothers were sisters. My great-grandfather had been a mining engineer, I told her. Shortly after coming to central Washington State from Italy he was trampled and killed when his team of horses spooked at a motorcar rumbling down the highway, or else it was a tumbleweed rolling across the road, no one is sure anymore of that detail. He left behind his wife and three children, the youngest just six months old. At fourteen, my grandfather became the man of the house.

Catterina's paternal great-grandfather, she said, had been a Russian gentleman. He had crossed the Alps into Italy on a white horse at the outset of the revolution, his panniers stuffed with Russian banknotes. After the Bolsheviks came to power he was left penniless, his money not worth the paper it was printed on. She still had a few rubles tucked away somewhere.

Catterina remembered meeting my grandmother during the 1960s, her great-aunt from America who smelled of rosewater. She remembered the Christmas packages arriving from Washington State, opened, rewrapped, and stamped in triplicate by the customs agents. Lace slips and nylon pantyhose, a wool coat just like Jackie Kennedy's. In exchange she had helped pack boxes of dried mushrooms and gianduiotti chocolates to send to my grandparents. I remembered the gianduiotti, Torino's signature confection. They are named for Gianduja, a marionette character and a mask of the Italian Commedia dell'arte depicting the archetypal Piedmontese peasant. Wedge-shaped chocolates blended with creamy hazelnut paste and enclosed in gold foil wrappers, my grandmother passed them around in a cut-glass crystal dish on special occasions.

Catterina shared a story about the first time Giuseppina made vin brulé as a young bride. She was at the home of her in-laws, and when she served up the steaming mugs her new relatives winced at the first sip. The spiced wine was mysteriously potent, with a strong odor that cleared the sinuses and made the eyes water. Mortified, Giuseppina enlisted the help of her mother-in-law, and they tried everything to repair it—another spoonful of sugar, an extra cinnamon stick, a squeeze of lemon, an extended simmer—but with no improvement. Finally, she gave up and started over again. She went back to the cantina to draw more wine from the cask and realized she'd mistakenly tapped the vinegar barrel the first time through. She made the second batch with her father-in-law's homemade red wine and received compliments all around, but she was teased about her vinegar brulé for years to come.

We talked and laughed and stayed up too late in spite of my cold. *Basta*, Catterina finally said. She had to work in the morning and my voice had gone hoarse. She gave me another spoonful of turnip syrup and sent me upstairs to bed. I fell asleep immediately, only to awaken a short while later, drenched in sweat from my fever. The next few hours passed fitfully as I tossed under my blankets, alternating between fever and chills. In the long stretch before dawn I fell into a deep, restorative sleep that lasted until morning. When I arose my fever had broken, my headache was gone. I took in a deep breath and felt my lungs expand effortlessly with air. The worst was definitely behind me.

I could hear rumbling from behind closed doors. Augusto had long since left for the bakery, but the children were starting to stir. I entered the kitchen to the smell of espresso and the sound of the moka coffeepot clamoring on the stove. Catterina was fixing herself a cup, and she poured one for me, too. *Buongiorno!* she said, then asked how I was feeling.

Much better, I said.

She was glad to hear it. I looked and sounded better, that was sure. But still, she said, coming at me with her spoon and turnip bowl, I should keep up with the syrup for good measure. One spoonful this morning, and another again tonight.

Had my cold simply run its course on its own, or had her turnip remedy actually worked? The cloying syrup had certainly lined my irritated throat, perhaps even bringing some relief, if only temporary, and the infusion of vitamin C couldn't have hurt. So I opened my mouth like a nestling sparrow once again. And I asked her to make me another vin brulé before bed that night as well. It might not have cured my cold either, but it certainly made it more pleasant to be sick.

❧

VIN BRULÉ

PIEDMONTESE HOT SPICED WINE

(Serves 4)

- 6 to 8 tablespoons sugar (depending on how sweet you like your wine)
- 2 large sticks cinnamon
- 6 whole cloves
- 4 bay leaves (fresh, if possible)
- 1 bottle hearty red wine (such as Barbera, Zinfandel, or Merlot—need not be expensive)

Combine all ingredients in a heavy saucepot and heat over a medium flame, swirling pot gently or stirring to dissolve sugar. Remove from heat just before wine comes to a boil. Carefully ignite wine with a long match to burn off the alcohol. When the flame subsides ladle vin brulé into mugs and serve hot. Makes an excellent après-ski drink or tonic for winter colds.

PASTA IN BRODO

PASTA IN CHICKEN BROTH

(Serves 4)

This simple soup is in almost every Italian cook's arsenal for curing colds, flu, even broken hearts. It also warms you from within after a day spent outdoors in the chill of winter. I save the end pieces when I make pasta and cut them into ¼-inch *quadretti* (little squares) or small, irregular *maltagliati* (badly-cut scraps). Left to dry on the cutting board for several hours, they will keep in an airtight container in the cupboard for months and are perfect in this soup. Packaged dried *pastine* (little pasta) such as *stelline* (little stars), *orzo* (barley) or *ditalini* (little thimbles) work perfectly as well.

- 6 cups homemade chicken broth
- kosher or sea salt, about ½ teaspoon, or to taste
- a 2-inch Parmigiano cheese rind, optional
- 1 whole clove garlic, peeled (also optional, but most cooks say it adds to the curative powers of the soup)
- 1 cup dried egg pasta squares, or small dried pasta for soup
- ½ cup Parmigiano cheese, plus additional for garnish

Bring the chicken broth, salt, optional cheese rind, and garlic clove to a rolling boil in a large, heavy stockpot over medium high heat. Add the pasta and cook until tender, about 3 to 5 minutes, or according to package directions, stirring occasionally to keep pasta from sticking. Discard cheese rind and garlic clove, if using, then stir in grated Parmigiano. Test for seasoning and add salt to taste, if needed. Ladle into soup bowls, garnish with additional grated cheese, and serve.

8

THE BAKER'S TRADE

On Saturday mornings Catterina and Augusto redoubled their pace at their panetteria. Augusto did not bake on Sundays, so he increased production the day before. His workday began at midnight instead of two in the morning to ensure enough bread to tide his customers over until Monday. At the front of the bakery the bell above the door chimed a steady beat as people entered and left, came and went. Its steady staccato rhythm and the contrapuntal tap and ring of an old cash register punctuated a stream of laughter and chatter in Piemontese dialect as Catterina and her assistant Rita exchanged greetings and bits of gossip with each shopper. The two women performed a pas de deux in the narrow aisle between the display case and bakery shelves, filling orders for loaves of bread and rolls, breadsticks and biscotti. The customers hurried off to complete their errands before the shops in the piazza shuttered their doors for the midday siesta.

I had returned to Rocca Canavese that October to work in the village trattoria and continue my explorations into the local cuisine, but my stint there would not start until the following week. I was staying once again with Catterina and her family, and since she and Augusto spent most of their waking hours at their bakery in Rocca's main piazza, I was spending a good deal of time there, too.

That morning Catterina had me peeling potatoes. She planned to roast them for *pranzo*, the midday meal. What she would prepare to accompany them, she didn't yet know, but she would think of something. There was always bread, I reminded her. A baker's family could always get by on bread. True enough. Still she hoped to make it to the market before it closed.

I was working a few steps away from the Saturday morning clamor, in the relative calm and quiet of the utility room off the back of the bakery. The room, a combination kitchen, laundry room, and office, was outfitted with a small stove, a sink, a file cabinet, a wooden worktable with a couple mismatched chairs, and an old couch. Catterina would disappear into the room during lulls between customers, accomplishing most of her domestic chores and the bakery's paperwork in fits and starts. She ironed sheets and pillowcases, mended socks and hemmed pants, paid bills and made jam. And she cooked the family meals, which she brought up the hill to the house a mile away at mealtimes.

That cluttered room is one of the pleasantest places I know. It greets the nose with a host of enticements even before entering. There is almost always something simmering on the stove in the corner—a pot of meat sauce or a soup, a braising chicken, stuffed cutlets of veal. Or else the coffeepot has just finished hissing and gurgling and the scent of espresso is rising up, permeating the interstices not already filled with the aroma of baking bread. I passed countless hours there during my visits, chatting with Catterina and assisting with sundry tasks amid the hubbub of the bakery. She knew that with my restaurant background I couldn't sit idly while others worked with food, and she always came up with something for me to do. Seated at her wooden table I rolled out gnocchi and cored peppers for preserving in olive oil. I canned tomatoes and pureed apples, stuffed peaches and pleated ravioli. While doing so, I met a steady stream of individuals whose lives have become intertwined with Catterina's as they've passed through her doors across the days and weeks and years for their daily bread.

The beaded curtain fluttered, making a musical clattering like bamboo wind chimes as Catterina entered to check on my progress. She grabbed a paring knife and helped me finish peeling and quartering the potatoes, then we tossed them with olive oil and chopped rosemary in a baking pan.

The curtain beads rustled again, and a frail-looking nun entered the room, a large black bag slung from the crook of her elbow. Catterina squeezed the nun's hands, greeted her with a kiss on each cheek. She

introduced me, *la cugina americana,* to Suor Marieangela, and I got a
kiss on each cheek, too. Suor Marieangela had an ageless look about her,
though she might have been somewhere in her sixties. She wore wire-rim
glasses, a black cardigan over a brown dress, and a habit. Catterina never
charged the sisters from the parish church across the piazza for their
bread. She wouldn't hear of it; after all, they'd taken a vow of poverty.
By way of thanks, Suor Marieangela came by the bakery every Saturday
morning to take Catterina's blood pressure. She pulled a blood pressure
cuff and stethoscope from her bag as Catterina took a seat, rested her
arm on the table, and pushed up her sleeve. The two women conversed
over the rapid *whoosh, whoosh, whoosh* as Suor Marieangela squeezed the
bulb to inflate the cuff, then held silent while the air hissed out. The nun
shook her head and clicked her tongue. Once again, Catterina's blood
pressure was too low. She was overtired, the sister explained to me, she
should put her feet up now and then and not work so hard.

Suor Marieangela loved to take blood pressures. She'd take anyone's;
you just had to ask. She pointed, almost covetously, to my arm. She'd be
happy to take mine, too. I obliged, taking a seat and removing my sweater
to expose my upper arm. She pumped up the cuff and let it deflate: 108/72.
I am an avid runner, which according to my doctor accounts for my low
systolic and diastolic numbers, but Suor Marieangela had made her own
diagnosis: I was overtired, too. It must run in the family. We should try
drinking an espresso mid-morning, she said. That would perk us up.

Catterina gave Suor Marieangela a sack filled with several loaves of
bread. The nun returned her black bag to the crook of her elbow. She put
her hand on Catterina's and gave it a squeeze. Wishing us *buona domenica,*
she disappeared through the curtain.

A few minutes later Catterina's brother Giacomo arrived carrying a
fishing creel. He'd had great luck that morning at his favorite fishing
stream. He lifted the creel's lid to reveal a basket full of trout. There
were more fish than he knew what to do with, he said, we should help
ourselves. Catterina rubbed her hands together greedily and transferred
six glistening brook trout to a colander in the sink. Giacomo said he
was sorry, he couldn't stay, not even for an espresso; he had to rush off.
Catterina handed him a loaf of bread and asked me if I would clean the
fish while she saw to another wave of customers that had just come in.

They left me alone to stare at the pile of trout in the sink. I could fillet a salmon, shell a lobster, and shuck an oyster, thanks to my various restaurant jobs over the years, but I'd never gutted a trout straight from the river. That had always been my father's job when I was a child. Not wanting to divulge this little gap in my résumé, I picked up a knife and reached for a trout. I had a vague recollection of my father cleaning rainbow trout off the side of the boat when we went lake fishing, which helped steel my resolve. And I had a very sharp knife, which helped even more. I inserted the knife in the opening at the anus and gently sliced up the belly to the gills. Real fishermen have a neat trick that involves making a notch just under the fish's mouth and creating a tab with which to pull and clear away the gills and entrails in one smooth downward tug. But I couldn't remember how to do it. So I poked around a bit with the tip of my knife until I finally had something to grasp, and cleared the entrails in a somewhat less elegant fashion. The hard work done, I rinsed the inner cavities clean of blood, finishing the last trout just as Catterina returned.

Accompanying her was a stooped, gray-haired woman in a floral print housedress. She had a basket of red bell peppers balanced on her hip. Her name, Catterina informed me, was Lina. She and her husband had moved into Torino years ago, but they kept their home around the corner from the bakery for summers and holidays. She was in the midst of closing the house up for the season. One of her final projects was to put up the bell peppers from her garden. Catterina was letting Lina roast them in the bakery oven. She would then pack them into jars and preserve them in olive oil for the winter.

Lina extended a hand. I placed the last trout in the colander, gave my hands a rinse, and hastily dried them with a towel before shaking her bony hand. *Piacere.* She motioned toward the colander and picked up a trout, appraising it with a learned eye. How did I plan to cook them?

I deferred to Catterina, and the two women embarked on a lively exchange in Piemontese, which I had trouble following. Finally, Catterina turned to me. Lina was a master of fish cookery, Catterina explained. Her husband had once owned a seafood shop in nearby Cirié, and Lina felt we owed it to our beautiful trout to roast them *al cartoccio*, wrapped in parchment paper. Lina said she had every ingredient we needed growing in her garden. She left her basket of peppers with Catterina and gave me a wave goodbye. Arrivederci, she would be back shortly to show us how it was done.

I helped Catterina arrange Lina's peppers on baking sheets and we carried them across the alley to the bakery ovens. We returned to find a white-haired man in clerical clothing at the bakery counter. It was Don Beppe, the priest from Barbania down the road, stopping in for his weekly visit. Catterina welcomed him warmly and introduced me, once again, la cugina americana. He had a broad frame and rugged features softened by a sonorous tenor's laugh and bright, clear eyes creased at the corners from smiling. We exchanged greetings and a few pleasantries and Don Beppe complimented me on my Italian. As always, this made me demur—no matter how badly you mangle their language, Italians will applaud you just for trying. Still, I felt flattered.

Since Catterina gave free bread to indigent nuns, I wasn't surprised to find she didn't charge priests either. Instead Don Beppe paid in *barzellette*. These are little stories with wry or funny endings—jokes, for lack of a better translation, and telling them is a time-honored part of the Italian oral tradition.

Don Beppe, Catterina informed me, was a master raconteur. He had a barzelletta or a story for every occasion. She filled his bag with bread and handed it to him over the counter. He tucked it under his arm, motioning to the window with his other hand. What a pleasure to see the sun after so many days of rain. One of his parishioners had been awakened during last night's downpour by a whining at the door. She opened the door to find a dog, soaking wet, sitting on the doorstep. The dog gave an eager bark, *woof woof,* and the woman slammed the door in his face. The dog tried again, *woof,* same response. On his third attempt, *woof,* the woman threw open the door and hurled a bucket of water at him. Undeterred, the dog put his paws to the window, peered in, and offered up a plaintive *meow.* The door opened and the woman ushered the dog in, gave it a bowl of food and a place to sleep by the fire. Don Beppe looked at me. Surely, he said, the cugina americana could attest to the moral of the story: If you want to get ahead in this world, it pays to know more than one language.

The bell above the entrance chimed again and a woman in a gray overcoat entered. She had come for her lasagne, which Catterina was baking for her in the bread oven alongside Lina's peppers. This was a traditional service of the village baker, Catterina explained. Most housewives do their cooking on the stovetop, as kitchens generally aren't equipped with an oven, especially in older homes. In appreciation the woman presented Catterina with a bowl of purple figs. I mentioned to Catterina that the barter system in Rocca Canavese still seemed to be going strong. Catterina was surprised it even struck me as noteworthy. She also traded bread with the butcher for a side of veal each year. A few customers gave her fresh eggs or young broiler chickens, while others swapped her for farmstead cheeses or homemade wine. She'd barter with everyone if she could; it made her customers feel like family. Besides, she said, her eyes taking on a sly glint, then she wouldn't have to give the taxman his cut.

When Lina returned later that morning she had with her a colander of washed lettuces and a handful of herbs. She led me by the elbow and I accompanied her to the utility room for a lesson in preparing trout al cartoccio. She seasoned the fish liberally inside and out with fine sea salt and filled each trout belly with generous sprigs of flat-leaved parsley and tarragon, along with a couple fresh bay leaves. Tarragon is not an herb generally associated with Italian cookery, though there are a few exceptions. It turns up in the traditional dishes of Siena in Tuscany, where it grows wild on the hillsides; legend holds it arrived with Charlemagne and his crusaders when they passed through on their way to Rome in the 12th century. Its presence in the Piedmont is a vestige of the region's interwoven history with France, where tarragon is a common kitchen herb. Along with parsley, chervil, and chives it is one of the four components of *fines herbs*, the classic herb blend used in French cookery. In Italian it is called *dragoncello*, from the Latin *Dracunculus*, meaning little dragon. Historians argue whether the name derives from the plant's serpentine root system, or from its traditional use in treating the bites of snakes and other venomous beasts.

As for the bay leaves, like many Italians Lina had a bay tree growing near the house. This small, Mediterranean tree, *Laurus nobilis*, is known to Italians as *alloro*, and to English speakers as bay laurel or Turkish bay. It has rounded, dark-green leaves that impart a nuanced vanilla-and-pine essence to foods. Fresh Mediterranean bay leaves bear scant resemblance to the dried leaves in dusty tins that most people keep in the spice cabinet for years on end, and they shouldn't be confused with California bay leaves, which are a completely different genus and species, *Umbellularia californica*. Leaves from this American shrub are longer and more slender than bay laurel leaves. While edible, they have a potent, medicinal flavor that some cooks find overwhelming.

Next, Lina tucked half a clove of garlic into the trout cavities, along with a couple thinly sliced rounds of lemon. She added a few drops of olive oil and placed each fish on a piece of baker's parchment large enough to encase it. Over each trout went two more slices of lemon, a sprinkle of pepper, and another thin drizzle of olive oil, and then Lina showed me how to wrap up the packets. She folded the paper up lengthwise over the fish, then turned up a corner about an inch at the base of one side and creased it well. Working her way around the edge of the parchment, she made a series of small pleats, each one sealing the one before it, then she tucked the last fold under the parcel to seal it completely.

The trout, Lina instructed, would need about twenty minutes in a moderate oven—350°F. The packets should be served on individual dinner plates so that each diner can have the pleasure of opening his own at the table. The first gift comes upon cutting open the parchment—carefully, so as not to burn the fingers. The escaping steam carries the scent of roasted herbs and trout straight to the nose.

For Americans accustomed to preportioned boneless fillets of fish, eating a trout with bones, head, and skin still attached can be a daunting proposition. But with a bit of determination and a steady fork it can be not only fun but delicious. The bones conduct heat to allow for even cooking, and their gelatinous proteins give the fish a succulent texture. The skin seals in flavor and bastes the flesh as it cooks.

You can remove the bay leaves, herb sprigs, and lemon slices to a separate plate before eating, or eat around them, as any fisherman would do. Likewise with the head, skin, and tail. (The eyeballs are considered a particular delicacy, though I've never tried them, but I find trout skin and cheeks very mild and tender.) Slice down into the flesh at the base of the tail until your knife touches the spine. Then, using a fork and knife held almost parallel to the trout, lift and tease the flesh away from the backbone. Use the same motion to lift the bone away from the flesh on the bottom half. Don't flip the fish over to eat the other side. In some cultures it is considered bad luck, the kind of thing that could capsize a fisherman's boat the next time he goes out on the water.

We put the trout on a baking sheet, where they rested comfortably in their packets, awaiting the oven up at the house for the midday meal. Lina gathered her things and went off to finish putting her garden to bed. She left behind a platter of roasted peppers. Dressed with olive oil, garlic, a few anchovies, and parsley we would have a fine antipasto. Our trout would be the main course, with roasted potatoes on the side. Next would come a salad of Lina's tender lettuces, and then the bowl of figs we had acquired for dessert. And of course there would be bread. Catterina's worries about what to fix for pranzo had been for nothing. In providing for her customers all these years they reciprocated in kind. The meal had taken care of itself.

TROTE AL CARTOCCIO

TROUT BAKED IN PARCHMENT

(Serves 4)

- 4 medium trout, cleaned
- fine sea salt
- 8 fresh bay leaves
- 4 sprigs fresh Italian parsley
- 4 sprigs fresh tarragon
- 2 garlic cloves, thinly sliced
- 1 to 2 lemons, thinly sliced
- freshly ground pepper
- olive oil

Preheat the oven to 350°F. Pat the trout dry with a towel and season liberally inside and out with fine sea salt. Place two bay leaves, a sprig of parsley, a sprig of tarragon, slices of half a clove of garlic, and two lemon slices inside the cavity of each trout. Drizzle a few drops of olive oil inside each trout and place on a piece of parchment paper large enough to encase it. Place two more slices of lemon over each trout, season with freshly ground pepper and another drizzle of olive oil.

Enclose the trout in the parchment paper: Fold the paper in half length-wise over the fish. Turn up a corner of the parchment about 1 inch, fold it over, and crease well. Work your way around the parchment, making a series of small pleats, each one sealing the fold before it. Tuck the last fold under the parcel to seal completely. Repeat with the rest of the trout.

Arrange the trout packages on a rimmed baking sheet and cook for about 20 minutes. Let diners cut open their own packages at the table to appreciate the aroma that rises up when the steam is released.

9

A BLISSFUL FEAST

The Piedmont in late autumn can be a dreary place. Fog settles into the mountain valleys and the Po River Plain, rain falls for days on end. I started traveling to the Piedmont during its gray months because the restaurant where I cooked in Vermont would close at the end of October for a few months, after the leaves had fallen and the tourists had gone home. I kept it up out of habit, visiting my relatives, exploring the countryside and cities, sampling the region's cuisine. During one of those late autumn visits, friends and strangers alike told me how fortunate I was to have come to Torino, the Piedmont's capital city, when I did, and they offered up two reasons why: Not everyone who comes to Torino gets to see the *Sindone*; or, not everyone who comes to Torino gets to experience a genuine *bagna cauda* feast. So when my cousin Giacomo and his wife Marina invited me to view the Sindone and eat bagna cauda on the same day, I considered myself fortunate indeed.

Most English speakers know the Sindone as the Shroud of Turin, making it one of the few products of the city that Americans recognize, along with the automobiles of Fiat and the soccer club Juventus. Considered by many to be the most important relic in Christianity, the Sindone is a fourteen-foot-long, bloodstained linen cloth bearing the faint image of a man, said to be the burial cloth of Jesus after the Crucifixion. According to custom, the Shroud belonged to a series of Byzantine emperors, was looted by crusaders during the Sack of Constantinople, disappeared for over a century, resurfaced in France in the 1300s, and was acquired by a Savoy duke. When the House of Savoy moved its capital from the French city of Chambery to Torino in 1578, the family brought the Shroud with them, and it has been housed there in the Cathedral of Saint John the Baptist ever since. Every few years a team of scientists cites new evidence based on radio-carbon dating or DNA sequencing or spectroscopy of some sort to alternately prove the Shroud's authenticity or unmask it definitively as a fake. One of the latest studies dates the cloth to the 14th century, which perhaps not coincidentally is when documentation of its existence begins. The Church has refrained from making an official pronouncement on the Shroud, though the Vatican is amenable to keeping the subject open to scientific inquiry. Most recently, Pope Francis declared it an image to be contemplated with awe.

The Shroud has endured flooding, fire, sieges, mildew, and mites over the centuries. To prevent further deterioration it is now kept in an atmospherically controlled case and brought out for public display only every twenty-five years or so to commemorate important events on the Catholic calendar. The Jubilee in 2000 at the start of the new millennium marked one such occasion, and it was on a Saturday in late October just before the exhibition closed that I paid a visit with Giacomo, Marina, and their infant son. With what I can best describe as claustrophobic anticipation we wound our way through the cathedral's cordoned maze with a thousand other visitors that day, from the truly faithful to the merely curious. During the course of the hour-long wait we saw German nuns and Australian backpackers and Japanese tour groups, and the cacophony of languages rising up around us lulled the baby to sleep in his stroller.

When we finally reached the head of the line and our allotted five minutes of viewing, Marina gave Giacomo a nudge. For years he'd worn his long, light brown hair in a thick braid that fell well past the middle of his back, but he'd recently cut it to just above his shoulders. He'd also grown a beard and moustache, and Marina thought he looked just like the image on the Shroud. Still, the relic, even with its discolored linen, its frayed edges and tears, projected an air of the miraculous. Around us people were moved to tears. It seemed like just the sort of handiwork God could work up with the wave of a hand. But to think of medieval knights errant or cloistered nuns or duplicitous nobles—to envision them with only the tools and technology of the time, fabricating the shadowy image of a man with a crown of thorns and a wound under his rib—that struck me as a miraculous possibility, too. The Pope was right, regardless of its provenance, the Shroud inspired reflection.

It was late afternoon by the time we returned to Giacomo and Marina's house in Rocca Canavese. Giacomo is Catterina's younger brother. Though I'll refrain from pulling out the family tree, our grandmothers were sisters, born and raised in a farmhouse just up the road from where he and Marina now live. On the way out of the city we'd stopped at an open market to pick up a few essentials for the evening meal. Without them, Giacomo informed me, you could not have a true bagna cauda.

Bagna cauda is the Piedmont's most celebrated dish. Pronounced "bahn-ya cowda" (and sometimes written *bagna caôda*), the name means "hot sauce" in dialect. In its simplest form it contains three principal ingredients: anchovies, garlic, and olive oil, which are gently simmered until the oil is infused and the anchovies and garlic have melted insepa-rably into one another. Variations exist, some cooks adding butter or cream or even a ladle of tomato sauce. The sauce is served in individual terra-cotta dishes kept warm by a Sterno burner or candle and accom-panied by an array of seasonal vegetables for dipping—some raw, others cooked. A prime example of *la cucina povera*, "poor man's food," it is a rustic dish of late autumn and early winter, once the standard fare of the region's vineyard workers. At pruning time in November they warmed themselves against the damp fog and frost with bagna cauda made over an open fire.

About bagna cauda the venerable Elizabeth David had this to say: "The Piedmontese do not usually serve the bagna cauda at meals, but at any time of the night or day they may feel hungry or thirsty, for it is a dish which essentially needs the accompaniment of plenty of strong, coarse red wine, such as the local Barbera. It is also excessively indigestible and is indicated only for those with very resistant stomachs. For garlic eaters it is, of course, a blissful feast."

On coming across this passage I assumed Ms. David was not a fan of garlic. But elsewhere she quoted Marcel Boulestin—celebrated French cookbook author, restaurateur, and 1930s BBC television chef—who famously declared, "Peace and happiness begin, geographically, where garlic is used in cooking." Likewise, Ms. David had nothing but nice things to say about anchovies, provided they were of good quality. So I don't quite know what to make of her dismissive remark, other than to say she was writing in 1954. She compiled her seminal work, *Italian Food*, for a British public eager for new delicacies after the food shortages and ration cards of World War II, but she might have thought her audience wasn't quite ready for two such potent flavors in a single dish. Regardless, she got one thing right. Bagna cauda is a blissful feast.

The Piedmontese think of bagna cauda not simply as a recipe, but as an event to which they attach the indefinite article: *una* bagna cauda. I've heard it called a choral ritual—an opportunity to celebrate moments of collective joy, with diners tucked elbow to elbow at a long table laden with a cornucopia of vegetables, terracotta chafing dishes lit by votive candles at each seat, open bottles of wine spaced within easy reach of all. Words like *convivialità, fraternità, amicizia, famiglia,* enter the conversation whenever bagna cauda is mentioned. Preparing una bagna cauda implies cooking for a group, in part because by the time you assemble all the requisite vegetables, you're cooking for a crowd. I suppose it's mathematically possible to reduce the proportions and prepare a meal for one, but it simply isn't done. Similarly, you can't order una bagna cauda off a restaurant menu, though occasionally a local *piola* or trattoria will close for the evening and hold una bagna cauda as a private event. In recent years, cities and towns across the Piedmont have hosted Bagna Cauda Day, a *sagra*, or local festivity, where bagna cauda is served. These can be delightful, and they help preserve tradition, but they lack the intimacy of una *vera* bagna cauda, a true bagna cauda, where friends and family break bread at the end of the day.

I grew up with my mother's bagna cauda, served in a fondue pot during the 1970s. My grandmother Teresa made it before her, counting out three anchovies, three cloves of garlic, half a wineglass of olive oil and a knob of butter per person. Lacking the proper earthenware servers, called *fujots*, from her native Piedmont, she simmered the bagna cauda in a heavy saucepot on the stove and the family gathered around the front burner to dip their vegetables.

There would be eight of us gathered at Giacomo and Marina's table that evening, which is a good size for a bagna cauda meal. Once we'd unpacked our provisions, Giacomo took charge of the sauce, starting with the anchovies. Most historians trace bagna cauda across the Alps to the *anchoïade* of Provence, an anchovy, garlic, and olive oil paste that fishermen and country-folk sopped up with coarse bread. This makes sense culturally, since the European anchovy (*Engraulis encrasicolus*) has been fished along the Mediterranean coast from Spain to Sicily since antiquity, and the Provencal seaport of Nice (*Nizza*, in Italian) shares a common heritage with the Piedmont, both of them having belonged to the House of Savoy. Still you might wonder how anchovies made their way into the bagna cauda of landlocked Piedmont, hundreds of miles from the sea.

They were brought there in wooden carts pulled by mules, along a network of trails traveled for centuries to deliver precious salt from the sea to the people of the mountains and inland plain. For most of history, commerce in salt was strictly regulated and heavily taxed, which naturally led to a thriving black-market trade. Legends tell of enterprising peddlers who outwitted the tax collectors by filling their carts partway with salt and topping them off with a layer of salted anchovies, which weren't subject to the tariffs. They sold the salt to the wealthy and the anchovies to the poor, who appreciated the savory note and the source of salt in their cooking.

There is little evidence to support the stories about smugglers and contraband, but researchers offer up equally swashbuckling theories involving Saracen invaders, British merchant ships, Catholic pilgrims returning from the Camino de Santiago in Spain. By most accounts, salt and anchovy merchants from Asti brought anchoiade home with them to the Piedmont during the Middle Ages, serving it with the vegetables of their region to make the first bagna cauda. But credit for the spread of the dish generally goes to the Jewish refugees who settled in the Val Maira (or Maira Valley) of the Piedmont after Ferdinand and Isabella cast them out of Spain in 1492. They brought a taste for anchovies with them and turned the Val Maira into a hub for trade in the salted fish. To supplement their meager incomes in winter after the work in the fields was done, peasant farmers descended the salt-roads to Nice and Genoa to trade wool, hemp, linen, wine, and other goods for anchovies, which they hauled back up to their villages and on to the cities of Torino, Asti, Cuneo, Alessandria, and beyond. By the 18th century the profession of *acciugaio*, "anchovy-monger" was well established, and not until after

World War II, with a surge in the economy and the arrival of the Auto-strade, did the itinerant anchovy vendors disappear.

Salt-packed anchovies are a world away from the tinned anchovies in oil familiar to most Americans. They are meatier and rounder in flavor, with a briny finish instead of a metallic one. They also come whole instead of in fillets, and they need to be cleaned before you can use them. Giacomo rinsed each plump anchovy under cold running water to remove the salt crystals and then rubbed away the skin. His rule of thumb was three anchovies per person, plus a couple more for the pot. He tore off the tail and dorsal fin of each fish, opened it like a book and teased out the backbone with his forefinger and thumb, then put the fillets in a bowl of cold water for about ten minutes to soak out the excess salt. He worked while seated at the kitchen table, a second chair pulled up beside him to elevate his leg. Years earlier he'd almost lost his life in a motorcycle accident, hit by a drunk driver at a crossroads on the way home from work. He'd met Marina in the hospital—a nurse in the trauma center, she'd been on his medical team in the weeks and months of operations and recovery fol-lowing the crash. The accident left him with a severe limp and a cane, but, he likes to say, it gained him a wife.

While the anchovies soaked, Giacomo broke several heads of garlic into cloves, peeled them, and removed the thin green germ in the cen-ters. Even the Piedmontese acknowledge garlic's indigestible reputation. They make jokes about halitosis or the scent of garlic oozing through their pores as they sleep, but they shrug this off, a small price to pay. One journalist insisted only the ignorant and prejudiced find the odor of garlic off-putting. Besides, he said, garlic is healthful, and the best cure for garlic-breath is a brisk walk in the countryside, thus doubling the salubrious nature of the dish.

A head of garlic per person is the traditional dose. It is the ratio recommended in the recipe registered with the Accademia Italiana della Cucina by delegates from the city of Asti, but even this canonical version allows the amount can be reduced to two to three cloves per diner. Many modern recipes not only cut back on the garlic, they include preliminary steps to tame it. Some cooks simmer the peeled cloves in milk or give them a quick blanch in boiling water; others advise a long steep overnight in wine, though purists decry these efforts. Giacomo counted out three plump cloves per person, sliced them paper-thin, then put them in a heavy terracotta saucepot. He poured in enough olive oil to float the garlic, added a spoonful of butter, and set the pot over a very low flame.

The olive oil in the bagna cauda comes from outside the Piedmont as well. People will tell you it's too cold for olive trees to grow in the region, but that's not exactly the case. Piedmontese landowners once cultivated olive trees and used their own olive oil for cooking, particularly in the hillsides around Asti. A series of cold snaps in the early 18th century killed off most of the olive groves, and oil production never recovered. The inhabitants turned to Liguria and elsewhere for their olive oil or substituted other cooking fats. In times of scarcity, which were frequent, walnut oil was used. Today some people garnish their bagna cauda with a few chopped walnuts to evoke the flavor of walnut oil, though I've never seen this done. As my mother tells it, Grandma Teresa refused to cook with walnut oil—although it has a certain boutique cachet today, it only reminded her of hard times. She always used olive oil, even in the early days when none of her American neighbors cooked with it and she had to buy it from the pharmacist, who recommended it steeped with onion for curing earaches, or infused with herbs to prepare balms and liniments.

Giacomo stirred the garlic from time to time to keep it from scorching. He kept the flame low and let the oil bubble languidly for about half an hour, until the garlic was tender and falling apart. He threw in the anchovies, mashing them with a fork to help them dissolve as he let the sauce simmer for another ten minutes. Next he poured in a few ladles of heavy cream and gave the sauce a final simmer, another ten minutes, until it thickened slightly. I hadn't expected this last step, as my grandmother's version didn't include it. Turns out all my relatives in Rocca Canavese make bagna cauda this way, as do the local trattorie. Depending on your source, this practice is considered yet another abomination, intended to force the garlic further into submission, or a refinement, elevating the dish from its meager origins and making it fit for bourgeois or even noble tables. In fact, Vittorio Emanuele II, Italy's first king, was known to dig into bagna cauda with gusto. The Savoy family's silver bagna cauda service is on display in Torino's Civic Museum.

Giacomo dipped a finger into the sauce, brought it to his tongue, and declared it done. Just then, eight-month-old Andrea—who had been remarkably well mannered and reverent at the cathedral—decided it was time to implode. Giacomo scooped him up, said he could use some rest himself before the evening's festivities, and the two of them headed upstairs for a nap. Not having children yet, I couldn't fully appreciate the luxury of having a fussy infant whisked away while trying to prepare for a dinner party, but it certainly allowed Marina and me to steamroll through all the vegetable slicing and cooking that remained to be done. We roasted beets and tiny cipollini onions, placing them in serving bowls alongside blanched cauliflower florets and boiled red potatoes. We sliced up carrot and celery sticks, strips of red and yellow peppers, wedges of savoy cabbage and peeled turnips, leaves of endive and radicchio, and arranged them in colorful mounds on ceramic platters.

We trimmed and prepared two vegetables unfamiliar to most Americans, though considered key to any proper bagna cauda: the cardoon and the Jerusalem artichoke. The former (*Cynara cardunculus*) is a thistle related to the artichoke, except instead of eating the flower buds you eat the stalks, which look a bit like celery or Swiss chard stems. At the market we'd found the prized *cardo gobbo di Nizza*, the "hunchback cardoon of Nice." Gardeners cultivate this labor-intensive vegetable by laying the stalks flat and covering them with soil to shield them from the sun for a few weeks before harvest. This process makes the stalks lose their chlorophyll, becoming white and crisp-tender, with a mild artichoke flavor. In addition, the stems develop a swollen "hunchback" where they were bent to the ground, hence the name.

The Jerusalem artichoke, meanwhile, is neither from Jerusalem nor an artichoke. It is a New World tuber (*Helianthus tuberosus*) that belongs to the daisy family and looks like gingerroot. In Italian it is known as *Topinambur*, the mispronounced name of a tribe in Brazil where Europeans thought the vegetable originated, although it is actually native to Northeastern America. This perennial plant grows wild here in New Hampshire and puts out dainty yellow flowers in late summer. It's a rampant spreader, though, and will quickly take over a garden bed once established, so it's best left to fend for itself along the roadsides. Jerusalem artichokes have a sweet, nutty flavor when roasted, and add a pleasing crunch served raw in salads. They are also served raw with bagna cauda, peeled and sliced into coins. Both cardoons and Jerusalem artichokes darken when trimmed and exposed to air, so Marina soaked them in water with a squeeze of lemon juice to help retain their color, and we drained them just before serving.

We set the table, placing the fujots at each seat. Giacomo and Andrea soon woke up and the guests arrived. When it came time to eat, Marina lit the votive candles and Giacomo ladled out the bagna cauda. This is a meal eaten not with knife and fork but by dipping a vegetable slice in the sauce with one hand and escorting it to the mouth with a piece of bread in the other to catch any drips. It is by nature informal and messy and lends itself to laughter. As the wine and bagna cauda flowed, a proud scent of garlic and anchovies rose into the air. It seeped into the deepest pockets of the lungs and penetrated the skin, strong enough to cure worms, the plague, all the poxes, and rid the house of malign spirits. The cream gave the sauce a velvety texture that offered a counterpoint to the earthy, autumn vegetables. I decided there was room for two versions of bagna cauda in my family recipe box.

Diners sometimes break an egg into the last of the sauce in their bowls and let it scramble or fry in the heat from the candle, though I've always been too full to partake in this ritual. With the plates cleared and the espresso poured, Marina brought out the grappa and Giacomo tuned his guitar. We sang the Partisan Song— *oh bella ciao, bella ciao, bella ciao, ciao, ciao*—and "Hey Jude" and "Piemontesina Bella" (the beautiful Piedmont girl), a waltz with minor chords that always makes me cry. A walk in the moonlight brought the night to a close; the prescribed *digestivo*. The evening had been bliss; I savored it with awe.

I returned to the States with a copy of Giacomo's bagna cauda recipe, written on a page from an old loose-leaf agenda notebook in Marina's looping, upright script. In addition to the cookbooks and linens, choco-lates and anise candies, coffee beans and moka pot I'd acquired during the visit, my relatives sent me off with a heavy shopping bag containing a set of six terra-cotta fujots and votive candles, a bottle of dolcetto d'Alba, a tin of salted anchovies, a bottle of Ligurian olive oil, and a braided strand of garlic (this last, alas, would be confiscated by the agents in Boston, as I was not crafty enough to check Nothing to Declare on my customs form).

Once on the plane, I wrestled my backpack and shopping bag through the aisle to get to my seat. A flight attendant asked if I'd like some help with my things; there was room up front. I handed the shopping bag to him and he broke into a smile when he saw the box protruding from the top, *fragile, Servito Bagna Cauda* printed on the top flap. "I see the signora is bringing a bit of Torino home with her," he said. He peered into the bag and took inventory: candles, olive oil, anchovies, garlic, wine. "*Che fortuna,*" he said—everything I needed for a bagna cauda feast.

BAGNA CAUDA ALLA CANAVESANA

BAGNA CAUDA, AS SERVED IN ROCCA CANAVESE

(Serves 6)

I have my own little theory about the presence of cream in this version of bagna cauda. The area known as the Canavese extends to the north of Torino up into the mountains—into dairy country where butter and cream are traditionally used in cooking and olive oil was once a luxury. Perhaps bagna cauda with cream is the authentic version of the region. Maybe my grandmother switched to olive oil when she came to America and her situation improved to the point where she could afford it.

- 10 to 12 salt-packed anchovies (or good-quality anchovy fillets in olive oil)
- 2 heads garlic
- 2 tablespoons butter
- ¼ cup extra virgin olive oil
- 2 cups heavy cream
- assorted raw and cooked vegetables for dipping

If using salt-packed anchovies, rinse in cold running water, remove the fin, tail, and backbone, and soak in cold water for 10 minutes. Peel the garlic cloves, removing the green-tipped germ, if needed, and slice paper-thin. Melt the butter and olive oil in a heavy saucepot (terracotta, if possible) over low heat. Add garlic and simmer gently until falling apart, about 30 minutes, stirring as needed to keep garlic from sticking or burning. Add the anchovies and simmer an additional 10 minutes, stirring with a fork to help them dissolve. Stir in cream and continue simmering until sauce is slightly thickened, about 10 minutes. Serve in individual terra-cotta pots kept warm by a candle or spirit flame.

Accompany with assorted seasonal raw and cooked vegetables for dipping.

Among the raw: sticks of celery and carrots; strips of sweet red and yellow bell peppers; thin wedges of fennel, turnips, and savoy cabbage; leaves of endive and radicchio; trimmed cardoons and Jerusalem artichokes (soaked in water with a squeeze of lemon juice to keep them from turning black before serving).

Among the cooked: roasted beets and cipollini onions; tender blanched cauliflower and boiled potatoes, cooked whole if small, or peeled and cut into wedges.

Serve with plenty of crusty hearth bread. If desired, break an egg into the pot and stir it into the last of the sauce, letting it cook over the flame to create a gray-yellow scramble that is as unappealing in appearance as it is delightful to mop up with your bread.

PEPERONI IN BAGNA CAUDA

ROASTED RED AND YELLOW BELL PEPPERS
WITH BAGNA CAUDA

(Serves 4)

The Piedmont is famous for its meaty, square-shouldered red and yellow
bell peppers, which are often roasted and served halved or quartered
lengthwise and topped with bagna cauda as an antipasto. The sauce, made
without cream, follows my grandmother's proportions. It is inspired by a
meal my husband and I shared with Giacomo and Marina in the village
of Serralunga d'Alba after a visit to the truffle market one Saturday in
November. It can be scaled up for a traditional bagna cauda feast with
assorted vegetables.

FOR THE BAGNA CAUDA:
- 3 salt-packed anchovies (or 6 good-quality anchovy fillets in
  olive oil)
- 3 cloves garlic
- 2 tablespoons butter
- ½ cup extra virgin olive oil

FOR THE PEPPERS:
- 4 sweet bell peppers (2 red, 2 yellow)

If using salt-packed anchovies, rinse in cold running water, remove
the fin, tail, and backbone, and soak in cold water for 10 minutes.
Peel the garlic cloves, removing the green-tipped germ, if needed, and
slice thinly. Heat the garlic in the butter and half (4 tablespoons) of
the olive oil in a small, heavy pot over very low heat. Let simmer, stirring as needed to prevent burning, until the garlic is soft and breaking

apart, 20 to 30 minutes. Add the rest of the oil and the anchovies, and continue cooking gently, stirring with a fork to help the anchovies break up and dissolve into the sauce, about 10 minutes.

Preheat oven to 425°F. Place the peppers on a sheet pan and roast in the oven, turning once or twice during cooking, until blackened and blistered, 20 to 25 minutes. Transfer to a bowl and let steam, covered, until cool enough to handle. Remove the peel, stem, and seeds from peppers, halve or quarter lengthwise, and arrange cut side up in a single layer in a casserole dish. (Can be prepared ahead and refrigerated. Reheat briefly before serving.)

To serve: Spoon hot sauce over the roasted peppers and serve immediately.

10

A SOUP FOR THE DEAD

I returned to Rocca Canavese at the end of October the following year, just in time for Halloween. Technically, that is not a holiday celebrated by Italians, though as festivities go, the day has gained some ground in recent years. In October many storefront windows now display ghoulish skulls, black cats, and jack-o'-lanterns. In some city neighborhoods children dressed as ghosts and witches scurry through the piazza after school, knocking on doors and crying, *"Dolcetto o scherzetto!"* Treat or trick, they say, perhaps because the phrase rolls off the Italian tongue more smoothly this way, but in reversing the order they seem to be offering a choice instead of issuing a threat. Few residents actually understand their role in this game, though some oblige the trick-or-treaters with a packet of cookies or a few coins. If anything, Halloween in Italy is less a holiday for children than a party for young adults, who head to the nightclubs and discotheques wearing elaborate makeup and bejeweled costumes the likes of which you'd expect to see in the wardrobe room at La Scala. This is, after all, a country known for its fashion designers and Carnival masks, so perhaps it is no surprise. The revelers have only a vague idea as to why they are partying, but they don't let that dampen their enthusiasm.

Italy's real holidays of the season come right on the heels of Halloween. Both are rather staid events in comparison, which might explain why they garner little attention in the States. The first celebration is Ognissanti on November 1, followed by Tutti i Morti the next day.

Ognissanti, also known as Tutti i Santi to Italians, or All Saints' Day to English speakers, is a day for commemorating the saints. Various Christian denominations throughout the world include All Saints' Day on their calendars, but it is a national holiday in Italy (which means municipal offices, schools, many businesses, museums, historic sites, and public transports are closed—pertinent information should you have plans to mail a package, sightsee, or travel by train that day). During the early years of Christianity martyrs were honored on the anniversary of their death. With the passage of time and martyrs the calendar became overloaded, so the Church set aside a single day to honor all the martyrs collectively, and eventually extended the solemnity to include all saints, martyred or not.

The rest of the departed have their day on November 2, the holiday Italians call Tutti i Morti, or else Il Giorno dei Morti, the Day of the Dead. In English it is All Souls Day. According to the Church, the souls laboring in purgatory can gain quicker entrance into heaven with the help of prayers from the living. On November 2, Italian Catholics can attend special services devoted to prayer for the dead. Families return to the cemeteries of their ancestors and loved ones to tidy the gravesites and leave candles or flowers, particularly white chrysanthemums, the traditional funeral flower in Italy.

Rather than a day of sorrow and gloom, the Italians manage to treat it as a celebration of life, an opportunity to maintain a connection to those who have passed on. Folklore holds that on the eve of Tutti i Morti the veil between the realms of the living and the dead is drawn back, and the spirits of the afterworld return to their earthly homes. Gifts left out for these meandering souls kept them from causing mischief, giving rise eventually to the trick-or-treating ghosts and goblins of Halloween—All Hallow's Eve—and the visits from the beyond on Tutti i Morti. In some regions, children wake to find gifts left for them by departed ancestors who have come to call during the night. In other parts of the country, people leave out food before heading to mass so the visiting souls won't go hungry, or they might turn down the beds so the spirits can have a place to rest.

So on October 31 that year in Rocca, I went to the market and bought a warty, yellowish winter squash, the closest thing I could find to a Connecticut field pumpkin, and I showed Catterina and her kids how to carve a jack-o'-lantern. The following day I accompanied Catterina to Rocca's tiny cemetery, which sits perched on a hill near the center of town. We passed through an iron gate with intricate grillwork and a patina of rust and walked through the graveyard to the mausoleum. I noticed headstones dating to the 15th century. Catterina put flowers at her parents' gravesites and showed me the resting places of my grandmother's parents and siblings. It occurred to me that my Grandma Teresa had made similar treks to the cemetery over the years. I envisioned her standing in the same spot, tracing her fingers over the stone inscriptions as she contemplated the past.

On the second of November, Catterina invited me to the bakery to help her make *zuppa dei morti*, soup of the dead. I should have known, like any proper holiday, Ognissanti and Tutti i Morti come with celebratory dishes for the occasion. Since the chestnut harvest reaches its peak at Ognissanti, many mountain villages in the Piedmont host roast chestnut festivals in honor of the saints. From late October through early November I have sampled *ossa dei morti*, bones of the dead, in pastry shops throughout the region. Crunchy, meringue-based cookies studded with almonds or hazelnuts, they are rolled into three-inch sticks and resemble knobby finger bones once baked. And in family homes and local trattorie, Catterina told me, you'll find versions of zuppa dei morti, hearty peasant soups that put the products of the season to good use. While some are based on chickpeas or fava beans or pumpkin, Rocca Canavese's soup of the dead is a bread and cabbage affair, steeped in broth and enriched with sausage and handfuls of cheese. It is often called generically *zuppa alla canavesana*—Canavese-style soup—because it didn't originally make an appearance just for the holiday. Rather it was served throughout the winter, a rib-sticking staple made with the region's distinctive Savoy cabbage.

Which is why it's also called *zuppa di verza*. Northern Italy distinguishes between *cavolo cappuccio*—the compact, smooth-leaved head of cabbage that is either green or purple, and *cavolo verza*, which has a crinkly head, its inner leaves creamy white, and the outer ones such a deep green as to take on an almost blue tinge. In America we know it as Savoy cabbage, named for the Savoy Dynasty that ruled the Piedmont from the Middle Ages until the end of World War II. I prefer Savoy cabbage to the smooth-headed kind when braised or sautéed, as it has a singularly mild, sweet flavor once cooked, though I'm fond of regular old cabbage, *cavolo* cappuccio, in cole slaw and other salads.

No matter the name, it is a zuppa in the original sense. Zuppa—along with our English "soup," French "*soupe*," and Spanish "*sopa*," among others—derives from the Latin *suppa*, which the Romans acquired from the Goths, who had to whip something up when feeling peckish between all the plundering and sacking. The word means "bread soaked in broth."

Until well into the Middle Ages the nobility ate from trenchers, large slices of hard, stale bread that served as plates. During the meal these trenchers became saturated with the juices of the meats and other foods placed upon them. If the sodden bread slices were not thrown to the dogs after supper (another word derived from *suppa*) they were offered as alms for the poor. Or else they were left for the servants, who boiled them in water to make meals of their own. The famous onion soup of France emerged from this same practice.

Italians today still differentiate between a zuppa, a soup thickened with bread or ladled over it, and a *minestra* (from the Latin *minestrare*, "to administer," because it was served forth at the table by the head of the household), which is a brothy mixture of vegetables with the occasional addition of pasta, rice, or other grain, and sometimes a little meat. Americans, however, just call everything soup.

After my morning run that day, I walked down to the bakery, entering through a side door to wait for Catterina in the cluttered utility kitchen off the shop. After a few minutes she took advantage of a lull between customers to join me. She made us each an espresso and pointed to a basket full of vegetables perched on a chair. Handing me a kitchen knife she set me to work dicing two onions and slicing a large head of Savoy cabbage into thin strips. Meanwhile she removed a couple links of mild sausage from their casings and crumbled them into a large soup pot set over a low flame. She stirred the sizzling meat from time to time to keep it from sticking, and after a few minutes, when it had lost its raw coloring, she swept in my cabbage and onions from the cutting board. Catterina told me that some people advise boiling the cabbage briefly before adding it to the pot to make it more digestible, but she never bothered with that step, and she didn't think the deceased in whose honor we were making the soup would mind in the slightest, either.

The pot simmered gently for several minutes, until the cabbage had cooked down and the onions were translucent. Then Catterina ladled in about a quart of good, rich broth, enough to cover the vegetables by about two fingers. Homemade broth, so thick and gelatinous you can scoop it out with a fork is essential for this soup, adding the requisite body and binding the other ingredients together. Beef or veal stock will work, but chicken stock is the traditional choice, as the country housewife of days past was apt to have plenty on hand at this time of year. With the colder days and waning light of early November, her chickens would have quit laying eggs. The oldest hens, those least likely to resume production in the spring, would end up in the stewpot, simmered with an onion, a carrot, a stalk of celery, and a sprig of parsley for an immensely satisfying meal. The resultant golden broth was the hen's parting gift. In Italian there's an old saying: *Gallina vecchia fa buon brodo.* An old hen makes good broth. In the Canavese part of the Piedmont, it often ended up in this soup. (If you've ever made a pot of stock from a barnyard hen, you'll appreciate how true this is, though I later learned it's a phrase most often used figuratively: with age comes experience. In particular, an older woman is better in bed than some pretty young thing.)

A bell jingled above the bakery's front door as a customer entered. Catterina adjusted the flame under the pot to maintain a lazy bubble and left me a few instructions before disappearing through the beaded curtain to the front of the shop. She broke into dialect as she greeted a matronly woman, and I listened to an incomprehensible rumble of chatter and laughter as I turned back to the zuppa.

Catterina had me finely grate a chunk of Parmigiano cheese, about a cup's worth, then I switched to the large holes on the grater and coarsely shredded a few ounces of Toma. Toma is a raw cow's milk cheese, produced in alpine villages throughout the Savoy region. In France it is called Tomme de Savoie. Originally made from milk after the cream had been skimmed off to make butter, it was once one of the primary sources of protein for mountain peasants who could not afford meat. Today it is considered a delicacy. You can buy quite a steak for less than the price of a wedge of good Toma. The best ones are farmstead cheeses, prepared in small batches from the morning and evening's milking by the same farmer who milks the cows. A wheel of Toma has a rough, brownish rind that sometimes shows traces of mold and smells of the cellar in which it was aged. The interior is pale yellow to ivory with tiny holes that develop as the cheese ferments. Toma has a mild, delicate flavor that becomes more savory with age. An excellent table cheese paired with fruit or country-style bread, Toma is also used in cooking throughout the region because it melts smoothly and retains its flavors when heated.

Many cooks substitute fontina for some or all of the Toma; it is a cheese much better known outside Italy, and certainly more readily available here in America. Fontina comes from the Val d'Aosta region on the Italian side of the slopes of Monte Bianco (called Mont Blanc in French). Prized since at least the 13th century, it once graced the tables of the dukes of Savoy. True fontina is an unpasteurized cheese made with milk exclusively from the Valdostana breed of cow. The cheese has a light straw color in winter when the cows feed on hay, and a darker, golden hue in summer when the cows graze in alpine meadows. Similar in taste and texture to the Swiss Gruyère, with which it shares a historical kinship, fontina has a woodsy, nutty flavor that develops during aging in mountain caves carved into the rock. Fontina is most noted as the principal ingredient in *fonduta*, the Italian version of fondue. It is also stirred into risotto, tossed with pasta, and added to many baked dishes because of its velvety texture when melted.

Once the cheese was grated Catterina gave me another job. In honor of the holiday, she informed me, Augusto would be building a bonfire in the courtyard to roast chestnuts. She hoisted a burlap bag onto the table, folded back the opening, and out tumbled a landslide of freshly collected chestnuts, dark as varnished mahogany and still smelling of the woods. The rounded edge of each nut needed to be scored to help the shell burst open in the heat of the flames. We could work on them while the soup simmered.

For the next twenty minutes I scored chestnuts, with Catterina popping back in to help me every so often between customers. I stirred the soup on occasion, and when the cabbage grew tender I summoned her. A few minutes later the curtain beads rattled and swayed as she emerged carrying a tray. She had cut the crust from a loaf of yesterday's bread, sliced it, and toasted it until golden in the bakery's oven. She set down the tray, opened a cupboard, and pulled out two earthenware baking dishes—one large, the other smaller. We would make the big one for ourselves, the smaller one for *i morti*.

I helped her line the dishes with the trimmed slices of bread. In order to make a respectable zuppa, you must use day-old artisan bread. A rustic loaf with irregular holes and a chewy yet delicate crumb. To use industrial processed bread is a waste of effort and good chicken stock. Commercial bread with its spongy, vapid middle will disintegrate in the broth and give you a gluey mess. Catterina covered the bread with a few ladles of soup, followed by a sprinkle of each of the cheeses. She repeated this layering three times, ending with ample handfuls of Parmigiano and Toma for the top.

After Catterina completed her end-of-day tasks she locked up the bakery and we brought the zuppa with us to the house to finish cooking. She let it bake for forty minutes at 350°F, then called her family to the table—*tutti a tavola!*—and served the zuppa steaming, straight from the oven.

The cheese had formed a crackled umber crust over the surface and the broth sputtered and hissed around the edges as it boiled and soaked up into the bread. Catterina spooned the zuppa into bowls and passed it round. It was hardly a soup in the American sense; I supposed we'd be more apt to call it a casserole, definitely something best approached with knife and fork. Regardless it was my favorite kind of winter meal, a hearty comfort dish to take the edge off a chilly evening.

Augusto brought the chestnuts to the table next, straight from the fire, roasted in a perforated cast-iron pan set over the coals. Almost too hot to hold, they stained our fingers with soot as we cracked them and extracted the sweet nutmeats. Next came an endive and arugula salad seasoned only with wine vinegar, lush olive oil, and a sprinkle of sea salt. For the final course, Catterina served misshapen russet apples, gathered from a tree below the house. We pared the coarse brown skins onto our plates and savored the crisp slices, washed down with the last of our wine.

After dinner Catterina and Augusto's children disappeared to their rooms to study. Augusto had nodded himself to sleep at the table, as he often did; baker's hours don't allow for long stretches of uninterrupted sleep at night. He awoke with a start and went upstairs to rest until three in the morning, when he would begin a new day at the bakery.

Once we had washed the dishes and cleaned the kitchen, Catterina began to prepare for i morti. Out came a fresh tablecloth, a pair of pewter candlesticks with beeswax candles, and a vase of white chrysanthemums. We laid the table anew, setting it for seven: Catterina's parents and grandparents, Augusto's father, and my maternal grandparents—special guests in my honor. We brought out the china and folded linen napkins, slipping them through silver napkin rings that had belonged to Catterina's mother.

As we arranged the dishes Catterina recounted a Tutti i Morti celebration from her youth. She and a couple friends had snuck into the kitchen of the neighborhood gossip, an elderly widow who had lost her husband in the First World War. They had spooned up servings of the signora's zuppa, poured themselves a bit of her wine, crumpled her napkins, and slipped away before she returned from mass. They overheard the old woman the next day at the market, telling anyone who would listen that the spirits had paid her a visit.

Catterina placed the second dish of zuppa in the middle of the table, and next to it a stack of grissini, which tumbled and spread across the table like giant pick-up-sticks. We put out wineglasses, but not for Catterina's mother, who didn't drink. She got a water glass instead, and Catterina draped an apron over the back of her chair. Her mother had never come to the table without an apron tied around her waist. Only then would she feel at home, Catterina explained, bouncing from table to kitchen, helping with the serving and clearing. We left a bottle of red wine at the head of the table for Catterina's grandfather, and a bowl of roasted chestnuts next to her grandmother's spot—her grandmother had always loved her chestnuts. We seated our grandmothers next to each other, since they were sisters. The wooden bowl of russet apples went in easy reach of both my grandparents—having left Italy for apple country in Washington State, surely they would appreciate an apple straight from the tree. Catterina pulled a cut-glass ashtray from the sideboard drawer and set it down above her father's plate. She knew he would want his after-dinner cigarette. As a final touch, she arranged a tray of porcelain cups, a moka coffeepot, and a bottle of grappa on the hutch so the guests could end the meal with espresso and a digestivo.

Catterina lit the candles and turned out the lights. We stepped back from the table to survey our handiwork, our shadows cast across the table in the flickering light. Silhouettes in motion, guests come to dine. As we stood in silence, Catterina squeezed my hand. I didn't need to wait until morning to see if the departed had returned for a visit during the night. I could already feel their presence in the room.

ZUPPA DEI MORTI

SOUP OF THE DEAD

(Serves 4 to 6)

- ½ pound mild Italian sausage
- 2 onions, diced
- 1 large head Savoy cabbage, quartered lengthwise, cored, and cut into thin strips
- 1 quart rich, homemade chicken broth
- 6 to 8 slices day-old country white bread, crusts trimmed, toasted until golden
- 4 ounces Parmigiano, finely grated
- 4 ounces Toma di Savoy, coarsely grated (can substitute fontina or Gruyère)

Preheat oven to 350°F.

Remove the sausage from the casings and crumble the meat into a heavy soup pot or Dutch oven. Cook over a low flame until sausage is browned, stirring to keep from sticking and breaking the sausage into smaller pieces, 3 to 5 minutes. Stir in the onions and cabbage and continue simmering until cabbage has wilted and onions are translucent.

Ladle in enough chicken broth to cover cabbage mixture by about two fingers, adding water if needed. Adjust heat to maintain a steady simmer and cook, stirring occasionally, about 20 minutes.

Line a deep baking dish or casserole with the toasted bread. Cover bread with a few ladles of soup followed by a sprinkling of each of the cheeses.

Repeat the layers three times, ending with ample handfuls of cheese for the top.

Bake the zuppa for 30 to 40 minutes, until the broth is bubbling and the cheese on top is well-browned.

Serve in bowls with a knife, fork, and spoon.

11

STIRRING UP ZABAIONE

Ayear later I spent the month of November helping out in the kitchen at La Piola, a neighborhood trattoria on the road heading west out of Rocca. Catterina had made arrangements for me with the *padrona*, Margherita, a stout, sixty-ish woman who ran the place with her two daughters. *Piola* is the Piedmont dialect term for a casual tavern or restaurant that serves simple, rustic meals. During my time there I learned to prepare some of the region's most well-known specialties, *piatti tipici* such as creamy fonduta; risotto stained deep red by Barolo wine; the beloved bollito misto with its seven cuts of beef, veal, and poultry; and the silky *bônet*, a chocolate-almond custard traditionally made in a metal mold that resembled an upturned hat—the name means "hat" in dialect.

That month at La Piola gave me an opportunity to experience firsthand the rhythms and pace of a Piedmontese family-run restaurant kitchen—the morning bustle at the produce market and the flurry of peeling, chopping, boning, stirring, and braising in preparation for pranzo; the afternoon lull between seatings, once the customers had gone home and the kitchen had been mopped clean; and then the frenzy again when an onslaught of diners arrived for the evening. On my first Friday night there, the pace in the kitchen was humming indeed. The dining room overflowed. Where all those people had come from, Margherita did not know. Only two parties had phoned for reservations; the city-dwellers escaping from Torino for the weekend were not due until the following day, and the famous November fog of the Po River Plain had blanketed the countryside since morning, casting an infectious gloom.

Margherita had assumed no one would venture out on such a night. Yet look at the dining room, almost every table full, and everyone had come at once, in accordance with that uncanny synchronization of inner circadian dinner clocks, a sort of harmonic convergence of appetites that manifests itself when restaurant diners are left to their own whims, unchecked by a reservation book.

Back in the kitchen, behind the expanse of a twelve-burner stove, stood Margherita, a lock of hennaed hair escaping from her hairnet, beads of perspiration on her brow, a splatter of parsley sauce across her apron. She presided over a battery of pots and sauté pans that simmered and sputtered and steamed as I helped her serve up platter after platter for the dining room. Roasted sweet peppers from Asti, veal carpaccio with shaved truffles, prosciutto and figs, porcini risotto, Gorgonzola ravioli with walnuts and cream, cotechino sausages with pureed potatoes, wild boar braised in Barolo wine.

Her daughters Marina and Daniela had planned a quiet evening of cards in the bar with the Friday night regulars. Instead they found themselves doing laps at a near jog from kitchen stove to dining room to keep pace with Margherita's platters. Daniela burst through the swinging wooden doors from the dining room. She stacked an armload of dirty plates by the sink, set out a tray of dessert goblets and announced she was in desperate need of five orders of *zabaione*.

Zabaione is a warm wine custard. It is a trattoria staple in the Piedmont, one of a vast array of desserts the Italians refer to collectively as *dolci al cucchiaio*, desserts you can eat with a spoon. Preeminently spoonable among these is of course gelato in its myriad flavors, but the category also includes puddings and custards, slushes and trifles, bavarians and frozen bombes. Zabaione is one of the simplest and most elegant of the lot. In its purest form it has but three ingredients: egg yolks, sugar, and wine, which when whisked together over gentle heat rise up into a voluminous, velvety fluff that melts on the tongue, delectable beyond anything intimated by each individual part.

Zabaione is the dessert's official spelling, but in a rare instance of orthographic tolerance, Italian dictionaries list *zabaglione* as an accepted variant. Curiously, this is the preferred spelling in most British and American cookbooks, while in France the dessert becomes *sabayon*.

According to my definitive French source, *Larousse Gastronomique*, the name comes from the Neapolitan dialect *zapillare*, meaning "to foam." The *Grande Dizionario Italiano* volleys the word back to France, saying it stems from *chaud bouillon*, "a warm drink," unless it derives from the Latin *sabaia*, an Illyrian ale. Ultimately the lexicographers throw up their hands and admit the word is of uncertain origin.

I have seen zabaione attributed to Florence and the cooks of the Medici court, to the Venetians in the days of the Most Serene Republic, and to a medieval army captain encamped in the countryside of Reggio Emilia. But in the Piedmont I learned a different story. The dessert, I was told, owes its name to the Franciscan friar Pasquale Baylón, who served in the parish of San Tommaso in the region's capital city of Torino during the 16th century. The friar prescribed the frothy concoction as a restorative for the weak and convalescent. He passed the recipe on to his lady penitents who lamented the lack of stamina demonstrated by their spouses in the boudoir. Word quickly spread of the uplifting results of the medicinal dish, and the gentle women of Torino soon found themselves atwitter discussing proportions and recommended dosages.

Friar Baylón was declared a saint in 1680 by Pope Alexander XIII. Although I could find no mention of his therapeutic dessert playing a role in the two miracles prerequisite for beatification and sainthood, the custard underwent likewise canonization, becoming *l'Sanbajon* in the Piedmontese dialect. In 1722 the Guild of Cooks and Waiters of Torino designated San Baylón their Saint Protector, and his feast day is still celebrated on May 17 at the Church of San Tommaso in Via Pietro Micca.

That gloomy night in the kitchen at La Piola I already considered myself something of an expert on zabaione. I'd read up on its history while researching the cooking of the region. My mother used to make it, and I'd prepared it countless times at home. I'd even paid a visit to the Church of San Tommaso in Torino's historic district just a few days prior, in hopes of corroborating the story of zabaione's origins. My cousin Giacomo and his wife Marina had accompanied me on my mission, and we knocked on one locked door after another at the various entrances to the dark, deserted church. An elderly signora with sparse white hair opened a window on the upper floor of the annex. Closed! she yelled down. No admittance! She gave an exasperated huff and shut the window with a crisp bang. I felt like Dorothy outside the gates of Oz. Giacomo interceded on my behalf, calling out to the unopened window in Piedmontese dialect, of which I understood snippets—American cousin, San Baylón, cooks and waiters. The window swung open again and the signora leaned out, her face lit with a toothless smile. I tried to look reverent and sincere. She would be right down, she said; her son the parish priest was out, but she had a key.

Minutes passed before she emerged from a side door on the ground level, her pace hindered by a dowager's hump and outworn slippers. She shook my hand warmly, unlocked the heavy wooden door, showed us into the vestibule. So, the *americana* wants to know about the famous friar, San Baylón? A cook and healer of great renown, she said. He lived right here at San Tommaso, his feet once trod these very floors. Of course we still celebrate his feast day—every May 17! And zabaione? She rubbed her hands together. Why San Baylón invented it! She thrust a brochure from an ornate display case into my hands. Her son had written it, she told me, it would tell me all I needed to know. Which was fortunate, because then she lapsed back into dialect, speaking with such a flurry of words I couldn't comprehend a thing.

In a corner of the dim antechamber I noticed a credenza covered with unlit candles. On it sat a velvet-lined basket for votive offerings, and I pulled a few bills from my wallet for a donation. The signora snuck a glance into the basket, then scurried back to the display case and gathered more pamphlets for me, pressing them eagerly into my hand—monographs on Torino's famous shroud, on the Sisters of the Third Order of Saint Francis, on the recently beatified railwayman, Paolo Pio Perazzo, entombed at San Tommaso after his untimely death from the bite of a mad dog. She ushered us out the door, saying *mille grazie*, do come again, thanks for your interest in our humble friar-cook, San Baylón! She spoke with such enthusiasm and conviction I didn't have the heart to bring up any of the competing theories I'd unearthed. In the face of such indisputable proof, what would have been the point?

I should mention you rarely find a genuine zabaione in American restaurants because chefs here tend to place a premium on efficiency and convenience when it comes to dessert. They prefer prefabrication—something that comes ready-made in a box, if they can get away with it, or at best something a pastry chef can turn out in the morning for service that night so as not to have an extra body in the kitchen taking up valuable space during dinner when the line-cooks are plating meals cheek by jowl. Here in the United States what chefs want are practical desserts. Desserts you can slip onto a plate, give a squiggle of raspberry sauce, a blop of whipped cream, and out the door they go.

But zabaione is not practical. It requires a good ten minutes of whisking, and in order to capture its full potential you must make it and serve it immediately, else it soon deflates. Like a helium balloon, as it loses its air it loses its charm. After a few hours it separates into a viscous mass that still tastes fine but looks rather unappealing, and therein lies the inconvenience. As a countermeasure, many cooks stabilize zabaione with flour or cornstarch, though at the expense of its exquisite texture, or else they fold in stiffly whipped cream after the custard has cooled, creating in essence not a warm wine custard but a chilled wine mousse, which might be satisfying, but it's not zabaione.

Fortunately for diners, practicality and efficiency are not descriptors that spring readily to mind when considering the Italians, and cooks are no exception, or they might have done away with zabaione long ago. In fact it is the leisurely pacing and spontaneous nature of the Italian meal that allow the Italians a spot for zabaione in their repertoire. A proper meal can unfold for hours, for not only are the courses multiple, but someone is always dashing off between them, trotting down to the cantina for another bottle of wine, a wedge of aged cheese, another salame or jar of preserved cherries to add to the repast. Or else the mamma of the house will head back to the kitchen to stir together one more little something the likes of which, she's decided, the pranzo cannot proceed without. If the convivial momentum is high enough after the meat, after the cheese and the fruit, she wouldn't think twice about reigniting the stovetop to whisk up zabaione. Likewise in restaurants; customers do not consider it a burden to wait a bit for the dessert. Rather, the interlude provides a welcome pause as the meal unfolds.

Still, I would not have blamed Margherita for denying her daughter's request that evening, for growling that the kitchen was out of eggs until further notice. But she did not throw a pan in protest, did not even roll her eyes. Instead she beckoned me to bring her the bottle of good marsala from the bar and the container of eggs from the back pantry.

As she cracked five eggs, separating the yolks into a thin, battered saucepot, she explained that most people make zabaione in a *bagna-maria*, a large metal bowl set over, but not directly in, a pot of simmering water. This nested set-up allows temperamental sauces and ingredients like eggs and chocolate to cook slowly without scorching. The French call the device a *bain-marie*, or "Mary's Bath," which depending on your source traces back to the 3rd-century alchemist Mary the Jewess of Alexandria, who is credited with its invention (along with a distillation apparatus considered the forerunner to the alembic still). Or else it is named for the Virgin Mary, the embodiment of gentleness, for the gentle heat it conveys. Americans refer to it as a double-boiler, shedding light on why we are not known as a nation of sauce-makers, since you want neither the water in the bottom of your bagna-maria (or bain-marie, suit yourself) nor the ingredients in the top to boil lest your sauce curdle or separate from excessive heat.

Margherita raised an eyebrow smugly, pointed to her dented saucepot, and said she preferred her *bagna-gesù*—her Jesus' bath. She burst into laughter, a hoarse smoker's guffaw, and as she whisked sugar into the pot she said a lesser cook would end up with scrambled eggs.

The classic formula for zabaione is one egg yolk, a tablespoon of sugar, and a half-eggshell of wine per person. This may seem a quaint approach to measuring, accustomed as we are to precision down to the eighth-teaspoon, yet in the days before eggs came graded and sold by standard size, counting by the half-eggshell allowed cooks to measure accurately by ratio. The method still works, with the added bonus of one less utensil to clean. Otherwise, a half-eggshell holds about two tablespoons, though Margherita simply upended the bottle and poured out the marsala by the glug, glug, glug.

Although the earliest printed recipes for zabaione called for sweet wine generically, purists have long insisted on marsala, the fortified amber liqueur named for the port city of Marsala in Sicily where it is made. One of Sicily's most important exports, it became fashionable among Torino's caffè society during the 19th century, and it made its way into belle époque cookbook recipes for zabaione as well.

Margherita ignited a low flame under the saucepot and asked if I would mind taking over, she had veal chops to sauté. I took the whisk from her hand, and as she walked away she mentioned casually that I must stir the zabaione *sempre a destra*, always to the right.

Huh?

To the right with the whisk, she explained. Clockwise.

But why?

She looked at me and shrugged. That was just what people say.

What people?

Another shrug, she didn't really know. Old people.

Oh.

I wanted to question her further, but she had already turned her attention to her veal chops. So I started to whisk. For left-handed people like me, stirring clockwise to the right is a rather awkward motion. The left hand seems better suited anatomically to circling the other way. Fortunately, I can make do in the kitchen with either hand in a pinch, so I transferred the whisk and started stirring with my right hand. Soon I felt my neck and shoulder grow tense, my heartbeat quicken. All the many times I'd made zabaione in the past, I'd never done it in a bagna-gesù, and the fear of curdling the eggs had overcome me. The harder I tried to calm myself, the more nervous I became. In order to redirect my thoughts I contemplated Margherita's little directive: Stir to the right. I'd once heard the same thing about polenta. Stir to the left and you'll end up with lumps. A superstition, surely, but what was the reasoning behind it?

I would not find an answer that evening; Margherita had told me all she knew. The next day I asked Zia Giuseppina. Having lived through World War II, she seemed sufficiently dated to qualify as one of Margherita's "old people."

Oh yes, it's true, she told me. Otherwise your zabaione is apt to seize. How come?

She smiled and shrugged her shoulders. She didn't believe it herself, but some cooks swore it was true.

I would have to bring the question home with me, along with my bottles of dolcetto d'Alba, my espresso pot and roasted coffee beans, my giandu-otti chocolates from Guido Gobino, one of my favorite chocolate makers in Torino. But my shelves of cookbooks contained no clues. So I took to the Internet, and then headed to the library, where I requested some musty books on European folklore. I discovered all this clockwise stirring has been going on since long before there were clocks.

Technically speaking, clocks don't move clockwise, they move sunwise. They rotate in the same direction as the moving shadow of a sundial, and they reflect in European culture a preference for motion from left to right that dates back to the sun worship of pagan times. Why left to right? The sun appears to pass directly overhead only at the equator. In northern latitudes you must face south to follow the sun in its diurnal path. As it rises in the east, the sun comes up on the left and it sets in the west, on the right. Actually it is we earthly inhabitants who do the moving. As Copernicus pointed out, the sun itself is staying put, but to the ancients this perceived sunwise motion represented natural order and harmony in the world.

By extension, clockwise movement became a charm throughout Europe to invoke good luck. You walked clockwise around a well to make a wish come true, likewise around an invalid in bed to drive disease away. Wedding processions advanced clockwise around the church to secure an auspicious start to the marriage, and pallbearers carted a coffin clockwise around the gravesite before lowering it into the ground to ensure the deceased a restful life in the sweet hereafter. And in the kitchen, tradition maintained you should stir to the right. Not just zabaione and polenta, but jams and jellies or they wouldn't set; cake batter, or your cake would sink as it baked; cream, or it wouldn't turn to butter in the churn; mayonnaise, or it would break; and egg whites, or they would never whip to stiff peaks. Stir the sugar into your coffee clockwise or risk stirring up a quarrel.

I didn't dare disobey Margherita's orders that night at La Piola, I wasn't brave enough to put the superstition to the test. Whisking dutifully and vigorously to the right, my zabaione billowed up obligingly at my command, much to my relief. I spooned warm custard into each goblet as Daniela gave me an approving nod and a definitive *brava*, Teresa! Then she hoisted the tray above one shoulder and disappeared into the dining room.

To stir eggs, sugar, and wine into the ethereal sea foam that is zabaione is to bring about an alchemical transformation that never fails to delight. This storied spoon dessert, I discovered, can be made in any tired old pot, but in my own kitchen I still prefer a bagna-maria for the control and subtle heat if offers. When I whisk, I must confess I alternate hands, and directions, in spite of customary wisdom. That way I can give each arm a rest as it tires. All this subversive stirring and I haven't curdled a batch of zabaione yet, but perhaps it's only a matter of time. And somewhere out there is a cook just waiting to shake her spoon at me and say I told you so.

ZABAIONE

ALSO KNOWN AS ZABAGLIONE

(Serves 4)

The classic formula for zabaione is one egg yolk, a tablespoon of sugar, and a half-eggshell of wine per person. To serve more than four people, scale the recipe up accordingly. A half-eggshell holds about two tablespoons.

- 4 egg yolks
- 4 tablespoons sugar
- ½ cup dry marsala

Fill the bottom of a bain-marie or a heavy two-quart saucepan with two inches of water and bring to a simmer over medium-low heat.

Combine egg yolks, sugar, and marsala in the top half of bain-marie, or in a metal bowl that will rest securely over the saucepan. Stir until smooth, then place bowl over saucepan, making sure it does not touch the water.

Whisk vigorously, checking occasionally to keep water at a moderate simmer and clearing the bottom and sides of the bowl frequently with the whisk so the eggs don't scramble. Continue whisking until mixture triples in volume and becomes thick and foamy, about 10 minutes. When done, the zabaione will form soft mounds that hold their shape for a few seconds when the whisk is lifted.

Remove from heat, continue whisking another 30 seconds, then spoon into goblets or bowls. Serve alone or with ladyfingers or fresh berries.

PART II

THE MAREMMA

12

THE KEY TO THE KITCHEN

All I wanted at first was to know enough Italian to read the menu in a good Italian restaurant. A handful of words and phrases would suffice—*penne ai quattro formaggi, pollo arrosto, fagiolini all'aglio, crostata alla marmellata.* Penne with four cheeses, roast chicken, green beans with garlic, jam tart. I didn't even care much about pronunciation, figuring all I had to do was point and the waiter would know what to bring. Then I began cooking in restaurants and decided to memorize a brief glossary of Italian culinary terms so I could study cookbooks in Italian and expand my repertoire. Terms like *stemperare a fuoco lento; montare i bianchi a neve; fare un soffrito di cipolla, sedano, e carote*—simmer over a low flame; whip the egg whites until stiff; fry diced onions, celery, and carrot in oil.

These phrases and others offered me the basics of Italian kitchen techniques. They also helped me decipher my grandmother's recipes, the ones written out in fountain pen on the backs of old agenda pages and in the margins of her *Mrs. Rorer's Philadelphia Cookbook.* She wrote in a combination of Piedmontese dialect and Italian before she'd mastered English. (One recipe mysteriously calls for two teaspoons of cement, though my mother thinks she surely meant cinnamon.) By learning just a few key phrases I was able to bring my grandmother's voice back from the page.

As I prepared for my first trip to meet The Family I picked up a couple grammar books and tapes and learned some adjectives and simple verbs—primarily infinitives, plus a few regular conjugations in the present tense—with the aim of attaining the bare minimum necessary to partake in the chit-chat of a family meal. Then came that formative first visit to Rocca Canavese and my subsequent desire to immerse myself in my grandparents' native cuisine. If I wanted to cook like an Italian it would require a better command of the language than I'd managed through my books and tapes. For starters, navigating the country on my own would be easier if I knew a past tense. I could probably even conquer some irregular participles, though I refused to learn the difference between transitive and intransitive verbs. That was simply asking too much.

With those modest goals in mind I began looking for language schools in Italy. I wanted something in Tuscany, the birthplace of Standard Italian, but not in Florence or Siena or any other popular city where English could be heard on every corner. Instead I sought out schools in quiet pockets of the region where few English speakers traveled, knowing I would be forced to use Italian, and I further whittled down my list to places renowned for their piatti tipici, or local specialties.

That is how I stumbled onto Centro di Cultura Italiana, a private language school for foreigners in the medieval hilltop village of Manciano, a town of some 7,000 residents in the part of southern Tuscany known as the Maremma. One of the least populated areas in Italy, it is a land of open spaces, of vistas by turns rustic and wild, a countryside ignored or dismissed by travelers for some eight centuries in favor of the cultural splendors of Florence to the north. The school's brochure promised all the incentives to bring about the language, culture, life, and style of Italy, and an intimate learning experience in the heart of the countryside, far from mass tourism, which might have been eloquent in Italian, but seemed so clunky in translation I was sure it had to be true. My guidebooks offered an added endorsement, describing Manciano as notable primarily for the network of intercity buses that stopped there to take you to more interesting places. So if any English speakers did turn up, they wouldn't linger for long. I sent in my application and took time off work one early autumn for a four-week course.

I had to take a train to Grosseto and a bus with two transfers to get to Manciano after I landed in Rome. I needed the extra bus because I'd been told the school was walking distance from the Bar Centrale. It was a Saturday afternoon, and I'd made arrangements through the school to stay with a host family (part of my plan to absorb the local culture, force myself to use the language, and experience Italian home cooking firsthand), but my room would not be ready until three o'clock the following day. The letter I'd received from the school's director informed me that a key would be waiting at the Bar Centrale. I had only to ask for it upon my arrival and I could spend the first night at one of the student apartments near the school.

The bus pulled to a stop shortly after a road sign pointing to Manciano, and there across the street was the Bar Centrale. I got off, dragged my luggage across the intersection to the bar as the bus sputtered out of sight, and went inside to ask for a coffee and the key. The barrista made me my coffee but seemed puzzled when I asked him about the school. I took a deep breath and repeated in my clearest, rehearsed Italian that I was the *studentessa americana*. I'd been told to ask at the Bar Centrale for the key to the *appartamento* that belonged to the Centro di Cultura Italiana. His brow furrowed and he shook his head in incomprehension. I tried again. *La scuola*, the language school for foreigners in Manciano. Was this not the Bar Centrale?

Sì, signora, the barrista responded. It was the Bar Centrale, but the town was not Manciano. Manciano was two towns away, another twenty kilometers down the road. Villages big and small throughout those parts had a Bar Centrale, I understood him to say. So I downed my espresso, dragged my luggage back across the street, and sat on the curb for an hour until the next bus came along.

It would be evening by the time I got situated in the apartment. I got off the second bus at the wrong stop as well, at the base of the hill on Manciano's periphery, and as I was hauling my luggage up the cobbled street two men in an old Alfa Romeo stopped to give me a ride. They hoisted my giant duffel bag into the trunk, and with the unclosed lid bobbing gently we trundled up the spiraling road to the center of town and its Bar Centrale. I thanked the men, mille grazie, and they sped out of sight. I retrieved my key from the owner of the bar, who would not allow me to carry my bags any farther up the road, no he simply wouldn't hear of it. He interrupted two men playing cards at a corner table, and they delivered me to the student apartment by the school in Via XX Settembre. Exhausted, I took a shower and collapsed into bed.

I slept late the following morning, awakened by the church chimes across the piazza. I rummaged through the apartment kitchen, found a canister of ground coffee and a moka pot to fix myself an espresso, then made breakfast out of a hunk of bread, a wedge of cheese, and a pear left over from my bus ride from Grosseto. The bell tower struck one o'clock and I set out for a walk through Manciano's historic center, a labyrinth of cobbled roads, narrow alleyways, and stone ramps and staircases impassable by car. I wandered past the 14th century Aldobrandeschi Fortress and sat for a while on the rim of the fountain in Piazza Garibaldi, taking in the view that extended to the sea on that clear September day.

The streets were empty at that hour, save for the occasional cat darting through a doorway or surveying its domain from a balcony railing. The storefront doors were locked and shuttered, the shopkeepers and patrons already at home for the Sunday midday meal. I wended my way through the maze of streets, enchanted by stone archways and iron grillwork, heavy wooden entry doors with ornate bronze knockers, travertine stairways lined with potted geraniums, stair-treads worn from centuries of passing footsteps. I noticed basil and parsley plants in terracotta containers positioned within easy reach of kitchen windows.

From these open, invariably unscreened windows came a flood of aromas and sounds. I inhaled bold scents of roasted meat and garlic and simmering tomato sauce and the sweet perfume of a cake just pulled from the oven, and I heard the metallic clang and plink of silverware on ceramic plates, the clinking of wineglasses, a serrated knife sawing through a loaf of bread. There was a chorus of voices—children's laughter, the wail of a baby, a smoker's hacking cough. Someone was singing in baritone, accompanied by an out-of-tune guitar. Above all came the sound of people talking. Voices deep in conversation—arguing, agreeing, chiding, consoling—others prattling lightly along.

All that talking, and I could barely understand a thing. Alone in those desolate streets all I knew was that I wanted in. I wanted access to those kitchens and dining tables and cantinas, and it struck me that unless I mastered Italian I would forever be locked out. The language offered me the key. In order to open the door I needed more than just a cook's glossary and a few traveler's restaurant phrases, more even than the advanced beginner's small talk I'd hoped to make with The Family after my monthlong session at the school. To make myself at home at the Italian table would require real fluency; only with a solid measure of proficiency could I gain entry to that world.

I finished my circuitous tour of the town and let myself back into the apartment, where I organized my bags and waited for someone from the school to accompany me to my new accommodations. I looked for something else to eat but found only a bag of stale breakfast biscotti in a kitchen cupboard, so I decided I was better off hungry. Instead I pulled out my grammar book. Might as well take the opportunity to read up on a few irregular intransitive verbs.

CANTUCCI

BREAKFAST BISCOTTI

(makes about 4 dozen)

These twice-baked cookies, called *cantucci*, or *biscotti di Prato*, are traditionally served with a sweet dessert wine at the end of the meal. The addition of dried apricots, almonds, and oats gives them all the ingredients you need for breakfast, too, served with an espresso or steaming mug of caffelatte.

- 2 cups flour, plus 1 tablespoon for tossing with apricot pieces
- 1 teaspoon baking powder
- ½ teaspoon salt
- 1 cup sugar
- 2 large eggs
- ¼ cup olive oil
- zest of a lemon
- 1 teaspoon vanilla extract
- ½ teaspoon almond extract
- 1 cup dried apricots, chopped
- 1 cup blanched almonds (whole or slivered)
- ½ cup old fashioned oats (not instant)

Combine 2 cups flour, baking powder, and salt in a small bowl and set aside.

Place sugar, eggs, and olive oil in the bowl of a stand mixer with the paddle attachment and mix on low speed until smooth. Add lemon zest, vanilla and almond extracts, and continue mixing, until combined.

In a small bowl, toss remaining tablespoon of flour with dried apricots to keep the pieces from sticking and set aside.

Add flour mixture to wet ingredients, stirring just until blended and making sure to scrape bottom and sides of bowl with a spatula to thoroughly incorporate dough.

Stir in chopped apricots, almonds, and oats. Cover dough and refrigerate 30 minutes (or up to several hours or overnight).

Preheat oven to 350°F. Grease a baking sheet or line with parchment paper. Divide dough in half, roll into logs (about 12 x 2-inches) and place on baking sheet a few inches apart. Flatten the logs into loaves about 1 inch high. Bake until golden brown, about 30 minutes, rotating pan halfway through.

Reduce oven temperature to 300°F. Let loaves cool slightly, then cut into ½-inch slices. Arrange cut-side down on baking sheet and return to oven until biscotti start to harden and turn golden (they'll still feel a bit soft, but will continue to harden as they cool), 15 to 20 minutes.

13

THE COOKED WATER
OF MAREMMA

My family homestay accommodations turned out to be with an unmarried woman in her sixties who took in boarders as a supplement to her income. Her name was Liliana, and as a cook she was more expedient than impassioned, so not quite the wooden-spoon-wielding Italian mamma I'd hoped to meet. Still she was kind, and maternal in her way, and the day I met her she prepared me a little something for the afternoon *merenda* that convinced me even perfunctory cooking can be satisfying. All she did was dice and sauté some fleshy, sweet bell peppers in abundant olive oil with a cut clove of garlic and a sprinkle of salt until the peppers were seared and frizzled. She served them hot over toast with a thin wedge of aged cheese, and I've been making the same dish for myself ever since.

Her niece Alessandra was the director of cultural activities at the school. In her thirties, she lived in the attic apartment in the same building as Liliana. She was the one who told me I probably shouldn't refer to Liliana as *una zitella*. Zitella was a new word for me, and when I tried it out Alessandra advised that even though my dictionary defined it as "an unmarried woman," the term implied a certain eccentricity and dottiness that single ladies tended not to appreciate. Best to reserve it for spinsters and old maids of literature and song like Miss Havisham or Eleanor Rigby.

The Sunday morning after my first week of classes I encountered Alessandra on the stairs of the apartment building. She was on her way out for a walk and invited me to join her. I went up to my room, changed my shoes and grabbed my sunglasses, and we set out along the dusty back road that led to the nearby village of Montemerano. The sun beamed down on us on that late September morning as we passed through vineyards already gleaned save an occasional overlooked bunch of shriveled grapes hanging limp on the vine and olive groves where twisted limbs on ancient trees held bushels of black-mottled, nearly ripe fruit.

As we walked, Alessandra and I discussed the region's specialty dishes, in part to satisfy my curiosity, but more because of my limited proficiency in the language. I could still comprehend far more than I could say, so the only topic on which I could converse at any length was food. She offered up a list of delicacies to try as I toured the towns throughout the vicinity—smoked eel or fried frog's legs from the lagoons of Orbetello, braised hare from the thickets near Capalbio, stewed saltwater snails in Porto Ercole, grilled thrush captured between the vineyard rows of Scansano. Then talk turned to our plans for the evening's meal. Alessandra had made reservations for several of the students that night at Passaparola, a family-owned trattoria in a former olive mill in Montemerano's Via della Mura. I had already studied the menu in the restaurant's window on an earlier outing, and I told her that I was torn between the tagliatelle with wild boar and the *acquacotta*.

Acquacotta is a hearty little stew, and I was familiar with it from my cookbooks and previous travels. The name means "cooked water." In general it is a dense tomato and onion soup ladled over toasted country bread and garnished with a poached egg, a drizzle of olive oil, and a dusting of grated Tuscan Pecorino cheese. But it did not start out that way. It is a stone soup of sorts, and as with most traditional country fare, recipes vary from village to village, cook to cook. Still I did not realize that even people who squabble over the soup's precise ingredients will concede you can only alter the dish so much before it loses its regional character, ceases to be acquacotta and becomes another dish entirely. A satisfactory dish, perhaps, but a soulless dish, a dish that no longer holds the story of the Maremma and its people.

The acquacotta? Alessandra looked at me, her eyebrows arched in surprise over her almond-shaped, dark eyes. Liliana said her niece's high cheekbones, her slender nose, the graceful curve of her long neck were definitive proof there was a branch of nobility somewhere on the family tree. The acquacotta? Alessandra repeated. Only a week in the Maremma and already I knew about the acquacotta? How could that be?

I couldn't help but feel a rush of pride, as though I'd succeeded, albeit inadvertently, in some unforeseen rite of passage. I had sampled it, I explained, at a restaurant on my first visit to Tuscany a few years earlier. I all but tasted the memory of it still. There was a sweetness to it, from the slowly simmered onions.

Yes, she nodded in agreement. It was an aspect of the dish she found particularly pleasing.

The tomatoes gave the soup substance, I said, and fresh basil leaves provided the perfect background note.

Indeed.

And there was an earthiness, I continued, my confidence growing as I listened to myself demonstrate my intimate acquaintance with the local cuisine; there was an earthiness from the porcini mushrooms.

Porcini? Her voice ascended a few notes in surprise. Yes, she'd heard of cooks who added mushrooms, but she'd never tasted acquacotta that way herself.

They were definitely there, I assured her, along with a bit of cabbage.

Cabbage? That was certainly an interesting variation. Far more common to use Swiss chard, or maybe spinach.

No, the soup had thin strips of cabbage, Savoy cabbage, I distinctly remembered. And shell beans, meaty ones.

Shell beans? Alessandra stopped mid-stride and turned to me. Impossible. Nobody puts shell beans in acquacotta.

But there were shell beans, I insisted. And artichoke hearts as well.

Madonna! Then it was not acquacotta. Not with artichokes. Acquacotta would be the death of them, their delicate flavors lost in such a robust stew. Lost.

She exhaled slowly, drew in another breath, and when she resumed speaking her voice had taken on a conciliatory tone. Obviously I'd mistaken acquacotta for some other soup; that was all. Not to worry, she understood my confusion, the cuisine of Tuscany possessed soups innumerable, a foreigner couldn't possibly be expected to keep them straight.

I started to stammer. The conversation had taken an unexpectedly sour turn and I wanted to set things right, but I'd almost run out of vocabulary. Memory hadn't failed me, I said. In fact, the restaurant where I'd dined was called Acquacotta, and the waiter had taken great pride in telling me that acquacotta was the specialty of the house.

Alessandra issued a disdainful *hmmph*. We walked in silence for several minutes before she managed to muster more of a response. She spoke slowly, her voice laced now not with curiosity but suspicion. Just where was this restaurant that called itself Acquacotta and served a concoction of shell beans and cabbage and artichokes that it called by the same name?

In Florence, I said. Surely this would lend me some credibility. Didn't Florence reign as the gastronomic capital of Tuscany? Of all Italy?

Florence? Her face flushed red. *Florence?* How could a restaurant in Florence know the first thing about acquacotta? She dismissed the idea with a wave of her hand. Aquacotta was her native dish, a dish not of Florence, not of northern Tuscany, but of the Maremma. The Maremma only!

Alessandra had had enough of those Florentines. Yes, Florence was the cradle of the Renaissance, home to Michelangelo's *David* and Botticelli's *Birth of Venus*. Yes, her neighbors to the north had only to gaze upward to the cupola of Brunelleschi's Duomo to prove they were arbiters of artistic style. And indeed, the Florentines were justly famous for the restrained elegance and purity of flavors of their cuisine. Even so, she was not about to let them dictate the ingredients in her ancestral soup. If they wanted to serve acquacotta, she had no objections in principle, but the least they could do was serve it *alla maremmana*!

Alessandra had abandoned the slow, elementary Italian she normally used with students and was speaking quickly, fervently. I couldn't begin to understand all of what she said, but I got the gist of it, and with a bit of research I would fill in the missing details once I returned home.

A dictionary will tell you that *maremma*, with a lower case "m," means "pestiferous swamp." I found this hard to reconcile with what I'd seen of the landscape thus far. On the bus from Grosseto I passed through one charming medieval hilltop town after another. I watched the road unfurl alongside fine sand beaches that give way to sheer rock cliffs, over thick holm oak hills and across scrubland plains punctuated by umbrella pines.

Through the window I saw tidy vineyards and silver-green olive groves, fields of wheat and artichokes, pastures home to grazing sheep and long-horn cattle. The bus came upon a tour group of naturalists decamped along the roadside with binoculars in hand, searching for who knew what, perhaps the endangered festoon butterfly or black-winged stilt. We got stuck behind a pack of bicyclists clad in brightly colored Lycra like so many blossoms in a bouquet of zinnias. They huffed up the hills, then swooshed the descents with chins to the handlebars, shapely bottoms to the sky. On the second day of classes I visited Saturnia with a group of students and encountered crowds of pallid German and British tourists, come with their dermatitis, their asthma, and their unwanted cellulite to bathe in the curative waters of the town's hot springs, renowned since antiquity. So many natural wonders to discover, yet not a swamp in sight.

Nonetheless, explained Alessandra, for most of its history the Maremma was not only a pestiferous swamp, it was referred to in the plural: *Le Maremme*, a network of pestiferous swamps. It was an unwelcoming land with low-lying marshes infested with mosquitoes, and impenetrable woods home to vicious wild boar and bear and venomous snakes. "*Maremma amara*" laments a popular folk song: Bitter Maremma. Dante used the woods of the Maremma as a model for the forest where the souls of the Suicides were banished in the seventh circle of Hell.

For the most part, inhabitants of the Maremma led a life defined by disease and poverty. They suffered from what they called endemic ague, with its paroxysms of chills, fever, and sweating, its weakness, headaches, and aching joints. Severe cases and repeated bouts of this ague were often lethal, and life expectancy in the region barely exceeded twenty years. Doctors attributed the pervasive illness to the miasmas rising from the region's many swamps, for they contained inhospitable air that permeated the body and sapped the life force from the veins. It was this diagnosis, this bad air of the Maremma, that gave the disease its common name. *Mal' aria*. Malaria.

To combat the bad air, physicians advised a harsh regime of bloodlet-ting, enemas, and induced vomiting to rid the body of corrupt humors, perhaps killing as many patients as the malaria itself in the process. Less torturous, but equally ineffective, tablets made from flour and urine were administered, or body rubdowns with wood chips shaved from a gallows pole after an execution. Should these remedies fail, said the doctors, try eating more garlic. The doctors did not yet understand that the ubiquitous malaria was caused by a mosquito. Or rather, by a single-celled organism called a plasmodium parasite carried by the mosquito and delivered into the bloodstream when it bit a human.

The ancient Etruscans who first inhabited the Maremma were not excessively bothered by mosquitoes. They had developed a sophisticated series of drainage channels to divert water from the swamps, rendering the bottomlands suitable for agriculture and effectively ridding the land of malaria. They tended vineyards, olive groves, and grain fields in the fertile soil; mined copper, tin, and silver from the hills; and established for some five hundred years a prosperous civilization. Then came the conquering Romans. In the 3rd century B.C.E. they wiped out the Etruscans in a particularly nasty fit of expansionism, and although they themselves were no slouches in the field of hydraulic engineering, their priorities lay elsewhere, on the continued conquest of territories to the north, east, and south. Through indifference and neglect, the waterways began to silt up, and with the decline of the Roman Empire the sea and the rivers reclaimed what they had once ceded.

The marshes returned, and with them the mosquitoes. The Maremma was abandoned but for a few isolated villages on the hilltops—at altitudes beyond the reach of the pernicious air, and not coincidentally outside the habitat of the mosquito. It was a fine life for the landed gentry, but the peasants lived in squalor. They eked out whatever living they could manage down on the flanks of the hills and did their best to avoid the lowlands during the summer months when the climate was most lethal.

From this bleak existence arose acquacotta, in a version appropriately paltry to warrant its name. It was the midday meal for generations of shepherds and *butteri*—the cowboys who herded the region's famous Maremmana cattle; for the charcoal makers who descended from the Appenines to overwinter in the valley floors; for the *mignattai*—the leech-gatherers who canvassed the swamps and peddled their wares for blood-letting. Among their provisions, these laborers carried an earthenware pot, which they filled with stream water and set to simmer over an open fire with a slice of stale bread and whatever edibles the land offered forth. A wild onion, a fistful of dandelion greens, a few woodland mushrooms. The fortunate ones flavored their broth with an itinerant ham bone, shared between workers and saved to reuse from one meal to the next.

Efforts to drain the marshes for agriculture met with little lasting success. As control of the fortressed hilltop cities passed hostilely from feudal lord to feudal lord, from Siena to Florence to the House of Hapsburg-Lorraine, there was too much swashbuckling and political upheaval to tend to the swamps. The Medicis of Florence made a few half-hearted attempts. They even tried repopulating the Maremma in hopes of driving out the insalubrious air, but the peasant farmers they imported stubbornly refused to survive. (In America, a similar misguided optimism would lead Horace Greeley to proclaim, "The rain follows the plow!")

Matters didn't change much until the mid–19th century with the commission of a series of reclamation projects by the Tuscan grand dukes. They brought in their engineers and mathematicians to design canals and sluice gates and sediment traps, to do whatever it took to dry up the marshes and create tillable land. Their efforts took on added urgency in the final decades of the century as physicians pieced together the true cause of malaria and the mosquito's role in its transmission.

These discoveries coincided with similar advancements in the treatment of the disease after quinine became readily available. Quinine, a powder derived from the bark of the South American cinchona tree, was first used to treat malaria in the 17th century when Jesuit missionaries in Peru learned of its curative properties from native healers. They brought it back to Europe, and the bark famously cured cardinals and countesses and kings of the dreaded ague. But it was too scarce and costly to prescribe to the masses until production and distribution increased in the late 19th century. (It was also too Catholic. In Protestant England, where malaria was endemic in the fens, quinine was disdained as a popish plot. Oliver Cromwell refused his physician's pleas to take it and died of malaria in 1658.)

Decades passed and the malarial tide began to ebb. The backwaters of the Maremma slowly transformed into lush green fields. Mussolini redoubled the reclamation efforts during the Fascist era in an effort to make the country less reliant on imported grain, although his men were perhaps more resourceful at diverting funds than diverting water, and the bombs of the Second World War left many of the projects in ruins. It wasn't until the early 1950s that the works saw completion and the disease was finally eradicated. Immigrants came streaming in all the while, up from Lazio, down from Lombardy and Veneto to farm the land. They came and they did not die. Anemic complexions took on a healthy glow thanks to pure air, square meals, and government-supplied quinine tablets. Babies grew plump and strong on sheep's milk cheese, and the farmer's wife took charge of the herdsman's acquacotta.

In her hands it became a substantial one-dish meal, enriched with an abundance of vegetables from her garden, eggs from her henhouse, and fruity green olive oil from the reestablished olive groves. This farmhouse acquacotta now appears in almost every trattoria in the region, served as a refined *primo piatto* in a multicourse meal. But it remains a soup of nostalgia—a soup that makes old women beam with pride at their ability to create something out of nothing, a soup that makes old men shed tears, bittersweet tears, for they remember their mother's acquacotta, rest her soul, just as they remember the bitter aftertaste of the daily dose of quinine administered by the nuns when they were schoolboys.

To my surprise, Alessandra confessed she herself had never made acquacotta. Italy, she told me, is full of women in their thirties and forties whose jobs are so demanding they barely have time to lift a spoon in the kitchen. Along with an assortment of siblings and spouses and offspring they take several meals a week in famiglia, congregating at their parents' tables where Mamma still does the cooking. But they grew up around simmering pots and sharp cleavers. They could whip up a meal for the Pope if pressed, and they rattle off recipes, describe techniques, and dispense advice as though they performed such culinary feats on a daily basis.

Naturally, Alessandra had watched her mother prepare acquacotta countless times. She knew precisely how it was done, and as we walked she rattled off the procedure. To serve four, start by finely dicing two onions and a couple stalks of celery, including the leaves. Put them in a heavy soup pot with enough of your best olive oil to coat the bottom of the pan, and simmer until they soften and grow fragrant. Add a minced clove of garlic, a pound of fresh plum tomatoes, peeled and chopped, and a handful of fresh basil leaves, gently torn into pieces. A few chopped leaves of Swiss chard or spinach at this point are permissible.

Cabbage leaves are not. Season with sea salt, a few turns of the pepper grinder, and a pinch of red pepper flakes and cook for a couple more minutes. Pour in water to a depth of two fingers above the vegetables and let the soup bubble lazily over a low flame until it thickens slightly, about half an hour. Stir the pot from time to time and add more water if it seems to be getting too thick.

Toast four slices of day-old, coarse country bread and place in soup bowls. Meanwhile, poach four eggs, and when they are cooked to your liking, lift them from the water with a slotted spoon and nestle them atop each toast slice. Ladle the bubbling acquacotta broth and vegetables into each bowl, shower freshly grated Tuscan Pecorino cheese, anoint with a drizzle of olive oil, and serve piping hot.

By this time we'd been to Montemerano and back. The dirt road reconvened with the main thoroughfare leading up to Manciano, and as we headed into town Alessandra insisted I forego the wild boar that evening. It was a delicacy best saved for another day. *Passaparola*, she said, served a genuine acquacotta, I should opt for it instead. The trattoria's name, incidentally, means "password," which was all the more reason I should sample acquacotta there. Because when you enter the Maremma on a culinary journey, no matter where you want to start or where you want to go, all roads will lead you back to acquacotta before you can move forward.

ACQUACOTTA ALLA MAREMMANA

BREAD AND VEGETABLE SOUP OF MAREMMA

(Serves 4)

- 2 small onions, finely diced
- 2 stalks celery, including leaves, finely sliced
- 6 tablespoons extra virgin olive oil
- 1 garlic clove, minced
- 1 pound plum tomatoes, peeled and finely diced
- 6 to 8 large leaves fresh basil, torn in pieces
- 3 leaves Swiss chard, stems removed and finely sliced, leaves torn in pieces
- 1 pinch red pepper flakes
- sea salt and freshly ground pepper, to taste
- 4 cups water
- 4 eggs
- 4 slices day-old country bread
- ¼ cup grated Tuscan Pecorino cheese (or substitute Parmigiano)

Place the onions, celery, and olive oil in a heavy soup pot over a medium flame and sauté until the vegetable are soft and fragrant, about 5 minutes. Add the garlic clove, tomatoes, basil leaves, Swiss chard leaves and stems, and red pepper flakes. Season with sea salt and freshly ground pepper and cook 2 to 3 more minutes. Add water and adjust heat to maintain a low simmer until soup thickens slightly, about 30 minutes, stirring occasionally and adding more water if needed. Taste and correct seasonings. Keep soup at a simmer.

Poach the eggs in a large pot of simmering water, 3 to 4 minutes (see note). Meanwhile, toast the bread. Place the toasted bread in four soup bowls. When eggs are cooked to your liking, drain with a slotted spoon and place on top of toast in bowls. Ladle the bubbling broth and vegetables into each bowl. Garnish with grated cheese, drizzle with additional olive oil, and serve immediately.

Note: Traditionally the eggs in acquacotta are cooked directly in the simmering pot, but another acceptable approach is to poach them separately, and over time I've learned a few tricks for the task. Most crucial is to use the freshest eggs possible. The older the eggs, the runnier the whites, which will spread dismally when cooked, resulting in a thin, amoeboid mass. (I've been told eggs thirty-six hours from the hen are ideal for poaching, but not even farmers market eggs are so precisely dated.) Crack each egg into its own teacup or ramekin, being careful not to puncture the yolk. Bring a large pot of water to a boil and add a spoonful of vinegar, which helps keep the whites clinging securely to their yolk. Gently slip each egg into the boiling water and adjust the flame to maintain a bare simmer. Spoon a bit of the poaching liquid over the yolks to hasten their cooking, then simmer until set—3 to 5 minutes total, depending on whether you like your eggs runny or firm. I prefer a 4-minute egg, with the yolk just beginning to set on the outside and runny in the middle.

14

INTO THE LAMONE WOODS

When I started writing about the Maremma, I didn't plan to mention the Selva del Lamone. It didn't enter into the narrative. This, after all, was to be a memoir about food and cooking, and save for a meal beforehand and a bottle of San Benedetto mineral water, the Selva del Lamone had nothing to do with either. Besides, it added a gratuitous element of drama and suspense that seemed unbefitting of a mild-mannered culinary memoir. But in a roundabout way the Selva del Lamone granted me the invitation into a Tuscan kitchen that I was longing for, gave me an honorary membership in a Maremman family that I wouldn't otherwise have received. Many of the kitchen experiences I've come to write about wouldn't have occurred without the Selva del Lamone, so in hindsight I should have known I'd end up bringing the story of the Lamone Woods to the table.

The Selva del Lamone is a 4,500-acre wilderness area rising up from a volcanic plateau some twenty miles east of Manciano, just outside Tuscany in the region of Lazio. Officially designated a nature reserve in 1994, it is noted for its dense, old-growth oak groves, abundant wildlife, Bronze Age ruins, and characteristic lava formations known colloquially as *murce*—enormous mounds of volcanic boulders scattered haphazardly (some say inexplicably) throughout the terrain. Legend maintains the murce arose after Hercules went out strolling in the woods one day. He was overtaken by a band of robbers, and Jupiter rescued him with a barrage of molten stones that killed the thieves in their tracks. This seems plausible enough, but apparently the geologists remain unconvinced. They continue to look to the extinct Vulsini volcano at the periphery of the reserve for answers.

Thieves reigned again in the Selva del Lamone during the 19th century, an era in Italian history when the bulk of the country's money, land, and power lay in the hands of a select few and the rest of the populace lived in varying degrees of poverty. Throughout the Maremma, brigands plundered the hilltop country estates of the landed gentry and hid out in the impenetrable Lamone woods, including the celebrated folk hero Domenico Tiburzi. A convicted murderer, on the lam since 1872 when he escaped his chain gang in the government salt mines, Tiburzi got his start as a highwayman, preying on pilgrims as they traveled to and from Rome. He rose to become the self-proclaimed "King of the Lamone," collecting taxes from area landowners in exchange for protecting their property against lesser thieves, and according to legend, sharing his profits with the poor in the manner of an Italian Robin Hood. To the State and land barons he was a bloodthirsty racketeer, but he was a champion of the oppressed to the peasants who received his largesse. Or was it simply hush money? Time has blurred the line distinguishing truth from myth. For almost twenty-five years Tiburzi made the Lamone woods his lair, abetted by local farmers, until 1896 when he was gunned down by the *carabinieri* near the town of Capalbio. They tied his body to a pillar outside the cemetery and photographed him with his gun in hand as a warning to other bandits, but the act had the unintended effect of making Tiburzi a martyr among the poor, and copies of the famous picture still hang on trattoria and storefront walls throughout the area.

A single dirt road passes through the reserve today, and from it branches an extensive network of over sixty miles of trails, including *Il Sentiero dei Briganti*, the Brigands' Way. Guided excursions on foot, horseback, and mountain bike can be arranged through the reserve's headquarters in the town of Farnese to the south; in fact a guide is recommended for inexperienced hikers, especially on the more difficult trails where the terrain is particularly rugged. Arrangements must be made in advance, because amenities are limited inside the reserve—there is no visitors' center, no restroom, no convenience store, no cell service.

On the crisp Friday afternoon in mid-October that concluded my first two-week session at the language school, Alessandra organized an excursion to the nature reserve. We were a small group, only five of us—Alessandra, a retired couple from Utah, a Swiss woman who worked as an interpreter (in Geneva, if memory serves), and me. The rest of the students had either returned home, their vacations ended, or opted to spend the weekend in Siena or Florence or some other tourist destination farther afield before the next session started on Monday.

Before heading into the woods we stopped off at I Due Cippi da Michele, a moderately priced restaurant that served classic Maremman cuisine in the village of Saturnia. While Saturnia is best known for its therapeutic hot springs outside the village walls—complete now with a modern spa and five-star hotel—the city itself is rich in history, Etruscan, Roman, and otherwise. The eponymous *cippi* are the ruins of two Roman columns that grace the piazza in front of the restaurant, which is located in a palazzo once home to the Marchese Ximenes of Aragon.

Our waiter brought an antipasti platter brimming with prosciutto and salame, salty black olives, and tiny marinated zucchini and eggplant. Then came *tortelli di castagne*, one of the most memorable dishes I would encounter during my stay in Tuscany. Tortelli is a regional name for ravioli. Generally meatless, these were gossamer pillows of hand-rolled egg pasta filled with pureed chestnuts, Parmigiano cheese, and a hint of cinnamon, then drizzled with melted butter infused with wild fennel seed. A salad of radicchio and endive leaves glistening with fruity olive oil followed, and for dessert, *la pignolata*, a pine-nut torte with vanilla cream filling.

The meal and two bottles of local Morellino wine made the idea of a walk in the woods less appealing for some. The retirees decided an afternoon nap in the lounge chairs at their beachfront hotel in Porto Ercole sounded more enticing, and the Swiss woman went in search of an enterprising and sympathetic butcher to vacuum-pack some prosciutto and salame for her. Ever since the outbreak of mad cow disease in Europe in the mid-nineties, the transport of meat products across international boundaries has come under tight restriction, but with ingenuity and shrink-wrap it is still possible to outwit the customs officers and their contraband-sniffing dogs at the airport.

So Alessandra and I set out alone in the sputtering red Fiat 127 that belonged to the school. A wooden sign emblazoned with a multicolored trail map marked the Selva del Lamone trailhead when we arrived at almost four o'clock. With only a few hours of daylight left, we were off to a late start after our multicourse meal. Alessandra chose one of the shorter routes, a two-mile loop she had last hiked with students in the spring. The narrow path wound through a thick forest just beginning to acquire the red and yellow and orange tints and dank aromas of autumn. We crossed moss-covered rock beds and fallen logs, while around us clumps of violets and ferns, blooming cyclamen, and box holly with ripe scarlet berries carpeted the forest floor. Green acorns littered the path, likewise spiny chestnut pods that had burst open upon hitting the ground to surrender their dark, shiny nuts. Overhead a thick canopy of lichen-covered holm oaks afforded only intermittent glimpses of a cloudy sky. The woods opened occasionally onto gray lava mounds—the evocative murce—with boulders heaped to the angle of repose, as if at any moment they might tumble to the ground, when in fact they've been motionless for fifty thousand years.

The going was easy at first, the terrain essentially flat, though the trail was muddy in places as it traversed the volcanic plateau. Soon, however, our progress slowed, the trail obscured by numerous downed trees and washouts from a recent summer storm and subsequent logging activity. Still, the way was well marked with red blazes painted on the trees lining the trail, and we persevered, often bushwhacking from one red marker to the next. Somewhere along the way the red blazes disappeared, but we'd picked up a string of yellow ones as we plodded along. This seemed a bit odd to me, accustomed to the Appalachian Trail that practically passes through my front yard in New Hampshire— for all of its 2,175 miles it is marked with the same symbol. But this was Italy, I thought, and Alessandra was striding so confidently onward. Naturally they did things differently here. We'd left the red trail, and the yellow blazes corresponded to the yellow trail on the map, that was all.

If we humans could sense the exact moment we wandered astray—the misguided step or, better, the footfall immediately preceding it—no one would ever get lost. Instead, most of us have only an inadequate internal compass or astrolabe, and without the sun to cast a shadow or a landmark on the horizon to fix our bearings, we invariably end up walking in circles, our inner compass needle spinning freely, its magnetic field disrupted. Which is exactly what happened to Alessandra and me. We realized we'd seen that rotten log, that twisted oak snag, that pile of rocks twice already before, now three times. We slowly understood the path that kept appearing in fits and starts was only a game trail. Those yellow stripes on the trees? Who knew what they were for; maybe just marks for loggers.

The sun had already set. With darkness falling we made our way back to a clearing we'd circled through and decided to stay put for the night. Alessandra started to cry, as much out of embarrassment and frustration, I sensed, as fear. How could such a thing have happened? If she'd been on this trail once, she'd been on it a dozen times, how could she have been so stupid? As for me, I remained calm, partly in an effort to console Alessandra—I certainly didn't hold her to blame. I should have spoken up the instant we lost our red blazes. And I truly wasn't worried yet. An avid hiker, I had logged hundreds, maybe thousands of miles on trails across America—the Cascades, the Sierra Nevada, the White Mountains, the Green Mountains. Any of my hiking companions will tell you my own sense of direction is none too keen. I am accustomed to temporarily misplacing myself on the trail. I didn't get lost; I just took circuitous routes. Spending an unplanned night out in the elements, now that was something new, but I had no doubt we would find our way in the morning. Turns out I had no idea the seriousness of our predicament.

The Selva del Lamone, I would learn, has been ensnaring travelers for centuries. Upon visiting the woods in 1537, the poet Annibal Caro wrote, "Thus we entered a forest, such as we were quickly lost, and found ourselves enclosed and stumbling around in circles." Folk songs and legends tell of lost shepherd boys and charcoal makers and hunters. Those who managed to emerge had usually been robbed at gun or knifepoint of their valuables. A few years ago a search party unearthed the forgotten wreckage of an American B-24 Liberator, shot down by the Germans in World War II.

Between sobs, Alessandra spoke of the wild boar and other dangerous creatures that lurked in the thickets, but I dismissed her fears as so much melodrama. I did not know about the scorpions and asps that infest the area, and I'd always thought of the wild boar as a rather good humored, comical fellow. In fact he possesses a much darker disposition, feared by farmers for his ability to tear a newborn lamb or calf limb from limb. Attacks on humans are not unheard of in the area, and hunters often protect their dogs with Kevlar vests when hunting boar. Every so often the local papers run yet another account of a search mounted by the forest service for some unfortunate hiker or outdoorsman lost in the labyrinth of the Lamone woods. Not all the stories end happily. Exposure, injury, starvation—people have died in those woods.

The writer Angelo Pellegrini—author of the classic 1948 memoir *The Unprejudiced Palate*; emeritus professor of English at the University of Washington; Italian immigrant, cook, gardener, and winemaker—once spent a night lost in the Cascade Mountains near Seattle while foraging for mushrooms. He passed the time by reciting passages from Dante's *Inferno* through the long hours until morning when the search and rescue team appeared:

> *Nel mezzo del cammin di nostra vita*
> *Mi ritrovai per una selva oscura*
> *Ché la diritta via era smarrita.*
> *Ahi quanto a dir era è cosa dura*
> *Esta selva selvaggia e aspra e forte*
> *Che nel pensier rinova la paura.*

> Midway upon the journey of our life
> I found myself within a forest dark,
> For the straightforward pathway had been lost
> Ah me, how hard a thing it is to say
> What was this forest, savage, rough and stern;
> Which in the very thought renews the fear.
>
> (tr. W. W. Longfellow)

Too bad I hadn't yet read Dante, for there I was, lost in his very woods, his *selva oscura*, right there 'twixt Cecina and Corneto, with the She-wolf and Harpies hiding behind every tree, and I didn't even know it. Blissfully unaware, I actually started to enjoy myself, once Alessandra was over her tears. Instead of reciting cantos, we came up with other forms of entertainment. I taught her how to swing dance, Texas-style, and she showed me a few tango steps she'd picked up. She taught me the regular and irregular conjugations of the present conditional. *Ci piacerebbe ritrovare la via diritta.* We would like to find our way again. *Sarebbe bello avere una lampadina tascabile.* It would be nice to have a flashlight.

We pulled up a log for a bench and in my Italian of limited tenses and her smattering of English we engaged in a lively conversation. In this, she broke a cardinal rule, for school policy required employees to speak to students only in Italian. Given the circumstances she granted herself an exemption. Our talk unfurled with the random turns and tangents typical of discussions at the midnight hour. We spoke of socialized health care and the immigrant crisis, of my Italian heritage and the immigrant experience in early 20th–century America, of cellulite and crow's-feet, career changes and biological clocks, remedies for hay fever and broken hearts. Two thirtysomething women in different cultures, one married, one not, both childless, we discovered that our dreams and fears, our frustrations and joys were remarkably similar, and along the way we ceased being just acquaintances. I was boarding with Alessandra's aunt Liliana, so the two of us had enjoyed an additional degree of familiarity from the start, but our relationship until that afternoon had been essentially a professional one. During the course of the night, after we'd talked and danced, laughed and cried, and ultimately run out of things to say, we had become friends.

Alessandra removed her windbreaker and spread it over the ground. We each took a swig from her bottle of San Benedetto, deciding it best to save the rest until morning. With a black, starless sky overhead, we huddled together in an attempt to doze the remaining hours until first light. Alessandra, in sweatpants and long sleeves, was marginally more appropriately dressed than I was. While daytime temperatures had remained pleasantly warm for October during my visit, autumn had been making its presence felt more acutely at night, with temperatures dropping into the upper forties. In my cotton pullover and khaki shorts, the earth felt damp, the air uncomfortably cold against my bare legs. The rocky ground and the noises of the night—the wind in the trees, the snuffling and rustling of unseen animals, the odd branch abruptly snapping, the screech of an owl—made sleep impossible.

Amid the eerie din, however, came two reassuring sounds: the low-pitched bark of a large dog and, just before daybreak, the crowing of a rooster. Somewhere nearby there had to be a farm, and as soon as it grew light enough to see, all we had to do was head toward the barnyard cries.

Just after dawn the sun pulsed faintly through a thick fog, too weak to take the morning chill out of the air. We drank the last of Alessandra's water and set out in the direction of the sounds we'd heard, scrambling over boulders and through the underbrush without so much as a game trail to follow, hoping the dog would bark, the rooster would crow again to guide us. But our beacons of the night had fallen maddeningly silent. After an hour the forest had grown thicker and thornier, creating an impassable barrier between us and the farm we hoped to find. We made one last effort, trying to force our way through the briars by sheer will, but the woods refused to cede us any more ground and we retreated, legs and forearms scratched and bleeding. We retraced our steps to the clearing and resumed our search for the trail, but soon found ourselves circling, once again, past landmarks by now too familiar.

On one of these laps I felt my first twinge of fear, realizing we were not going to up and walk out of there with the ease I had envisioned during the night. My heart started to race, and I noticed my hands shaking. I made myself take a few slow, deep breaths, let the fear pass over me, and then forced it to leave, for Alessandra's spirits had improved measurably. She was certain her father and brothers would be looking for us. They would put together a search party, she just knew they would.

I knew how long it took a group of Italians just to decide on a restaurant for dinner. To expect them to organize a search party so quickly seemed too optimistic even for me. I started looking at the forest floor with a new eye. We could gather plenty of dead branches and downed tree limbs and make a lean-to for better protection against the elements if we had to spend another night. My throat felt parched. I didn't recall coming across a stream during our wanderings, but we'd have to find one and take our chances that the water was good to drink. We had tramped through patches of violets and wild sorrel, which were edible, and so were the chestnuts scattered on the ground, if we could figure out a way to pry them from their capsules. I wasn't particularly hungry yet, but our chestnut tortelli and Morellino wine seemed a distant memory, as did the pleasantly sated, mildly euphoric state in which we'd left I Due Cippi only an afternoon ago.

By midmorning the fog had burned off to reveal a brilliant blue sky. Overhead in the distance we heard the drone of an engine, a small plane perhaps. Someone was out for a pleasure flight, if only we could get to higher ground we might be seen. We plowed our way back to an enormous hill of bare boulders, one of Jupiter's murce that we'd previously skirted. I clambered to the top with Alessandra following behind me. We could hear the plane but couldn't see it, so we sat down to wait. Minutes later, a helicopter came into view, making a pass on the horizon then turning around to sweep back again. We jumped to our feet and started waving our arms. *"Aiuto! Aiuto!"* Alessandra shouted. "Help! Help!" I heard myself scream. The engine roar grew louder, the helicopter made a closer pass. I switched to Italian, *"Aiuto! Aiuto!"* believing, I suppose, it would be more productive to shout into the void in the mother tongue of the land.

We watched in disbelief as the helicopter sped away, disappeared from sight. I learned a new Italian expletive and yelled a couple American ones of my own. We sank to the ground, there on the summit of the boulder mound, too devastated to speak. Five minutes passed in silence and then the low drone returned. The helicopter reappeared on the horizon, closer this time. It flashed its lights, banked abruptly, started moving in our direction. We sprang to our feet and resumed our *aiuto* chorus, our voices going hoarse as we jumped and waved our arms and hugged each other.

The helicopter drew in close, hovered as low as it could—it belonged to the carabinieri, the Italian military police. Amid the deafening roar of the engine and wind churned up by the blades, two grinning pilots pantomimed that we should wait there, a search party was on its way. Only then did I comprehend they'd actually been *looking* for us. This was Italy, after all, country of infuriating bureaucracy and municipal documents stamped in triplicate. Far more logical to think the pilots had stumbled on us by accident, out on a training flight, than to imagine they'd organized a rescue operation on such short notice. In fact the search had been launched the previous evening, immediately after Alessandra's father reported us missing to the police. More than thirty people had joined in the effort; I'm embarrassed now to have ever harbored doubts.

After a wait that seemed interminable but actually lasted little more than an hour, the rescue squad arrived—several carabinieri officers,

Alessandra's father and two brothers, and a middle-aged man with sun-creased skin, a green cap, and a dog of undetermined breed. I didn't pay much attention to the man and his dog at the time, overwhelmed as I was by lack of sleep, the language barrier, and my relief at having been found. Alessandra would later explain he was a well-known poacher in the area. Hunting in the reserve was prohibited, a fact that only made the pursuit more sporting for many locals. He'd been enlisted by the rescue team—a kindhearted outlaw in the spirit of Tiburzi himself, who knew the Lamone woods more intimately than any park official. To his chagrin, the helicopter had spotted us first. Turned out he only had his second-best dog with him. While this dog had been given articles of our clothing to sniff, he was an inexperienced tracker, still in training. The hunter's number-one dog was out on maternity leave, home with a week-old litter of puppies. If she'd been along, she would have picked up our scent, the hunter had no doubt.

A flurry of embraces and handshakes and mille grazies ensued. Were we all right? Yes, fine; no injuries, just a bit thirsty. Our rescuers offered us water and a packet of biscotti and proceeded to escort us to safety. We walked out of the Selva del Lamone easily, leisurely, in a fashion almost surreal, or perhaps just quintessentially Italian, for we stopped twice—once while a couple officers took a cigarette break and again while the poacher foraged for wild mushrooms. In my muddled state I didn't notice who led the way, maybe the poacher, maybe a ranger. While at first we walked without the benefit of a trail, one soon appeared. Not the red-blazed trail we'd been looking for, but an obvious trail all the same, as if the woods had decided it was finally time to let us pass. The forest that had so tightly closed in around us obligingly released its hold. *Che miracolo!* said Alessandra. Like the Red Sea parting for Moses.

Our helicopter was waiting at the edge of the woods when we emerged less than an hour later, along with an assortment of carabinieri, forest rangers, cameramen, and reporters—we made the local television news that night and two papers the following day. Liliana was there, making the sign of the cross. Beside her stood a small, dark-haired woman in her sixties, fingering a rosary. She rushed to Alessandra, threw her arms around her, clutched her with eyes closed in that silent, still embrace of gratitude and relief universal to mothers even of children long since grown. She turned to me, placed her hands on my shoulders and planted a kiss squarely on each cheek.

Alessandra laughed. "Teresa," she said, *"Ti voglio presentare mia madre."* I'd like you to meet my mother. Indeed we hadn't yet met. But now that we'd been formally introduced, Franca insisted I join her family that afternoon at the midday meal, surely I must be famished. She and her husband, Eraldo, would take me home once the thank-yous to our rescuers had all been said. After I'd had a chance to shower, she informed me, I should descend the stairs from Liliana's apartment to theirs. No need to knock, the door would be open. She would set a place for me.

TORTELLI DI CASTAGNE

CHESTNUT TORTELLI

(Serves 4)

The wonderful book *La Cucina Maremmana* by Aldo Santini contains culinary lore, commentary, and recipes for traditional dishes served at restaurants throughout the Maremma, including the delectable chestnut tortelli that sustained Alessandra and me through the night in the Lamone woods.

Santini wonders if these tortelli might trace their origins back to the Etruscans who first settled in the region, the cradle of Italy's most ancient civilization. Eating this dish by candlelight, there in Saturnia with its thousand-year-old ruins, its necropolises, the atmosphere certainly seems evocative enough to support the claim. Santini tells his readers to think whatever they'd like; the Etruscans have been credited for far grander accomplishments on even less evidence.

Like most Italian cookbooks, *La Cucina Maremmana* lists ingredients, but doesn't give quantities. Here are the proportions I've worked out to recreate I Due Cippi's signature pasta dish in my own kitchen each autumn.

FOR THE PASTA DOUGH:
- 3 large eggs
- 300 grams (about 2½ cups) all-purpose flour

Santini says to prepare the pasta as you normally would. If you don't know how, he recommends you turn the page, or content yourself with merely reading the recipe to stimulate the appetite. Or you can scoop the flour onto a dry cutting board, make a well in the center, crack in the eggs, and stir with a fork until you can no longer whisk. Use your hands and a dough scraper to incorporate the rest of the flour, knead 8 to 10 minutes, until smooth, and set aside for about 30 minutes, covered with an upturned bowl or wrapped in plastic.

FOR THE CHESTNUT FILLING:
- 450 g (1 pound) fresh chestnuts
- 50 g (½ cup) grated Pecorino or Parmigiano cheese, or a combination of the two
- ½ teaspoon wild fennel seeds (or regular dried seeds, lightly crushed)
- 1 egg
- pinch of ground cinnamon
- sea salt, to taste

Cut a slit across one side of each chestnut with a sharp knife, then place in a pot and cover by about two inches with water. Bring to a boil and cook until chestnuts are tender when pierced with a knife, 20 to 30 minutes. Let cool and peel, which according to Santini, requires the patience of a saint, though peeling goes faster with practice. Pass the chestnuts through a food mill or puree in a food processor with the fennel seeds, grated cheese, egg, cinnamon, and salt.

TO MAKE THE TORTELLI:
Divide the dough into four pieces, working with one piece at a time while keeping the rest covered. Roll the pieces into strips with a pasta machine, working down to the thinnest setting, or perhaps the next to last setting, depending on your machine. The dough should be thin enough to see your hand through, but not so thin it tears when you make the tortelli. Cut the pasta into 3-inch squares, place a tablespoon of the filling on each square, fold in half as you would a book, and press the edges with your fingers, allowing any air to escape as you seal the tortelli. Transfer the tortelli to a flour-dusted baking sheet and keep them covered with a dishtowel as you work.

TO COOK THE TORTELLI AND SERVE:
- 50 g (4 tablespoons) butter
- 1 teaspoon fennel seeds

- sea salt
- additional freshly grated Pecorino or Parmigiano cheese

Bring a large pot of water to a boil over high heat and add a heaping tablespoon of salt.

Melt the butter and fennel seeds in a large sauté pan over high heat until the foam subsides and the melted butter begins to brown around the edges. Remove from the heat.

Boil the tortelli until tender and cooked through, about 4 minutes (don't be afraid to test for doneness by cutting into one and tasting it). Drain the tortelli, then add them to the sauté pan with the fennel-infused butter and a spoonful of the pasta cooking water. Stir carefully over high heat for a minute and test for salt, adding more if needed. Transfer to a warmed serving dish and garnish with additional cheese. Serve straight away.

ABOVE LEFT: Giacomo harvesting figs from his new tree. ABOVE RIGHT: Marina with the day's harvest of heirloom *cuor di bue* (oxheart) tomatoes. BELOW: Augusto and Catterina's bakery in Rocca Canavese.

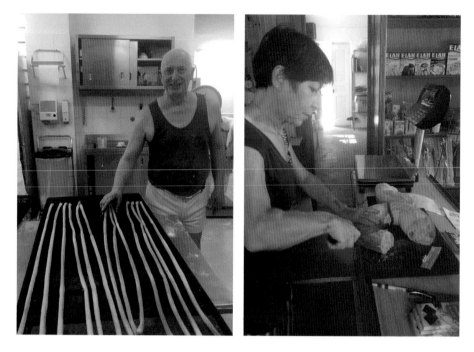

ABOVE LEFT: Augusto surveying his *grissini*. ABOVE RIGHT: Catterina slicing bread for a customer in the bakery. BELOW LEFT: Suor Mariangela checking Catterina's blood pressure. BELOW RIGHT: Felice's corn drying in the open air for polenta.

ABOVE LEFT: Felice descending the stairs to work in his garden. ABOVE RIGHT: Giuseppina and her sister, Maddalena, in front of the house in Case Perrero. BELOW: Giuseppina and my mom, Darlene, in the garden.

ABOVE LEFT: Giacomo roasting chestnuts for a neighborhood feast. ABOVE RIGHT: Margherita pouring a glass of wine at La Piola. BELOW LEFT: Margherita's husband Domenico stirring polenta (to the right) at La Piola. BELOW RIGHT: Alessandra (foreground) and her mother, Franca, cooking with students from the language school.

ABOVE: Newspaper article from the *Corriere di Viterbo* with the headline, "Lost in the Lamone Woods, Found after a Night of Fear." BELOW LEFT: Clara (left) and her friend's daughter Sara at La Stellata's end of harvest celebration. BELOW RIGHT: Manlio (right) and his friend Giovanni (left) loading grapes into the hopper to be de-stemmed and crushed.

ABOVE: Harvesting procanico grapes at La Stellata.
BELOW: Wheels of Pecorino Toscano cheese and salumi.

ABOVE LEFT: Conero Park in Le Marche. ABOVE RIGHT: Cinzia making *cappelletti*, "little stuffed hats" for Sunday *pranzo*. BELOW LEFT: Francesco leading the descent of the talus slope to his asparagus grove. BELOW RIGHT: Francesco scaling the monument on Monte Revellone.

ABOVE: Dining on *stoccafisso* with Rebecca, Cinzia, and her daughter Angelica at Trattoria La Cantineta in Ancona. BELOW LEFT: Bianca, "*la sfoglina*," cutting tagliatelle by hand at Trattoria Strologo in Camerano. BELOW RIGHT: A late summer fig, ripe for the picking.

Interior images courtesy of Margot Davis, Nancy Lust, David Picatti, and Teresa Lust.

15

A GOOD COOK

Seated on a log under a starless sky that night in the Selva del Lamone, the conversation eventually turned to food. Hunger had nothing to do with it; our lavish pranzo at I Due Cippi had been enough to tide us over till morning. Perhaps after we'd exhausted all the other topics I could discuss after my few weeks at the school—family, home, work, relationships—food just came up next on the list. Or maybe, as I heard someone once say, Alessandra and I talked about food because Italians enjoy talking about eating as much as they enjoy eating itself. They like to talk about what they are eating at the moment, what they've eaten in the past, and what they intend to eat in the future. While these discussions ideally take place around a crowded dinner table, an open meadow in the midnight hours was as good a place as any.

Well into the night, hands shoved in pockets, collars turned up against the damp air, Alessandra gave me a private lesson in the local cuisine. The cooking of the Maremma was, and remains, a *cucina casalinga*, rustic home cooking, deeply rooted in the land and the seasons, prepared by the wives of fishermen and woodsmen, shepherds and cowhands, sharecroppers and charcoal makers. Fish and seafood specialties still prevail in the coastal villages along the Tyrrhenian Sea, but just a few miles inland you will find farm dishes based on lamb or pork, or on wild boar, hare, and other upland game, as hunting remains a popular pastime. The Maremman housewife rounded out her meals with vegetables and herbs from her garden, sheep's milk cheeses from her neighbor's dairy, olive oil and wine from nearby groves and vineyards, and wild mushrooms, greens, and chestnuts foraged from the woodlands.

Traditional Maremman cooking is elemental. Though there are peas to be shucked, beans to be shelled, artichokes to be trimmed, it is not an ornate or excessively labor-intensive cuisine. Who could spare time to prepare fussy meals, what with laundry and mending and children underfoot? Rather than spend hours at the stove, the casalinga cooked in catches and snippets, often in just the time it took for the pasta water to reach a boil. Or else her dishes sputtered away on the back burner, untended while she devoted herself to other tasks.

Alessandra described the region's specialties with mouthwatering and technical detail. She discussed the finer points of roasting wild boar whole on a spit, and which cuts of domestic pig were best salted and spiced for salame. She told me how cooks hand-cut *pappardelle*, the wide pasta ribbons of the area, served with a slow-simmered sauce of wild duck, and she spoke with nostalgia and reverence of the housewives of Manciano who still made *ciaffagnone*—gossamer crepes browned in a skillet, showered with Pecorino cheese, and folded in quarters like a handkerchief. She had me examine a few spiny outer husks of the chestnut pods littering the ground near our site. With October drawing to a close, vendors were turning up on street corners selling hot roasted chestnuts, and aromatic chestnut flour would soon appear at the markets for the region's *castagnaccio*, a dense chestnut cake infused with rosemary and studded with golden raisins.

Alessandra enjoyed cooking. She considered herself accomplished to a degree, but her job kept her busy, and she didn't yet have a husband or children to cook for, so she spent less time in the kitchen than she otherwise might. Her mother, Franca, though, was a true cook. She knew the piatti tipici of the Maremma, all the old recipes and then some. A better teacher would be hard to find.

Though a native of Pistoia in northern Tuscany, Franca moved to the Maremma with her family in the 1940s at the age of five, and she experienced firsthand the forces that shaped the area's traditions. Her father, like many young Tuscan men in those days, came seeking work. He found a job as a lumber foreman, coordinating timber cutting for the production of charcoal. Her family spent early autumns through winter in a logging camp in the shrublands, living in a cabin made of sod and straw and sleeping on mattresses stuffed with cornhusks. Her teachers gave her homework over the winter months and she kept up her studies with her mother's help. In spring, before the mosquitoes hatched and brought malaria back to the lowlands, the family returned to Pistoia and Franca returned to school. Her father eventually moved the family to a new home in Manciano. In the same building lived a handsome boy named Eraldo, who would become Franca's husband. The two started a family together, and Eraldo eventually opened an insurance business in town.

When I returned to Manciano the following year for another session at the language school, Alessandra invited me to stay with her. She had spoken with her mother about my interest in Maremman cuisine. Though flattered by my request to watch her cook, Franca initially resisted. Shouldn't I find a more qualified instructor? Surely there were professional chefs out there who taught cooking lessons to foreigners, maybe even expats who gave classes in English. Doubtless there were, and good ones at that. But those weren't the lessons I sought. I wanted a more familial experience, an informal apprenticeship in the kitchen of a good home cook. Home cooks, I'd learned, tend to be generous with their time; good home cooks even more so. They share their knowledge eagerly, all you have to do is ask, and the more you want to learn the more they have to teach you. Franca was no exception.

After my morning language classes I would make the ten-minute walk from the school in Manciano's historic center to Alessandra's attic apartment in a brick palazzo on the town's periphery. Liliana had switched apartments since my previous visit, to the one directly beneath Alessandra, and her parents and two of her three brothers lived two floors below, in her childhood home. Seated at my desk in the spare bedroom I would immerse myself in verb tenses and conjugations, comparatives and superlatives, double object pronouns and the use of the subjunctive in hypothetical situations until I heard Franca calling up the stairs, "Teresa! Teresa, *vieni!*"

She would have been in her mid-sixties then, her close-cut curls streaked with gray at the temples and above her high forehead. She spoke in a smooth contralto voice, soft but clear. Tuscans have a saying: *Lingua senese in bocca pistoiese.* It refers to the blend of Tuscan dialects that laid the foundation for Standard Italian in the 13th century. Linguists have

long considered *la lingua senese,* a variant spoken in Siena in southern
Tuscany, to be the purest expression of the Italian language, and when
spoken with the accent of the people of Pistoia in the region's north it
is said to be the most pleasing to the ear. Franca certainly lent credence
to the expression. Her voice had round tones and a lilting cadence that I
could listen to for hours. Even when I was first learning the language,
I could somehow always understand her.

"Teresa, *sono pronta!*" She looked up from the landing below, drying
her hands with a dishtowel, a floral print apron tied over her somber
housedress. She was ready for me. From Franca I learned the Maremma's
legendary acquacotta and the chestnut flour castagnaccio Alessandra
had described so vividly in the Lamone woods. I helped Franca prepare
chicken breasts stuffed with artichoke hearts, stewed roebuck and braised
endive, octopus salad and risotto with tiny shrimp, veal scallopine and
fennel gratin.

I don't remember Franca ever starting a meal from a completely blank
slate. She incorporated ingredients from one season, one week, one meal
to the next with a fugue-like rhythm and an agrarian sensibility. As every
farmer or gardener knows, nature gives up its abundance in bursts of
profusion rather than in measured portions. The Maremman casalinga,
who could ill afford waste, has long put up this bounty—dried in the sun,
cured in salt, preserved in olive oil or vinegar—to capture both flavor
and sustenance for use during nature's more parsimonious times of the
year. Franca practiced careful economy out of habit rather than necessity
anymore, but her cooking remained the better for it. Jars of her marinated
vegetables graced the antipasto platter. Homemade preserves of summer
fruits filled her tarts and cakes. Crisp, dried slices of yesterday's bread
held chicken liver or pureed olive spread to become crostini. Moistened
stale breadcrumbs helped bind the stuffing for her rolled chicken breasts.
The rest of the roast turned into a filling for baked zucchini or sweet red
peppers, pan drippings enriched a soup or coated potatoes before they
went into the oven, and the gleaned carcass went into the stockpot, sur-
rendering the last of its flavor for broth.

Compare this to the tired, re-warmed pot of last night's dinner that is
so often the American leftover. Even the Italian word suggests a different
attitude, a more positive take: *Gli avanzati.* It refers not to leftovers, but

to something made in advance, an essential ingredient to enrich the meal rather than add to the monotony.

And cookbooks? Franca had a few on the shelf for decoration, copies her sons had given her as presents. She pulled a couple out one afternoon in case they might interest me, their spines still stiff, pages crisp and white from little or no use. She relied not on written instructions and diagrams, but on memory, on practice and intuition, her skills honed by years at her mother's side. With time she had developed a discerning palate, which she used diagnostically, assessing whether her tomato sauce needed more salt or a few more basil leaves. Like the best cooks everywhere, she brought not just her taste buds but all her senses to bear in the kitchen. She knew by sight the shimmer of the oil when the frying pan was hot, or the deep lacquer of a cutlet's underside when it was ready to be flipped. Essential, too, were smell, touch, and hearing, to recognize the scent of a finished cake in the oven or the particular way it springs back under the touch of a finger, to discern by the quickening sound of the simmering pan juices that it is time to add a splash more wine to the pot.

I have a vivid memory of the first time I ate at Franca's table. I was invited for pranzo on the afternoon Alessandra and I emerged from the Lamone woods. The meal opened with platters of Maremman salame and prosciutto, hand cut by Franca's son, who said the butcher's slicing machine is the death of good prosciutto. Sure, the paper-thin slices are beautifully uniform, but the diner is robbed of the pleasant toothsomeness of the meat. Alongside these, Franca served her marinated artichokes and slender green beans *sott'olio*, preserved in olive oil. Next came tagliatelle *paglia e fieno*. Straw and hay. Long strands of golden yellow pasta, made from flour and eggs, combined in a tangle with bright green strands, made by adding pureed spinach to the pasta dough. A classic combination, Franca served hers with a sauce of fresh porcini mushrooms and a grating of Pecorino cheese.

Our pasta bowls cleared, Franca brought a platter of roast chicken, its burnt umber skin glistening, steam rising up from where she had cut it into portions. Nestled underneath like so many bantam eggs were thickly sliced potatoes flecked with rosemary and redolent of garlic. Alessandra's father served up slices of the region's unsalted bread, cradling a large, crusty loaf in the crook of his elbow and drawing a serrated knife across it as if playing a violin. One slip, I mused, and he could sever an artery. I've since learned it's a point of pride among Tuscans to master the technique.

After the roast, Alessandra and her mother started clearing the dishes. I rose to help, but no one would let me; I was still a guest that day. One of Alessandra's brothers topped off my wine and Eraldo passed a bowl of pears. I followed his lead and used my table knife to trim the skin from the pear, savored the slices as they dripped ripe juices onto my fingers. I pushed my chair back from the table, wondering if I would need another night out in the woods to be hungry again, but I knew there was more to come. Franca passed wedges of a delicate golden ring cake. Scented with lemon, not too sweet, it was dense and moist like the best home-made pound cakes. Finally came the rumble of the moka pot and a cup of espresso to settle the stomach. The cold forest floor and rustlings of the night seemed a distant past.

I once recounted that meal to a friend after returning to the States. I described its aromas and tastes in full detail, tried to capture Franca's actions as she wielded paring knives, stirred her pots, bustled from table to stove. "My goodness," said my friend. "What a spectacle. She must have been cooking all day!"

No. After my time spent under Franca's tutelage, I knew she could pull a meal like that together without so much as a splatter on her apron. Franca hadn't been cooking all day. Instead she'd been cooking all her life.

※

FAGIOLINI SOTT'OLIO

STRING BEANS PRESERVED IN OLIVE OIL

(Makes 2 pints)

Preserving garden vegetables, either *sott'olio*, in olive oil, or *sott'aceto*, in vinegar, was a summer chore for every farm family in the days before refrigeration. Jars of marinated beans, artichokes, onions, eggplants, peppers, and other produce would keep for months on a cool, dark shelf in the cantina. These vibrant vegetables, seasoned with custom blends of herbs and spices, still form a traditional part of the antipasto platter throughout Tuscany and other parts of Italy. Franca seasoned hers with fresh bay leaves and black peppercorns.

- 2 cups good quality white wine or apple cider vinegar (approximately)
- 2 cups water (approximately)
- 1 teaspoon kosher salt
- 2 pounds slender, freshly picked green beans, ends trimmed
- bay leaves
- peppercorns
- pinch red pepper flakes, if desired
- extra virgin olive oil

Place equal parts vinegar and water (enough to cover the green beans) and the salt in a medium saucepot and bring to a boil. Add the beans and boil for 3 to 5 minutes, until just tender. Drain the beans in a colander, then spread them out on a cloth tea towel to dry completely.

In the meantime, sterilize two pint-size Mason jars by boiling them according to standard canning directions. Pack the beans into the jars.

Add two bay leaves and a few black peppercorns to each jar along with a pinch of red pepper flakes, if using. Cover the beans completely with olive oil. Insert a chopstick or knife down into the oil and wiggle it around in a couple spots to get rid of any air bubbles. Wipe the rims and sides of the jars clean and seal. Transfer to a cool dark place for at least a day or two to let the flavors meld. Store in the refrigerator once opened, but bring the beans to room temperature before serving. The oil is a precious commodity itself—use it as the base for salad vinaigrettes, or drizzle it over cooked vegetables, meats, or fish.

Note: Italian housewives will keep fagiolini sott'olio in the pantry all winter long, though in America we're squeamish about these things. Most home economists and county extension agents advise to process home-canned pickles in a water bath or with a pressure cooker to avoid spoilage.

TAGLIATELLE PAGLIA E FIENO

STRAW AND HAY PASTA

(Serves 4 to 6)

- 1 pound fresh tagliatelle paglia e fieno (or ½ pound dry egg fettuccine and ½ pound dry spinach fettuccine)
- 1 heaping tablespoon salt, for cooking the tagliatelle
- 4 ounces pancetta, cut into small dice
- 2 tablespoons olive oil
- ½ small onion, minced
- 1 whole clove garlic
- 8 ounces sliced fresh mushrooms, about 2 cups (Franca used porcini, but crimini or regular button mushrooms are also nice.)
- ½ cup homemade chicken stock
- ½ cup heavy cream
- salt and freshly ground pepper, to taste
- ½ cup grated Parmigiano cheese, plus additional for garnish
- fresh parsley, chopped

Bring a large pot of water to a boil over high heat for cooking the pasta.

Render the pancetta with the olive oil in a large, heavy skillet over a medium flame until browned, about 5 minutes. Add the onion, garlic, and mushrooms and sauté another 3 to 4 minutes, until the onions are translucent and the mushrooms are tender.

Add the chicken stock and cream, and simmer another 3 to 4 minutes, until the liquid is slightly thickened. Add salt and pepper to taste, and remove the garlic clove.

Meanwhile, add a heaping tablespoon of salt to the boiling water and cook the pasta until just al dente. (If needed, remove the sauce from the heat until the pasta is ready.) Drain the pasta, add it to the skillet, and toss to coat well with the sauce. Continue stirring over high heat for another minute until the liquid reduces and becomes creamy. Remove from the flame, stir in the cheese, and transfer to a serving dish. Serve immediately, garnished with parsley and additional grated Parmigiano.

Note: Franca can purchase fresh tagliatelle at the market. The commercially packaged fresh pasta I've tried here in America is rubbery and bland, though artisan shops making wonderful pasta are springing up in some places. For a special occasion, you can prepare your own paglia e fieno from two two-egg batches of pasta. Make one plain, for the straw, and add two tablespoons of cooked, finely minced spinach to the eggs before combining them with the flour for the hay. Both De Cecco and Bionatura make dried egg fettuccine and spinach fettuccine that work beautifully in this dish.

16

UNDRESSED FOR DINNER

One Sunday morning I heard Franca calling my name up the stairs. "Teresa! . . . Teresa!" I walked out onto the landing and leaned over the railing to see her looking up at me as she dried her hands on a dishtowel. She announced she was starting the preparations for Sunday pranzo and asked if I wanted to join her.

Pranzo is the most substantial meal of the day for most Italians, served at about one in the afternoon, and Sunday pranzo is the most important meal of the week. It is a hallowed institution, a multicourse, multigenerational event that can last for hours. It has a leisurely pace because most shops are closed, so no one has to hurry back to work, Sunday being a day of rest. It is abundant because it traditionally marked the end of the fast prescribed by the Catholic Church from midnight Saturday until after mass on Sunday.

Catholics, by the way, haven't been skipping breakfast before church since the Second Vatican Council of 1962, because in addition to doing away with mass in High Latin and letting nuns jettison their wimples, Pope Paul VI reduced the Sunday fast to only an hour. This loosening of strictures came as a relief to many a parishioner, my mother included. Come Sunday morning she fed us a ploughman's breakfast of eggs and bacon or a stack of pancakes. If we stood in the back of the communion line, she reckoned, the full sixty minutes of abstention would elapse before we received the Host, and she wouldn't have to worry about us growing irritable or fidgety, sitting through the homily on an empty stomach.

Even so, plenty of Italian Catholics must still feel peckish by the end of Mass, for the prodigious Sunday pranzo endures. I've heard complaints it has seen a decline in recent years, fallen prey to the faster pace of modern times, but by American standards I assure you it is going strong. *Il pranzo della domenica* is hardly a day of rest for the women though, as they generally have all the cooking to do. A saucepot had been simmering on Franca's stovetop since early that morning, and when I arrived around eleven, she was pulling out ingredients and utensils to make her famous *gnudi*.

Gnudi are little ricotta dumplings, usually flavored with spinach or Swiss chard and served as a first course. They are currently enjoying a certain cachet here in the States. You'll find celebrity chefs who send them steaming from the kitchen, garnished with microgreens or black truffle essence or cappuccino foam. Diners raise a fork, savor each bite rapturously, and write odes or haiku or rap songs in their honor. Such fanfare, yet their origins trace to the peasant cooking of the Maremma, part of the tradition of la cucina povera.

Alessandra had included gnudi on the list of Maremman delicacies she'd enumerated during our night in the Lamone woods, and she'd all but composed her own sonnet describing her mother's light hand with them. As poverty goes, gnudi fall among the poorest of the poor. Until well after World War II the average housewife used the little flour she could afford for making bread, sparing enough for pasta only on special occasions—weddings and funerals, Christmas and Easter Sunday. Gnudi are essentially lumps of ravioli filling cooked without their pasta wrapper. They come to the table undressed. Or nude, as the name suggests, though the "g" isn't silent, as in *gnat* or *gnome*. It's pronounced instead like the "gn" in lasagne.

Franca unwrapped a package of ricotta, purchased from the creamery in town, and started spooning it into a large bowl set on her kitchen scale. Like most Italian cooks, she measured in kilos, but a pound of good quality fresh ricotta will make enough gnudi for six people as a first course.

Ricotta is one of the gems of Maremman cuisine. From antipasti to dolci it turns up at every course in the meal, spread on crostini, as a filling for stuffed pastas or crepes, in cakes and pastries both savory and sweet. It is also the ultimate in peasant thrift, a testament to what the combined forces of ingenuity and frugality can accomplish on an empty stomach. Made from the whey that remains after skimming off the curds for cheese—think of Miss Muffet and her tuffet—ricotta is something delicious coaxed from leftovers that others would discard. When reheated, proteins in the whey coagulate and float to the surface. This ricotta—the name means "re-cooked"—is scooped from the vat and strained in perforated baskets. Technically it's not a cheese since it doesn't derive directly from milk; Italians classify it as a *latticino*, or dairy product.

Ricotta's history is as cloudy as the whey used to produce it. Known since classical times, the ancient Roman Cato mentioned it in his manual on farming. It originally came from sheep's milk whey after making Pecorino cheese (*pecora* means "sheep" in Italian) and it formed a mainstay of the peasant diet, slathered while still warm on a crust of dark bread. Since ricotta was ready for market within hours, it provided a welcome source of income for farmers whose wheels of Pecorino took months to mature. Actually, few farmers had the luxury to enjoy their own aged Pecorino cheese. Under the *mezzadria* sharecropping system in place in Tuscany until well after World War II, half of a farm's production went to the landowner, while the tenant who worked the land kept the remaining half. These farmers often sold or bartered their shares of Pecorino for cloth or shoes or other goods needed throughout the year.

Ricotta is still made from ewe's milk whey in Tuscany and other regions that produce Pecorino, though some dairies now add fresh milk to increase yields. Cheese-makers also use whey from the milk of cows (the ricotta of Parma, a by-product of Parmigiano cheese, is especially billowy and flavorful) as well as goats and even water buffalo after making mozzarella.

Traditionalists deem the texture and taste of sheep's whey ricotta to be superior to any other, and they'll say it is especially delectable in spring. After winter rations of dry, baled hay, the flocks are turned out on the hillsides. The sheep graze avidly on tender new grass and wild-flowers made sweet by the sugars stored in their roots. This change in diet enriches the sheep's milk, giving the resulting ricotta a seasonal creaminess and floral perfume.

But Franca and I made gnudi on a gray day in November. I'd looked forward to my cooking lesson that morning if only for the burners on

the range. Tuscans don't go in much for central heating as they rarely
have the need for it, but Manciano was in the midst of a cold snap like
nothing they'd seen in years. The pots bubbling away on the stovetop
created an inviting warmth. Franca scooped up a spoonful of ricotta and
motioned for me to try a taste. Snowy white, with a fine, nubbly texture,
it had a mild sweetness and a subtle taste best described as barnyard-y,
though in a pleasant way.

Franca next had me remove the stems from a market bag filled with
spinach, then I rinsed the leaves in a basin and set them to drain in
a colander in the sink. Spinach (*Spinacia oleracea*) is a member of the
goosefoot family, so named because its leaves, with the proper sense of
fancy, resemble the webbed foot of a goose. Its relatives include two other
gardener's favorites, beets and Swiss chard, along with quinoa, the noble
grain of the Incas, and lamb's quarters, which most American gardeners
consider a weed even though farmers in Asia and Africa cultivate it in
large tracts as a valued food crop. Botanists generally credit the ancient
Persians for bringing spinach under cultivation, domesticating it from a
species that still grows wild in parts of the Middle East. The Saracens
introduced it to Sicily in about the 9th century and its cultivation spread
throughout Italy, brought by either returning Crusaders or invading
Moors, depending on whom you believe. Recipes containing spinach
appear in some of the earliest Italian cookery books, including the late
medieval manuscripts *Libro della Cocina* by the Anonymous Tuscan and
De honesta voluptate et valitudine by Vatican librarian Bartolomeo Sacchi.
Sacchi's work, known in English as *On Right Pleasure and Good Health*,
praised spinach for relieving the heat of summer, reviving those who
were disinterested in food because of squeamishness, and filling nursing
women with plentiful milk. In country medicine, the juice from the
boiled leaves was considered useful for scorpion and spider bites.

Like ricotta, Italians have long considered tender young spinach leaves
a spring delicacy. One of the first greens of the season, spinach offered a
welcome respite from the starchy root vegetables that sustained most
families through the winter. Spinach bolts and sets seed during the heat
of the summer, but crops sown once the weather cools off again will
produce well into autumn, and it was this late-season spinach that Franca
had brought home from the market.

Franca transferred the spinach into a large saucepot and began cooking it with just a pinch of salt and the water that clung to the leaves. It was a mountain of spinach, surely enough to feed the multitudes, but it started to wilt immediately and after a few minutes of light stirring it had reduced to a small heap in the middle of a green puddle of cooking liquid. Franca transferred the mound to a colander in the sink. Once it cooled she gathered it into a ball, squeezed it forcefully several times to remove the excess juices, and then minced it finely on a cutting board before adding it to the bowl with the ricotta.

She broke an egg into the bowl, added half a cup of grated Parmigiano, a handful of dried breadcrumbs, and a spoonful of flour—about a quarter cup and two tablespoons respectively. Next came a sprinkle of salt, some pepper, and a grating of nutmeg. Nutmeg and spinach form a classic pairing in the cooking of Tuscany. With its sweet, musky notes, nutmeg softens the mineral edge of spinach and similar leafy greens, and it affords gnudi their only hint of luxury.

Nutmeg is the kernel of an apricot-like fruit from the evergreen tree *Myristica fragrans*. (The tree generously offers up two delicacies; the bright red webbing that encases the kernel is the spice known as mace.) Known since antiquity, nutmeg was originally prized as a potent medicinal. Doctors used it to treat everything from toothaches, boils, and impotence to the plague. Nutmeg entered Italy in the 12th century, brought by Venetian merchants, who procured it from Arab traders, who took great pains to keep the nutmeg's true source a mystery. They motioned vaguely eastward, told tales of distant lands guarded by leviathans and winged dragons. Some said the spice came from the Garden of Eden itself. Actually it came from the Banda archipelago, a remote group of ten tiny volcanic islands forming part of what was once known as the Spice Islands in Indonesia. With every change of hands the price of nutmeg went up severalfold.

The quest for the riches of the Spice Islands sparked the Age of Discovery, sending Christopher Columbus across the Atlantic to stumble upon America, and Vasco Da Gama around the Cape of Good Hope. Magellan's crew stopped at the Banda Islands on their way to circumnavigating the globe. The Bolognese adventurer Ludovico Di Varthema published an account of his travels to the islands in 1507, and his descriptions of nutmeg trees flourishing on the hillsides had seafaring nations battling for dominion of the archipelago and the nutmeg trade for over a century. By 1667 the Dutch needed only the minuscule British-held island of Run to gain complete control of the Bandas. In exchange they offered up one of their colonial outposts half a world away: a marshy, mosquito-infested island called Manhattan.

Their monopoly over the spice established, the Dutch went to great lengths to maintain it, uprooting nutmeg trees in areas they could not police, treating the kernels with quicklime to keep them from germinating, and burning warehouses full of nutmeg when stores grew too high. The price of nutmeg soared, fortunes were made. A single kernel was worth an oxen, a daring ship-hand could purloin a small bag of nutmeg kernels, purchase a house, and retire from sailing for good.

Meanwhile the spice moved from the apothecary's dispensary to the kitchen. To serve dishes laced with nutmeg brought status to any house, and every fop and dandy carried a silver nutmeg grater in his waistcoat pocket to impress the ladies at dinner parties. On various occasions British and French agents managed to smuggle nutmeg saplings off the islands. They established groves in Mauritius, Granada, and other more hospitable locations, loosening the Dutch stronghold on the trade. The spice market collapsed during the Napoleonic wars, but it wasn't until the 20th century that the average casalinga could afford a tin of nutmeg for her pantry.

Franca stirred the ricotta mixture together, then dropped it by the tablespoon onto a plate dredged with flour. I watched as she coated the mounds with flour, then rolled them into balls the size of a walnut. Working together we formed all the gnudi in short order, setting them aside on a semolina-dusted baking sheet. Franca turned her attention to the rest of the meal, bringing up wine from the cantina, grating cheese, stirring pots on the back burner.

Alessandra came down from her apartment and helped me set the table. Her two younger brothers filed into the kitchen, followed by her father. Next arrived her older brother with his wife and their toddler son. After the chicken liver crostini, the platters of salame and prosciutto, the marinated string beans and olives, Franca cooked the gnudi. She added a handful of salt to a large pot of boiling water and simmered the gnudi in batches, waiting a few minutes for them to float to the surface and bob about while the water gently boiled. She transferred them to a serving dish using a slotted skimmer, added a drizzle of melted butter infused with fresh sage leaves and a garnish of freshly grated Parmigiano cheese, then brought the dish to the table.

Other courses followed. A roast, or maybe cutlets, and then fruit. Doubtless everything tasted sublime, but somehow none of it made it into my journal, and all of it has been eclipsed in my memory by Franca's gnudi. Tender ricotta pillows, whispers of nutmeg and sage, each bite a voluptuous delight.

After the meal I helped Franca with the dishes and offered her my compliments yet again. She gave a dismissive shrug of the shoulders. Now that her sons were grown and had jobs, they sometimes took her cooking for granted. They preferred to eat in restaurants, she said, wringing out her washcloth. She supposed they would eat out every night if they could. They occasionally suggested she broaden her repertoire, try re-creating some of the restaurant dishes they'd discovered. Franca motioned to the platter that had held the gnudi, empty but for a few wilted sage leaves glistening with butter. Her boys had enjoyed the gnudi well enough, though, hadn't they? She sighed. She had no interest in the latest restaurant fad. Her casalinga's cooking suited her just fine.

GNUDI CON BURRO E SALVIA

SPINACH AND RICOTTA "GNUDI" WITH BUTTER AND SAGE

(Serves 4 to 6)

FOR THE GNUDI:

- 16 ounces ricotta (Choose a variety made without gums or other stabilizers, or make your own.)
- 8 ounces fresh spinach
- a pinch of sea salt
- 1 egg
- ½ cup grated Parmigiano cheese
- ¼ cup dried breadcrumbs
- 2 tablespoons flour
- freshly ground black pepper
- freshly grated nutmeg
- about 2 cups semolina flour, for shaping and coating the gnudi

Set the ricotta in a strainer lined with a double layer of cheesecloth and let drain for a few hours or overnight to remove excess liquid.

Rinse the spinach, discard stems, and place in a large pot over high heat with a pinch of salt and the water that clings to the leaves. Cover pot and cook 3 to 5 minutes, until wilted, stirring a few times to help the spinach cook evenly. Let cool, gather into a ball and squeeze forcefully several times to remove excess juices. Mince finely.

In a large bowl combine the drained ricotta, minced spinach, egg, Parmigiano cheese, breadcrumbs, flour, a pinch of salt, and a few grindings of black pepper and nutmeg.

Drop mixture by tablespoonsful onto a plate of semolina flour, dust with additional flour, and shape into balls the size of a walnut. Place on a baking tray dredged with semolina flour while you form the rest of the gnudi.

TO COOK THE GNUDI AND SERVE:

- salt, 1 heaping tablespoon for boiling the gnudi, plus additional, to taste
- 50 g (4 tablespoons) butter
- 10 to 12 fresh sage leaves, coarsely chopped
- freshly grated Parmigiano cheese

Bring a large pot of water to a boil over high heat and add 1 heaping tablespoon of salt.

Meanwhile, heat the butter and sage leaves in a skillet over medium-high heat until the foam subsides and the melted butter begins to brown around the edges. Remove from the heat.

Working in batches so as not to crowd the pot, drop the gnudi into the pot of boiling water and cook gently, about 3 to 4 minutes, until they float to the surface and are cooked through. Transfer with a slotted spoon to a heated serving dish and keep warm in a low oven while you cook the remaining gnudi. Drizzle with the melted sage butter and garnish with freshly grated Parmigiano cheese. Season with salt to taste and serve at once.

17

IN THE WHEY

Ricotta turned up in more than just gnudi at Franca's table. It made occasional star appearances in dishes, other times it played just a cameo role, but Franca used it frequently, from the first course to the last. One of my favorite preparations has become a weeknight staple in my own home, a pasta dish I first sampled one afternoon in September after an overnight flight from Boston. I'd taken the train from Rome, and Alessandra met me at the station. We wedged my duffel bags into the hatchback of her Fiat Panda and drove the twenty miles to Manciano. As we pulled into her family's palazzo she asked if I was tired. If I liked, I could go straight upstairs and have a nap in her attic flat. Otherwise, we'd arrived just in time for pranzo.

I felt rested enough. But in between the layovers and time zone changes I'd lost track of the days. Was it Sunday already? What a pleasure to be invited to Sunday pranzo for my first meal back in Manciano. Alessandra helped me haul my luggage up to her attic apartment, and we descended the two flights to her parents' home. Instead of the aroma of roasting meat and simmering tomato sauce that wafted up the stairs during previous Sunday meals with Alessandra's family, a pine-laced, antiseptic odor greeted me in the entryway.

My befuddled inner clock found a reference point in the scent and recalibrated itself. It was Saturday, not Sunday. Unlike Sunday, with its lavish multicourse meals, Saturday was for domestic chores—for shopping, errands, laundry, and mopping. Franca focused all her energies on bringing the house into order; she wasn't going to work herself to the bone with cooking, too. For pranzo she almost always served what she called a *pasta del sabato*, a Saturday pasta, something quick, tossed together with a few pantry staples and prepared with as little effort and cookware as possible.

As Alessandra escorted me down the hall to the kitchen she shouted, "Mamma, *butta la pasta!*" Throw in the pasta. It's a phrase Italians often use to announce their arrival. Or else they phone from the road to say they'll be there shortly, *butta la pasta!* It means I'm home, or I'm minutes away, go ahead and start the final preparations for the meal. And woe betide them if they're late. Italians are adamant on that point: once the boiling pasta is *al dente* it should be drained, tossed, and served straight away, lest the toothsomeness the cook has so carefully attained be lost. *La pasta non aspetta nessuno.* Pasta waits for no one.

Franca dropped a box of spaghetti into the pot of water boiling on the stove and wrung her hands in her apron. She greeted me with a tight embrace, looked me up and down, said the year had been kind to me since my last visit, and promptly turned her attention back to the stove. We would be having *spaghetti con la ricotta,* she informed me, a dish whose ingredients can be counted on one hand, and a Saturday pasta I'd never eaten before. Only fifteen minutes into my visit and Franca was giving me another cooking lesson.

Alessandra brought another place setting to the table as I watched Franca scoop ricotta into a serving bowl. She threw in a handful of Pecorino cheese, added a stream of olive oil, a few grinds of black pepper, and mashed the mixture in the bowl with the back of a fork until smooth. Just before the spaghetti finished boiling, Franca added a ladle of the salted cooking water to the ricotta and stirred to make a creamy sauce. She drained the spaghetti, tossed it with the ricotta, and garnished the dish with grated Pecorino cheese. An informal Saturday pasta for family, yes, but it has a spare elegance fit for special occasions, too.

One weekday after my language classes I helped Franca prepare a main dish with ricotta, *polpettone di tacchino e ricotta*, turkey meat loaf. Italians eat a great deal of turkey; it is readily available fresh from the butcher, ground or in various cuts, sold alongside chicken breasts and thighs, veal chops and ribs. Every Italian seems to know that Americans roast a whole turkey for Thanksgiving, and with their small home ovens this seems to them oddly medieval, like roasting a wild stallion on a spit. To serve four you will need a pound of freshly ground turkey and a cup of ricotta. Combine these in a bowl with an egg, a tablespoon of freshly chopped Italian parsley, a minced clove of garlic, a handful each of grated Parmigiano cheese and dried bread-crumbs, salt, and freshly ground black pepper. Mix the ingredients well with your hands, form into an oval, dust with flour on all sides and brown in olive oil in a skillet. Transfer the polpettone to a baking dish, pour in half a glass of white wine, and bake at 325°F until done, about an hour. A meat thermometer, if you have one, should register at 160°F. Allow the meat loaf to rest for five to ten minutes and serve hot with braised kale or other greens, or let cool to room temperature to serve on a summer evening with a salad. Leftovers are wonderful cold in a sandwich.

The simple golden cake served at my first pranzo *da Franca* turned out to be her *torta del tre*. This "cake of threes," like our traditional pound cake, is named for the quantity of the main ingredients in the recipe. The "three" stands for three *etti*, or hectograms, a standard unit of baking in Italian kitchens, and the amount of ricotta, sugar, and flour needed for the cake, along with three eggs and the juice and zest of an orange.

Once again I must point out the Italians measure by weight rather than volume, and they've long ago switched over to the metric system. In American units this translates to a cake of two and two-fifths, one and one-third, one and one-third, and three, which doesn't have nearly the same nice ring to it. In addition, volume measurements are fraught with inaccuracies. Flour, for example, settles during storage and doesn't have a constant density. A cup of sugar weighs more than a cup of flour, and a cup of brown sugar weighs more than both, though by how much depends on how firmly you pack it down.

Cookbook authors and recipe writers offer all sorts of tips to help surmount the shortcomings of measuring by cup and tablespoon: Always fluff the flour with a spoon to aerate it before measuring. Spoon flour into the cup to the brim, then level it gently with a straight-edge spatula. Dry measuring cups for dry ingredients, clear liquid cups for liquids, and don't just stand there, crouch down, view your liquids at eye level to ensure the meniscus rests right on the line of the measuring cup. (Don't remember what a meniscus is? Time to dust off that old high school chemistry book.)

Such machinations and gymnastics feats. Still, you'll never get the same results twice. Our quaint American system with its cups and tablespoons, pounds and ounces is inherently imprecise. It is fine for cooking, but too often it lets the baker down. Baking is mathematical. It relies on proportion and precision for success, and volume measurements allow too much variability, which makes for fallen cakes, tough crusts, and cookies that spread across the baking sheet. No wonder so many Americans think they can't bake. It's not that they can't bake; they just can't measure. And they can't measure because our American system doesn't provide the right tools.

Home bakers, the hour is now! Lay down your measuring cups and spoons, go out and buy a kitchen scale. You can get a decent one for twenty-five bucks, which you will more than recoup in the ease and convenience a scale brings to this recipe alone. Not to mention the long division and rounding of irrational numbers you will be spared when scaling recipes up or down. With enough outcry, recipe writers won't be able to skirt the issue any longer. They'll have to start listing their ingredients by weight in the same manner as bakers across the rest of the modern world. I'd like to press them even further, into converting outright to the metric system with its kilos and grams so easily divisible by ten, but a revolution of this nature is best started with baby steps.

Franca admitted the torta del tre isn't her recipe exclusively. All the ladies in Manciano make it. With its moist but tender crumb it is at once homespun yet refined, delectable and special enough for Sunday pranzo, even better with fresh berries to serve on the side. It comes together in a snap, and it keeps well, too. Franca's husband, Eraldo, likes a leftover slice with his caffelatte in the morning for breakfast.

To make it, bring 300 grams best-quality ricotta and three eggs to room temperature. If the ricotta and eggs are cold, the batter will curdle, separating into liquid and fat, and the cake will have a dense texture. Preheat the oven to 350°F. Lightly grease and flour a ten-inch cake or Bundt pan and have your ingredients, mixing bowls, and baking utensils at the ready. Combine the ricotta in the bowl of an electric mixer with 300 grams sugar and beat on medium speed until smooth and fluffy. Scrape down the sides of the bowl with a spatula. With the mixer on low speed, add the eggs, one at a time, mixing well after each addition, and stir in the zest of an orange. In a separate bowl sift 300 grams all-purpose flour with two teaspoons of baking powder. Add the flour to the batter in three installments, mixing just until smooth. Gently stir in the juice of the orange. Turn the batter into the prepared pan and bake until golden brown, forty-five minutes to an hour. When done, the cake will slowly spring back when you press it lightly with your fingertip. A toothpick inserted in the cake's center will come out clean, with no batter or moist crumbs.

Let the cake cool on a wire rack. Run a knife around the edges of the pan to loosen, then invert onto another rack or plate. Place a serving platter on top (actually, on the cake's bottom), flip it back upright, and allow the cake to cool completely. Serve unadorned, or with a dusting of powdered sugar.

Now for one last note on ricotta itself. My early attempts to duplicate Franca's ricotta-based recipes in my New Hampshire kitchen met with disappointing results. My gnudi dissolved in the pot. My meat loaf seeped. My spaghetti con la ricotta came out gummy, my torta del tre, even worse. American supermarket ricotta is runnier than its Italian counterpart. To increase the yield American producers don't drain off as much whey. They often use gelatin or guar gum or other stabilizers to compensate, and they sometimes add preservatives to improve shelf life, since Italian-style ricotta only keeps for a few days. The result is a soggy, tasteless paste that can't take the place of genuine ricotta. I've since found a few dairies making farmstead ricotta without any additives, and I've come across specialty cheese counters that sell ricotta in bulk, scooped off from a larger piece unmolded from a basket. These are a marked improvement over commercial products, but you usually still need to strain the ricotta for several hours in a colander lined with a double layer of cheesecloth to attain the consistency of Italian ricotta.

Another solution is to make your own ricotta. It's effortless and tastes fresher than anything you can buy in a store. Since I don't have a ewe in the backyard or a ready supply of whey, I make ricotta from cow's milk. It is cream line Jersey milk from a dairy the next town over. If you have a source for fresh local milk, by all means use it, but any grocery store whole milk will do as long as it doesn't have any additives. Technically, I don't make true ricotta, since I use milk rather than whey, but it is luscious and flavorful, and it performs beautifully in traditional recipes calling for ricotta.

To try it yourself, pour half a gallon of fresh whole milk and two cups cultured buttermilk into a stainless saucepot. Set the pot over a medium-low flame, stirring occasionally to keep the milk from scorching and sticking to the bottom of the pan. Meanwhile, rinse a piece of cheesecloth in water, wring it out, fold it in half, and line a large colander placed over a large stockpot. The buttermilk provides the acid needed to coagulate the milk, and it adds a pleasant, tangy flavor reminiscent of sheep's milk. After a few minutes curds will start to separate from the whey and float to the surface. Reduce the heat to low to keep the milk from boiling and cook another two to three minutes without stirring, until the curds and whey are fully separated, then turn off the heat and let the curds rest undisturbed for about fifteen minutes to allow the flavors to develop. Skim off the curds into the colander with a slotted ladle. Carefully pour the whey into the colander to catch the remaining curds (you may have to do this in batches as it takes a while for the whey to drain). After about five minutes gather the ends of the cheesecloth around the curd and tie at the top like a knapsack. Hang the bundle from a long wooden spoon handle set across a pot and let the curds continue to drain until the dripping stops, about fifteen minutes.

You can mix in chopped herbs and a little salt, and spread the ricotta while still warm over fresh bread with a few drops of olive oil for an incomparable appetizer. Or skip the herbs and serve it with a drizzle of honey on toast. To use the ricotta for cooking, let it continue draining for a couple hours. Store in the refrigerator and use within a day or two for the best texture and flavor. In the spirit of Maremman thrift you can save this whey, even freeze it, and substitute it for the liquid when making bread or pastry dough (this last comes out especially flavorful and tender). Add it to smoothies, or use it to cook potatoes for mashing, or to make polenta or oatmeal. My chickens adore whey sopped up in table scraps, and it makes a nutrient-rich addition to a compost pile. In Franca's kitchen I came to appreciate the versatile role ricotta plays in the cooking of the Maremma, and whenever I use ricotta in my own home today, I can almost feel her presence beside me.

SPAGHETTI CON LA RICOTTA

SPAGHETTI WITH RICOTTA

(Serves 4 to 6)

- salt, 1 heaping tablespoon for cooking the spaghetti, plus additional, to taste
- 1 pound spaghetti
- 8 ounces best-quality ricotta
- 2 tablespoons freshly grated Pecorino cheese, plus more for garnish
- 2 tablespoons olive oil
- freshly ground pepper
- 1 small ladle pasta cooking water (about 2 tablespoons)

Put a large pot of water on to boil. Once the water boils, add 1 heaping tablespoon of salt, then add the spaghetti and cook until al dente, about 10 to 12 minutes.

Meanwhile, combine the ricotta, Pecorino cheese, olive oil, and a few grinds of pepper in a large serving bowl. Mash with a fork and stir until smooth. When the spaghetti is almost done, add a little of the salted cooking water (about 2 tablespoons) to the ricotta mixture and stir to create a creamy sauce.

Drain the spaghetti, toss with the ricotta mixture, and garnish with additional grated Pecorino cheese. Serve straight away. *La pasta non aspetta nessuno!* (Pasta waits for no one!)

POLPETTONE DI TACCHINO E RICOTTA

TURKEY AND RICOTTA MEAT LOAF

(Serves 4)

- 1 pound ground turkey
- 1 cup best-quality ricotta
- 1 egg
- 1 tablespoon finely chopped Italian parsley
- 1 minced clove garlic
- 1 handful grated Parmigiano cheese (about 2 tablespoons)
- 1 handful dried breadcrumbs (about 2 tablespoons)
- ½ teaspoon kosher salt
- freshly ground pepper, to taste
- 1 tablespoon olive oil
- flour, for dusting polpettone
- ½ glass white wine

Preheat oven to 325°F. Combine turkey, ricotta, egg, parsley, garlic, Parmigiano, breadcrumbs, salt, and pepper in a large bowl and mix well. Form into a large oval. Heat a thin layer of olive oil in a skillet over a medium flame. Dust the polpettone lightly with flour and add to skillet, browning on all sides in the oil. Transfer to a baking dish, pour in half a glass of white wine and bake until done, about an hour. A meat thermometer will register at 160°F. Let rest 5 to 10 minutes before serving.

TORTA DEL TRE

MANCIANO'S CAKE OF THREES

(Serves 8 to 10)

- 300 grams all-purpose flour
- 2 teaspoons baking powder
- 300 grams best-quality ricotta, at room temperature
- 300 grams sugar
- 3 large eggs, at room temperature
- zest and juice of an orange

Preheat oven to 350°F. Lightly grease and flour a 10-inch cake or Bundt pan.

Sift together the flour and baking powder and set aside.

Have ricotta and eggs at room temperature to ensure the lightest texture. Combine ricotta and sugar in the bowl of an electric mixer and beat on medium speed until smooth and fluffy. Scrape down sides of bowl with a spatula. With the mixture on low speed, add eggs one at a time, beating well after each addition. Stir in the zest of an orange.

Add the flour to the batter in three installments, mixing just until smooth. Gently stir in the juice of the orange.

Transfer batter to prepared baking pan and bake until golden brown, 45 to 60 minutes. When done, the cake will slowly spring back when touched with a fingertip, and a toothpick inserted in the cake's center will come out clean, with no batter or moist crumbs.

Let the cake cool in the pan about 10 minutes, then remove to a wire rack to finish cooling completely. Serve by itself or with fresh berries.

RICOTTA FATTA IN CASA

HOMEMADE RICOTTA

(Makes about 2 cups)

- ½ gallon fresh whole milk
- 2 cups cultured buttermilk

Combine milk and buttermilk in a large stainless saucepot and set over a medium-low flame. Stir occasionally to keep the milk from scorching.

Meanwhile, rinse a piece of cheesecloth in water, wring it out, fold it in two, and line a colander set over a large stockpot.

After a few minutes, the curds will start to separate from the whey. (If you have a thermometer, the milk will reach about 190 to 195°F.) Reduce the heat to low to keep the milk from boiling, and continue to cook 2 to 3 more minutes without stirring, until the curds begin to clump together and the whey becomes almost clear. Remove from heat and let the curds rest 15 minutes to allow the flavors to develop.

Skim off the curds into the colander with a slotted spoon. Carefully pour the whey into the colander to catch the remaining curds. Work in batches, allowing the whey to drain if necessary.

Gather the ends of the cheesecloth together and tie at the top like a knapsack. Hang the bundle from a long wooden spoon handle set across a pot and let the curds drain another 15 minutes, or until dripping stops. Serve while still warm, mixed with chopped fresh herbs and a pinch of salt, or drizzled with honey, slathered on toast or fresh bread. For use in cooking, continue draining ricotta for 2 to 3 more hours or overnight.

18

MARRYING WELL

My session at Cultura Italiana that first year came just at the end of the grape harvest in Manciano. Which meant, Alessandra lamented, that there wouldn't be time for a dinner at La Stellata. *Peccato*, what a pity. La Stellata was the winery just below the outskirts of the town. During quieter stretches of the year, the owners gave a *seminario sul vino* in conjunction with the language school, each course accompanied by a wine from their estate. A meal to remember, Alessandra assured me, always a high point for the students.

I was familiar with the winery because I'd passed its gates most mornings on my daily run. One of my homework assignments had been to read a few passages from an article in a regional magazine featuring local wineries, and Alessandra had filled me in on the rest.

So I knew that owners Clara Divizia and Manlio Giorni were living the dream of many an urban professional. They had left behind the frenzy of urban life, the traffic and smog, the crowds and noise and office hours. They had quit the city, fled to the countryside, and opened a winery. A winery in Tuscany, no less, risen up from the debris of a dilapidated farmstead. It was the stuff of dreams on a Hollywood scale.

It was not Clara and Manlio's dream, though. When they said *arrivederci* to Rome in their rearview mirror in the early 1980s and drove off to their newly purchased fixer-upper and overgrown plot of land just outside Manciano, they had ambitions of a more bucolic bent. They left behind successful careers—she an interior designer, he the proprietor of an antique automobile restoration business. They entertained romantic notions of a new life, of a more relaxed pace and a more fulfilling vocation in concert with the land and seasons. But wine did not figure into the plan. Instead they intended to raise sheep. They wanted to raise sheep and earn their living from sheep's milk cheese in the venerable tradition of the region.

Clara grew up in Manciano and her mother lived there still, so it was a homecoming of sorts. With his mechanical background and her flair for design they were well equipped to gut the house and outbuildings, to repair farm implements, modernize wiring and plumbing. They restored, renovated, and updated in judicious measures to create an inviting house infused with a harmonious blend of the modern and traditional. Terracotta floors, antique furnishings, arched entryways, sleek fixtures. In clearing the surrounding pastures of blackberry canes and stinging nettles they discovered the vestiges of a hillside vineyard. Clara spent her evenings looking out the farmhouse picture window at the sprawling vines. Such a shame to pull them out, and yet—and yet they needed the pasture for the sheep. And yet they knew nothing about making wine. And yet that was precisely as much as they knew about making cheese.

An elderly neighbor paid a visit, curious about the recent commotion on the *azienda* that had lain quiet so many years. Did they realize their thirty-acre plot of land was dry, rocky, inhospitable—in short, perfect for growing grapes? Advice was offered, trellises repaired, vines pruned and trained to mind their manners once again. Clara and Manlio refashioned their dream and invested the last of their savings in winemaking equipment. The die had been cast, the vines had begun to exert their fascination. *Abbiamo scelto la vita e le vite*, Clara likes to say. We chose our life and our vines. You could argue their vines chose them.

As gambles go, a cheesemaking enterprise would have been a surer thing. Artisanal Pecorino Toscano is one of the finest table cheeses in Italy, and its center of production is right there among the rolling hills of the Maremma. Creamy and mild when young, pleasantly sharp with the essence of hazelnuts when aged, Pecorino Toscano has a proud history stretching back to the Renaissance—it was a personal favorite of Lorenzo the Magnificent. Today it stands a world apart from the salty commercial Pecorino Romano known to most Americans.

As for wine, the area was considered a denomination of dubious merit. According to the byzantine regulations of the government, Clara and Manlio's land officially belonged to the winemaking zone of Pitigliano, a place allowed by decree to make only an insipid *vino bianco*. A blended white wine based primarily on the trebbiano grape, in those days it was produced on an industrial scale in a heavy-handed fashion that yielded an indestructible wine, and a lot of it, but one stripped of varietal character and depth. But Italy was in the throes of a winemaking revolution, and the Maremma just happened to be at the heart of it. A group of mavericks to the north in the town of Bolgheri had recently garnered international acclaim for wines made using nontraditional techniques and unsanctioned blends of grapes, including—horrors!—popular French cultivars like cabernet sauvignon and chardonnay. All this, in defiance of the archaic rules of the government, which the iconoclast vintners dismissed as too restrictive, too much an impediment to realizing the true potential of their vines. These wines, dubbed "Super Tuscans," were attaining cult status, fetching extravagant sums, and proving wines of distinction could come from Maremman soil. Just a stone's throw from Clara and Manlio's farm in the vineyards surrounding the village of Scansano, winemakers had followed suit and were earning accolades of their own for a jammy red wine called Morellino di Scansano.

Clara consulted, studied, tasted. And she took particular note of the goings on in Scansano. Fueled partly by nostalgia and partly by practicality she decided to stick with her ancient vines, a jumble of native grapes little known or else dismissed outside the region. Trebbiano, malvasia, greco, grechetto, verdello, sangiovese, ciliegiolo. No need to plow them under and replant with chardonnay and merlot. What was needed was a new approach. Not the overprocessed industrial path, not the haphazard, foot-stomping practices of the contadini of the past, but a blend of modernity and tradition. An artisan's approach in the field and the cantina, with hand-harvested grapes and small-scale production, stainless steel fermentation tanks and temperature control.

They called the winery La Stellata, the name of both the original farmstead and the sinuous creek that flows along the foot of the property. The word means "starry," an allusion to the star-filled skies over the open, quiet valley. With another nod to the night sky, in 1984 they christened

their first wine "Lunaia," in honor of the luminous moon that reigns
during the harvest season. The wine was released with little fanfare and
whispered skepticism from the locals. The oenologist from the provincial
capital of Grosseto was doubtful, too, until his first sip, which revealed
a wine of excellent quality: flaxen-hued, dry and delicate, with a hint of
ripe pears and the slightly bitter finish characteristic of grapes grown on
volcanic soil. Positive reviews from the critics soon followed, even the
doubters came around. By 1986 their Lunaia, Bianco di Pitigliano, had
distinguished itself as an exceptional wine above the sea of white swill
that had previously characterized the zone, and Clara and Manlio had
carved out a satisfying life for themselves in the midst of their vines.

So as my language course drew to a close, Clara was up to her elbows
in grapes and had no time for preparing leisurely wine dinners for foreign
students.

Sensing my disappointment, Alessandra arranged for the next best
thing, an informal visit after the school session had finished. It was an
afternoon in late October, and Clara and Manlio were enjoying a lull,
the grape harvest behind them and the olives in their small grove not yet
ready to be gathered and pressed.

Wine tasting at all but the largest estates in Italy is a much more
casual event than in the great châteaus of France or the sleek wineries
of California. No tasting rooms, no sommeliers, no wine glasses or
corkscrews or tote-bags emblazoned with the winery's logo. Instead
Alessandra and I spent the afternoon at Clara's kitchen table—an
antique farmhouse table with a Carrara marble top, its surface worn
from years of kneading bread dough and rolling out countless batches
of pasta by hand. Outside the temperature had fallen and the wind
had come up. A tattoo of rain pelted the windows, quenching the dry,
cracked red earth and settling the dust.

Clara had brought out an armload of bottles, which she uncorked
and lined up like sentinels in the middle of the table. We were playing
a little wine tasting game—Clara, a friend of hers visiting from Rome,
Alessandra, and I, while Manlio puttered in the garage, repairing something on his tractor in preparation for the upcoming olive harvest. (Like
many wineries in Italy, the property had a few rows of olive trees that
Manlio and Clara harvested for their own use.) The object of the game

was to take a sip of wine, identify the predominant flavors detected, and suggest a complementary food with which to pair it. Among certain aficionados this can be a pretentious and annoying game, but with the right sensibility and company it can educate and sharpen the palate. And it's entertaining to boot.

I was faring poorly, handicapped in part by the vestiges of the head cold I'd come down with after my night in the woods, but more by my lack of proficiency in the language. Although my newly developed ability to conjugate regular verbs in the future and imperfect tenses had added considerably to my powers of conversation, I still became self-conscious and tongue-tied when trying to make a good impression, a condition that only grew worse with every error I heard fall from my lips. "Fresh peaches," I had intended to say upon sampling one of Clara's white wines. Instead of pronouncing *pesche* with a hard "c," I said *pesh-ay*. A painful instant of silence followed, and then Alessandra started to laugh. She explained my mistake, and Clara good-naturedly suggested the wine would indeed marry perfectly with pan-fried sole with lemon, but I shuddered to think I had just told an accomplished winemaker her award-winning vino bianco tasted like fish.

We moved on to her red wine. Blackberry and mint, Alessandra pronounced confidently. Clara concurred, but her friend thought it was more like black currants. Had it not been for my shaky Italian, I might have been able at least to weigh in, but I mistook Alessandra's *mora*, which means "blackberry," for *muro*. So while the three of them debated whether the wine was better suited to braised rabbit or roast veal I was stuck pondering how such a fruity red wine could possibly taste like a stone wall.

Clara suddenly remembered a dessert wine she wanted to share. She rose from the table, disappeared into the cantina, then returned with a dusty bottle in hand. It was a Recioto di Soave, a gift from visiting friends that she'd tucked away, waiting for the right occasion to present itself. Made from dried grapes, Recioto is produced in Northeast Italy near Verona. The name stems from the dialect *recie*, or "ears," because only the ears—the sweetest grapes from the tips of each cluster—are used in its making. It is an ancient wine, with origins tracing back to the Romans. In the 5th century the statesman Cassiodorus first described the process of drying the grapes on racks in sheltered rooms during the winter months and then vinifying them to yield a beautiful clear wine that seemed an evocation of lilies. Clara had just uncorked the bottle and poured a finger's worth into four fresh glasses when her cell phone sounded from within her handbag on the kitchen counter. She excused herself and motioned to us to continue without her.

We lifted our glasses to examine the brilliant amber liquid in the waning gray afternoon light. I brought mine to my lips and detected a familiar scent, perhaps of vanilla—an indication of aging in oak casks? I took a tentative taste. The wine washed over my tongue, filled my mouth, rich and honeyed. Spectacular. "*Fichi!*" I heard myself say. Figs. The flavor and the word were fresh in my mind because just a few days earlier while exploring the dirt roads leading down from Manciano I had chanced upon a gnarled, untended fig tree laden with ripe fruit in a hedgerow. I scrambled up the bank and plucked a soft purple fig to eat, still wet with dew. I ate another, then gathered up my shirt by the hem and filled my makeshift pouch with as many figs as I could carry away. I took another sip of Recioto. Yes, the wine had a pronounced note of figs, but what to serve with it? My years as a pastry chef told me that such concentrated flavors would only do battle with a sugary, heavy dessert, so I focused instead on the Italians' beloved cheese course. "I taste figs," I said, holding up my glass, "and I would serve this with Gorgonzola cheese."

Alessandra's dark eyes opened wide. She reexamined her glass, then swirled another sip around in her mouth. Figs, indeed, she tasted figs. But with Gorgonzola? She wasn't so sure. Don't misunderstand, she was a fan of Gorgonzola, the blue-veined cow's milk cheese named for the village outside Milan where it was originally made. (Alas, no one makes Gorgonzola in Gorgonzola anymore as the village has been engulfed by suburban sprawl. Production has shifted to Novara and other nearby agricultural areas.) The cheese comes in two forms: *dolce*, which is mild and creamy, and *piccante*, sometimes called "mountain," which is aged longer and has a crumblier texture and more pronounced flavor. Italians like to stir Gorgonzola, both kinds, into pasta or risotto dishes, or melt it over polenta, or serve it after the meal with fresh fruit or nuts. But Alessandra tended to think it better suited to a red wine. She had a point, it's a classic pairing—the inspiration for the estimable Gorgonzola sandwich and glass of burgundy that Leopold Bloom had for lunch at Davy Byrne's Pub in James Joyce's *Ulysses*. It's still on the menu at the pub in Dublin; maybe someday I'll stop in and give it a try. Maybe someday I'll read *Ulysses*.

Just then Clara returned to the table. We waited silently as she studied her wine, her forehead furrowed in concentration, her angular cheekbones accentuated as she savored a second taste. "*Fichi secchi!*" she declared. Dried figs. And she could think of nothing better to pair this recioto with than a wedge of ripe, bold cheese. Something like Gorgonzola. In fact, Gorgonzola above all others, and she sprang to her feet to make another trip to the cantina. She happened to have a piece of Gorgonzola in the house, and if we were to drizzle it with some local wildflower honey and serve it with the Recioto we would have a marriage of flavors made in heaven. Upon returning she refilled our glasses and brought out dessert plates, cut into the cheese and spooned a thin filigree of honey over each wedge. It was a seductive and intriguing interplay of flavors unlike anything I'd ever experienced. Salty and sweet, musky and floral, earthy and ethereal.

Clara's friend gave a nod. She, too, had had her doubts about the pairing, but *si sposano bene*. They married well. Her comment had nothing to do with social class, she didn't regale us with a tale of two peasants mustering enough of a dowry to send their daughter to the altar with a duke. What she meant was: Gorgonzola and Recioto marry well *together*. Italians often proclaim this when they come across particularly harmonious flavor combinations. *Si sposano bene,* they'll say, when considering tomatoes and basil, spinach and nutmeg, garlic and lamb, Sauternes and foie gras, as if the ingredients were made for each other. And as with any good marriage the members in the union play upon each other's strengths, buffer each other's weaknesses, express themselves more fully together than alone.

Alessandra broke into a broad smile as she toasted me with an upraised glass. "*Brava*, Teresa!" she said. "*Complimenti!*" Clara and her friend lifted their glasses as well, and a feeling of unbridled delight spread over me, a sensation not fully explained by the lubricating effects of the wine. It was precisely the dose of validation I needed. My tongue suddenly seemed more supple and agile, words flowed with much less effort, and as the conversation and laughter continued I cast off my worries about whether or not my articles and nouns were agreeing with each other in gender and number, or whether my past participles required transitive or intransitive auxiliary verbs. Instead I just let myself speak. I'd come to Italy to study the language in order to learn more about the country's cuisine, and there I was, my knowledge of cuisine helping me speak the language. *Si sposano bene*. It was a perfect match.

BRUSCHETTA CON FICHI E GORGONZOLA

BRUSCHETTA WITH FIGS AND GORGONZOLA

(Serves 4 to 6)

I don't often find myself with a bottle of Recioto in the house—it's hard to come by in New Hampshire. Likewise, I'm too far north to find decent fresh figs. But this bruschetta, with its interplay of earthy cheese and sweet dried figs, always reminds me of Clara. It makes a wonderful addition to an antipasto platter. I've also been known to have it for breakfast. If you live near a source of fresh figs, by all means use them here.

- 12 slices day-old baguette
- olive oil
- 4 ounces Gorgonzola dolce, rind removed
- 6 dried or fresh figs, stems removed, cut vertically into thin slices
- 2 to 3 tablespoons good-quality honey

Preheat oven to 350°F. Toast the bread slices in the oven or on a grill until browned. Brush lightly with olive oil. Spread each baguette slice with Gorgonzola and arrange sliced figs on top. Place bruschetta on a baking sheet and bake about 10 minutes, until cheese is melted. Drizzle with honey and serve.

19

HARVEST TIME AT
LA STELLATA

I talians refer to the two weeks each September when the wine grapes are gathered as *la vendemmia*, but the word encompasses far more than just picking grapes. The cultivation of the vine dates back thousands of years, and time has given the harvest a mythical dimension. Like no other agricultural act in Italy, a palpable air of exuberance surrounds the grape harvest each year, fueled by anticipation of the resulting wine and fortified by a glass or two of last year's vintage. The vendemmia has its share of unpleasantries—long hours and heavy lifting, blistered hands and sticky, purple-stained fingers, wasps and fruit flies. But it remains, especially in the smaller wineries, as much a celebration as a labor of the land, a communal gathering of family and friends, of neighbors helping neighbors—fourteen days of festivity.

Providing meals for the picking crews was once the obligatory responsibility of the winery, a task that fell to the matriarch of the estate and any daughters, sisters, aunts, or grandmothers able to lend a hand. Day after day during the vendemmia these women laid out hearty, multicourse meals featuring regional products and the prodigious output of the September garden. The aim was not only to provide sustenance for the day's labors, but to entice paid workers to return from one year to the next rather than drift to another winery down the road in search of tastier fare.

Today many of the larger estates have phased out this practice and rely instead on caterers and boxed meals. Some workers even have to pack their own lunches. This might seem perfectly reasonable to any American farm laborer, but in Italy it is viewed as yet another sign of the demise of civilization, a loss of integrity and decency wrought by globalization and corporate greed. At La Stellata the tradition of home-cooked meals still reigned. While a few seasonal employees helped out with the harvest each year, Clara and Manlio's picking crew consisted primarily of relatives and friends, who looked on the annual event as a reunion and vacation, a chance to convene in the countryside during its most bountiful season. And Clara welcomed the opportunity to cook for a crowd. If pressed, she'd say it was her favorite aspect of the vendemmia and a point of pride; she'd let her grapes rot on the vine before she would hire someone else to prepare her harvest meals.

I learned all this from Clara as I sat at her marble-top kitchen table peeling carrots and snapping beans for supper. Two years had passed since the wine tasting when we'd first met. As the tasting drew to a close on that gray afternoon in October, Clara had escorted me to the door. Come back next year for the vendemmia, she said. It was an impromptu remark, uttered merely as a courtesy, but I took her at her word. And when I grasped the two bottles of wine I'd purchased in one hand so I could shake her hand with the other, I did not say goodbye. I said, "*Ci vediamo presto.*" We'll see each other soon.

That hour spent at her table had offered a tantalizing first taste. Listening to Clara I became increasingly curious to see her at work in her kitchen. Looking around the room I knew, from the clusters of tomatoes and stalks of wild fennel drying in the rafters, from the glass crocks of baby zucchini and string beans preserved in olive oil on the side table, from the salt cod soaking in a basin on the counter, that here was a cook I wanted to see in action. I wanted a tour of her cantina, that mysterious inner sanctum of provisions, into which all devoted Italian cooks surreptitiously slip and then reappear with homemade delicacies—jams and preserves, vinegars, liqueurs, cured meats and cheeses, each one more tantalizing than the next. I wanted a glimpse inside her recipe file, a black loose-leaf binder stuffed with stained and tattered scraps of paper that lay at the ready on her cookbook shelf. And so I considered her offer an official invitation.

I had too many other commitments to return to the Maremma the following September, but a year later I sent a letter to Clara asking if her offer to work the vendemmia still stood. I would love to help out in the kitchen, I wrote, but I'd happily do whatever needed to be done. It seems quaint now to think how anxious I was waiting for a reply in those days before email and texts. Come, she wrote back. By all means, come.

In the intervening two years I had audited a few college Italian courses and returned several times to language schools in Italy. I could conjugate the historic past perfect and use the imperative with relative ease. More important, I could book a hotel and haggle with the cab drivers outside Stazione Termini in Rome. A docent at the Borghese Gallery mistook me for an Italian, from Umbria perhaps, he couldn't quite place my accent. It gave me a smug sense of satisfaction, even if it was a line he used with all the girls.

By that September I was also four months pregnant, a little matter I forgot to mention in my correspondence with Clara. But pregnancy hadn't slowed me down much (at ten weeks, I'd climbed Mount Rainier with my three sisters). And as Alessandra's mother said when I expressed doubts about making the trip, *"Meglio in pancia che in braccia."* Far easier in your belly than in your arms.

An August heat wave brought the harvest on early, and I arrived in Manciano on the first weekend in September with the vendemmia already underway. The cloying smell of fermenting grapes greeted me as I walked the narrow, cobbled side streets of the town's historic center. Old men driving rusty Ape pickups—Italy's iconic three-wheeled trucklet—sputtered their way down crowded alleys, their cargo holds heaped with pressed grapes and swarming with yellow jackets. Through cantina doors open to the street I watched men dumping grapes into hoppers, siphoning must from one barrel to another, dipping a finger into a vat to sample the fermenting juice.

In the vineyard at La Stellata early the next morning, as the vines shimmered with dew and the sun gained strength overhead, Clara gave me a pair of pruning shears and a ten-second lesson on harvesting grapes. She motioned up and down the row to indicate the baskets that had been placed intermittently throughout the vines, and assigned me to a row with her friends Paola and Giovanni, a couple in their early fifties who came each year from Viareggio to help with the harvest. She told Giovanni to carry my baskets for me—she didn't want me doing any lifting in my condition.

Incidentally, a moratorium on heavy lifting was one of many perks of "my condition" while in Italy. People put out their cigarettes or stepped outside to smoke when I walked in the room, and whenever I traveled by car I was given the front passenger seat instead of a spot in the back, lest I should suffer from *la nausea*. I felt a twinge of guilt taking advantage of this last concession, as I went my entire pregnancy without so much as a pang of *la nausea*, but many Italian automobiles lack seatbelts in the back, and driving in Italy is perilous enough even with a seatbelt firmly fastened, so I acquiesced. Perhaps best of all, when I announced my pregnancy to Clara upon my arrival, she opened a cabinet and pulled out a bottle of champagne to celebrate. Wonderful news, congratulations! she said, handing me a glass. I hesitated, explaining that American doctors frowned on drinking during pregnancy. What? Not even wine? She had never heard anything so absurd, of course an expectant mother could enjoy an occasional glass of wine. What did I think Mary drank when she was pregnant with Jesus?

I tell you, Italy was a great place to be pregnant.

We were picking white procanico grapes that morning, a traditional Tuscan variant of the more widely known trebbiano grape, and the main constituent in Clara's prize-winning Lunaia wine. As instructed, I snipped off clusters at their base and placed them in my basket after cutting away any unripe or rotted fruit. I found the going easy—the workload light, the discourse pleasant as Giovanni, Paola, and I made our way down the rows, although Giovanni scolded me more than once when he caught me carrying my own basket through the vines. The percussive snip of garden shears punctuated any lulls in our conversation, along with the rustle of leaves being nudged aside to better access a stem, the soft plop of grapes landing in a basket.

Clara picked with us until midmorning, then announced she was slipping away to the market; she would be back within the hour and I was to meet her in the kitchen. My vendemmia routine had begun. I harvested grapes in the morning, helped prepare pranzo, headed back to the vineyard after the meal to gather grapes until late afternoon, then returned to the kitchen to lend Clara a hand with the evening supper, *la cena*.

Each day Clara returned from the market laden with bags of local produce and cheeses, cured and fresh meats. And the meals she made!

Each pranzo was a multicourse study in abundance, from antipasto to
dolce, served to twenty or so workers at an extended wooden table on
the terrace. Salt cod salad, stuffed squash, hand-shaped pasta or gnocchi,
braised rabbit, lamb chops, eggplant and zucchini grilled over an open
fire, lemon tart, ricotta torte. Evening meals were less prodigious, though
prepared with equal care—platters of prosciutto and salame, olives and
wedges of Pecorino cheese, a vegetable dish of some sort or a green salad,
always accompanied by coarse unsalted bread. Suppers were also more
intimate, usually half a dozen of us or fewer at the table, as most of the
pickers were neighbors who went home at the end of the day.

Clara's cooking had a vibrancy and simplicity that was classically
Tuscan but infused with her own flair. Seasonal ingredients being a
hallmark of the region's cuisine, it didn't surprise me to learn that grapes
figured into many vendemmia specialties. Over the course of the harvest I
watched Clara incorporate them into one dish after another, their appearance each time as unexpected as it was delicious. Braised duck legs with
muscat grapes; whole turkey breast simmered with Prosecco, fresh bay
leaves, and sultana raisins; carrots sliced into thin coins, blanched and
served al fresco with an oregano and raisin vinaigrette.

On my first evening at La Stellata she served a slightly sweet flatbread
studded with ink-dark grapes to accompany our celebratory champagne.
Called *schiacciata con l'uva*, it is a local variant of what many Americans
know as focaccia. With origins dating back to the Etruscans, *schiacciata*
is a classic harvest dessert made in the tradition of la cucina povera,
with ingredients any housewife was sure to have on hand: bread dough,
olive oil, a little sugar, and wine grapes. *Schiacciata* means "flattened"
or "smashed," and refers to the way the dough is pressed flat with the
fingertips. The baker brushes the dough with olive oil, presses *uva*, or
grapes, into the surface, and sprinkles the top generously with sugar,
maybe a little rosemary or aniseed, before loading the schiacciata into
the oven, where the olive oil pools in the dimples of the bread and the
juices ooze from the grapes, forming a syrup with the sugar as the crust
turns golden.

The traditional topping for schiacciata con l'uva was the canaiolo
grape, an ancient varietal used as a blending grape in Chianti and other
regions of Tuscany. It has particularly small seeds, which some say add

a satisfying, nut-like crunch to the bread. Others will tell you the canaiolo grapes ended up on the schiacciata because farmers considered them of lesser value than the prized sangiovese—the region's noble wine grape—so they passed them on more readily to the ladies in the kitchen. I have a hard time finding wine grapes of any sort in New Hampshire, though if you live in wine country you might be able to talk a grower out of a couple clusters. Instead I look for dark, seeded table grapes in the grocery store in September. You can take the time to seed them, but purists might not approve. Another option is regular red table grapes, though they aren't quite as flavorful as their seeded cousins.

Clara, like most Italians, used bread dough purchased from the bakery. Since artisanal bread dough isn't available to me, and I enjoy baking, I've come up with my own dough, which I use for Clara's schiacciata and focaccia alike. It incorporates my preference for breads made with a small amount of yeast and a long, slow rise. Although it takes two days from beginning to end, you only spend a few minutes in active work. Time and patience do the rest. I usually start the dough in the late afternoon or early evening to serve the schiacciata the following day.

Combine 450 grams (3½ cups) all-purpose flour (I use King Arthur), 30 grams (¼ cup) whole wheat flour, 1 teaspoon kosher salt, and ¼ teaspoon dried yeast in a large mixing bowl. Though not exactly authentic, I often add a little whole wheat flour to my dough for the nutrients and earthy sweetness, and the resulting bread more closely resembles those made with the less refined flour once used by country bakers. You can omit it and substitute another ¼ cup of all-purpose flour if you prefer.

Dissolve a teaspoon of honey in 350 grams (1½ cups) room temperature water. Add this liquid to the flour and stir with a sturdy spatula to combine. Once the dough forms, it will be wetter than what you're probably used to—not quite batter-like, but much too sticky to turn out onto the counter and knead. Still you must resist the urge to add more flour. Instead hold the side of the bowl with one hand and use the other hand or the spatula to scrape the dough from the side and fold it into the center, rotating the bowl a few degrees with each stroke. Don't despair about the gloppy mess you seem to be making. Take heart in knowing that you only have to work the dough for a few minutes, three to four are plenty. You can also opt to use an electric mixer, starting on low speed with the paddle attachment until the ingredients are combined, and switching to the dough hook for about five minutes total, until the dough starts to pull away from the sides of the bowl. You might have to stop the mixer midway through to scrape the dough from the sides of the bowl or the top of the hook. Cover the dough with plastic wrap or a large, upturned bowl, and set aside at cool room temperature for about three hours, after which it should have risen nicely and be full of bubbles.

Brush a large stainless or glass bowl with good quality olive oil, then rub some more oil on your hands to keep the dough from sticking. Slip your fingers underneath one side of the dough, lift and stretch the dough up and out to about twice its length, then fold the flap back onto the dough, like folding a business letter. Repeat this action with the other side of the dough, then the top edge, and finally the bottom. Rub a bit more olive oil on your hands if needed, and repeat this stretch-and-fold operation on all four sides. This is a technique used by artisanal bakers to create the irregular holes and billowy texture you can only get from a very wet, or slack, dough; you'll notice the unwieldy blob becomes better mannered and more agreeable each time you perform the procedure. Flip the dough seam-side down, place it in the oiled bowl, and cover with plastic wrap (I use a kitchen-sized garbage bag). Let it rise at cool room temperature overnight. In the heat of summer, you can put it in the refrigerator; give it a couple hours to warm up to room temperature before proceeding.

The next morning, oil your hands and give the dough another stretch-and-fold session. Don't press out the air bubbles that have formed—they add to the airy crumb and charm of the finished schiacciata. Turn the dough seam-side down and let it rest for thirty minutes at room temperature. Oil your hands again and perform one more stretch-and-fold, this time incorporating about a cup of grapes. Brush an 11 x 17-inch rimmed metal sheet pan with olive oil and dust with semolina or corn meal to keep the schiacciata from sticking. Gently transfer the dough into the pan, spreading it out slightly, and let it rest for ten to fifteen minutes. Some of the grapes might tumble out of the dough, but you can press them back in later. Drizzle about two tablespoons of olive oil over the dough and then brush it over the surface. Use your fingertips to dimple the dough and spread it out evenly in the pan as best you can. Don't worry about extending the dough completely into the corners. Sprinkle a tablespoon of coarsely chopped fresh rosemary over the dough and dot the top with another cup of grapes, pressing them in firmly. Let rise at room temperature for about an hour, until the dough has roughly doubled in height.

In the meantime, preheat the oven to 425°F. Sprinkle the schiacciata with two tablespoons of sugar and dimple it once again with your fingertips just before sliding it into the oven, then bake for thirty to thirty-five minutes, until deep golden and the bread sounds hollow when tapped in the middle. Let cool slightly and serve warm or at room temperature. If you'd like to serve the schiacciata straight from the oven for dessert in the evening, you can put the dough in the refrigerator after the first stretch-and-fold and leave it there until about three hours before the meal. Let it warm up for a couple hours before continuing with the recipe.

Enjoy the schiacciata with the last of your dinner wine, or celebrate and open a bottle of champagne to pour all around. And if you're pregnant? Well, I'm sure Clara wouldn't mind if you have half a glass. After all, the vendemmia only comes once a year.

SCHIACCIATA ALL'UVA

GRAPE SCHIACCIATA

(Makes 1 loaf)

- 450 grams (3½ cups) all-purpose flour
- 30 grams (¼ cup) whole-wheat flour
- 1 teaspoon kosher salt
- ¼ teaspoon dried yeast
- 1 teaspoon honey
- 350 grams (1½ cups) water, at room temperature
- 2 tablespoons olive oil, plus additional for oiling your hands and the baking sheet
- 1 pint red wine grapes, if available (can substitute seedless black or red grapes)
- 1 tablespoon fresh rosemary, coarsely chopped
- 2 tablespoons sugar
- semolina flour, for baking pan

Combine all-purpose flour, whole-wheat flour, salt, and yeast in a large mixing bowl.

Dissolve honey in water and add to flour mixture, stirring thoroughly to combine with a sturdy spatula or spoon. Once the dough comes together, finish working it with your hands: Hold the side of the bowl with one hand and use the other to scrape the dough from the side and fold it into the center, rotating the bowl a few degrees after each stroke. Continue until dough is smooth, 3 to 4 minutes. (You can also use a heavy-duty electric mixer, starting on low speed with the paddle attachment until the ingredients are combined, and switching to the dough hook until the dough starts to pull away from the sides of the bowl, about 5 minutes.)

Cover the dough with a large, upturned bowl or plastic wrap and set aside at cool room temperature for about 3 hours, after which the dough should have risen nicely and be full of bubbles.

Brush a large stainless or glass bowl with good quality olive oil, then rub some more oil on your hands to keep the dough from sticking. Perform what bakers call a "stretch-and-fold": Slip your fingers underneath one side of the dough, lift the dough up and away, stretching it out to twice its length, then fold the flap back over the dough, like folding a business letter. Repeat this action with the other side of the dough, then the top edge, and then the bottom. Flip the dough seam-side down, place it in the oiled bowl, and cover with plastic wrap or a kitchen-sized garbage bag. Let rise at cool room temperature overnight. (In hot weather, or to delay baking until the next evening, dough can be refrigerated. Let it warm up for 2 hours at room temperature before proceeding and allow about 3 hours total before serving.)

The next morning, oil your hands and give the dough another stretch-and-fold, leaving any air bubbles that have formed, to the extent possible. Turn dough seam-side down, return it to the bowl, and let rest 30 minutes.

Oil your hands again and perform one more stretch-and-fold, this time incorporating half the grapes, and let rest for 10 to 15 minutes.

Brush an 11 x 17-inch sheet pan with olive oil and dust with semolina. Transfer the dough to the prepared pan, spread it out slightly, and let rest for 10 to 15 minutes.

Drizzle about 2 tablespoons olive oil over the dough and then spread it across the surface. Use your fingers to dimple the dough and spread it out in the pan. Don't worry about extending the dough completely into the corners of the pan. Sprinkle with chopped rosemary, dot with another cup of grapes, pressing them in firmly, and add any fallen grapes back into the dough. Let rise at room temperature about 1 hour, until the dough has roughly doubled in height.

In the meantime, preheat oven to 425°F. Just before sliding the schiacciata into the oven, sprinkle it with sugar, dimple it again lightly, and bake for 30 to 35 minutes, until deep golden and the bread sounds hollow when tapped in the middle.

TACCHINO RINASCIMENTALE

RENAISSANCE TURKEY WITH PROSECCO, WHITE RAISINS, AND BAY LEAVES

(Serves 6)

Although Clara had no idea the exact origins of this recipe, it certainly evokes the flavors of Renaissance Italy with its use of dried fruits and exotic spices, its slow-simmered melding of savory and sweet.

FOR THE TURKEY:
- 1 boneless turkey breast (about 2½ pounds)
- 375 ml Prosecco (half a bottle)
- 1 small onion, peeled and roughly sliced into crescents
- 6 whole cloves
- 1 thin slice lemon
- 4 to 5 bay leaves (preferably fresh, or freshly purchased, and not from a jar that has been on the shelf since you moved into the house)
- salt
- freshly ground pepper

Rinse the turkey breast and pat dry. Place in a large Dutch oven and add the remaining ingredients. Bring just to a boil on a medium flame, then adjust the heat and cook turkey uncovered at a low simmer, turning occasionally, about 1 hour, or until turkey is cooked through. (A meat thermometer should register 160°F.)

FOR THE SAUCE:
- zest of a lemon
- juice of half a lemon

- 3 tablespoons white raisins
- ¼ cup extra virgin olive oil
- braising liquid from cooking the turkey
- salt
- freshly ground pepper

Combine lemon zest, juice, raisins, and olive oil in a small bowl and let soak while turkey braises.

When the turkey is done, transfer it to a carving board, saving the braising liquid, and let rest 10 to 15 minutes while completing the sauce.

Remove the lemon rind and bay leaves from the braising liquid. Pass the remaining liquid and solids through a food mill or puree in a food processor. Add to the raisin mixture and season with salt and pepper. Transfer to a small saucepot and heat gently, just to warm.

Carve turkey breast and arrange on a heated platter. Spoon sauce over the meat and serve. Can be served hot or at room temperature.

CAROTE CON UVETTA E PIGNOLI

CARROTS WITH RAISINS AND PINE NUTS

(Serves 4 to 6)

Clara served these carrots for dinner one evening with a platter of prosciutto and salame, wedges of aged Pecorino cheese, and a loaf of bread. They make an elegant *contorno* (side dish) for roasted meats and fish. Prepackaged, trimmed "baby carrots" have a stale, chemical aftertaste that doesn't do this dish justice.

- 1 pound fresh carrots
- 1 clove garlic
- olive oil
- salt
- 2 to 3 tablespoons water
- white raisins (about 3 tablespoons)
- pine nuts (about 3 tablespoons)
- fresh oregano or mint, stripped from the sprig and chopped

Trim and peel the carrots and cut into thin coins. Heat the whole garlic clove and the olive oil in a sauté pan over a medium-high flame and cook until fragrant. Add the carrots and sauté for a few minutes, until they start to soften. Season with salt and add a splash of water. Cover the pan, reduce the heat to low, and continue cooking until carrots are just tender, stirring occasionally and adding more water if needed to keep the carrots from sticking or scorching.

Stir in the raisins, pine nuts, and oregano or mint, sauté another minute or two to heat through, and serve.

20

SOUR GRAPES

N ear the end of my stay at La Stellata the picking crew split in two. Half the group stayed at the winery to bring in the last of the morellino grapes, while the rest of us piled into the back of Manlio's truck and headed to a neighboring estate, the vacation home of a German couple who had made arrangements with Clara and Manlio to have their grapes harvested in their absence in exchange for a share in the wine. The home was a lavishly restored villa with a sparkling swimming pool and stone loggia half-hidden by wisteria. Formal gardens inside a manicured boxwood hedge overlooked a vineyard partly shrouded by the dissipating morning mist. Harvest bins had already been distributed throughout the rows, and we tumbled out of the truck with shears in hand to set to work.

Clara pulled a garden trug from the front seat of the truck. She beckoned me with a wave of her hand and asked me to follow along. She led me along a peastone path lined with shrub roses in their last flush of bloom, then we passed through an opening in the hedge to a pergola covered in still more vines with dark, tight grape clusters dangling through the cross posts. Clara motioned to the grapes and raised an eyebrow. We might as well take some of these, too, she said. No sense leaving them all for the birds. She reached overhead, snipped a cluster, and held it out to me. Signorina americana, you should be familiar with these, she said, and motioned for me to try one.

I pulled a round, deep-blue grape from the cluster and polished off the dusty bloom on my shirtsleeve. The thick skin burst between my teeth, followed by a rush of sweet juice and a flood of memories. An enamel colander full of grapes draining in my grandmother's kitchen sink. Clusters of grapes plucked on the sly from the neighbor's arbor. Grapes held to pursed lips to extract the morsel within, pulpy flesh sucked from tough skins and swallowed without chewing so as to savor only fruit untainted by bitter seeds. I identified it as a Concord grape, and Clara nodded, grinning. They were a rarity in Italy, she explained. Italians call them *uva fragola*, "strawberry grapes," because they have a taste reminiscent of strawberries. Concord grapes. What a surprise to find them growing in a Tuscan villa; and more surprising still, to find a vintner eyeing them covetously.

Of the several thousand named varieties of grapes, the ones traditionally used for wine-making all stem from a single species, aptly named *Vitis vinifera,* "the vine that bears wine." While the juice of any fruit can be fermented into wine, only the vinifera grape has the perfect yet serendipitous balance of acid and sugar to create a palatable wine—even an exquisite wine, given the right conditions—that will not spoil. From aligote to cabernet sauvignon, morellino to zinfandel, *V. vinifera* is not only the winemaker's grape par excellence, it has given rise to most of the world's table grapes and raisins. It is an Old World grape, native to the Caucasus in Central Asia, or thereabouts, and if the Bible is correct it was first husbanded by Noah, who perhaps not coincidentally happens to be one of the first drunks on record. He planted a vineyard, drank of the wine, and was drunken, the Book of Genesis sums up in a couple lines, as though it were the work of an afternoon.

When the earliest settlers arrived in America they found wild grapevines wending their way across the landscape. Botanically speaking this New World vine was a species apart from *V. vinifera.* The taxonomists, evidently short on imagination that day, or at least feeling more pragmatic than poetic, dubbed it *Vitis labrusca,* which means "wild grape vine." The colonists rubbed their hands together gleefully, seeing in the dark blue fruit not only another symbol of the promised land, but a potential in viticulture to rival the riches they were already pocketing by turning standing timbers into ship's masts for His Majesty the King. But attempts to turn the wild grapes into wine failed dismally. "They be fatte, and the juyce thicke. Neither doth the taste so well please when they are made into wine," reported Captain John Smith of the Jamestown colony in Virginia in 1606.

The captain was not the only disappointed connoisseur. While fresh labrusca grapes have a pleasant taste, wines made from them have a pronounced musky component that people accustomed to Old World wines tend to find unpalatable—somewhere between dirty socks and a dead skunk on the road. The offending flavor came to be described as "foxy," either for its striking similarity to the scent of a wet fox or because wild labrusca grapes are a favorite food of foxes, depending on your source. Regardless, oenophiles consider the trait an intolerable flaw.

Undeterred by the unsavory results from labrusca, the colonists next planted European vinifera grape vines along the eastern seaboard. These endeavors failed miserably, too, for those vines that did not perish in the harsh winters or suffer from viral and fungal diseases during the humid summers were ravaged by the grape phylloxera, a tiny insect that feeds exclusively on grape vines. The grape phylloxera has a complex life cycle and in its varying forms it prefers either the leaves or roots of grape vines. Damage to the leaves generally does little harm to the vines, but infestations below ground cause the roots to decay, ultimately killing the plant. The insect is native to the eastern United States, and American species have a natural resistance to it, secreting a toxin in their roots that keeps the insect at bay. The vinifera vine, lacking this innate defense, is mortally susceptible.

In the 1860s the grape phylloxera was inadvertently introduced into France on a shipment of American vine cuttings imported by a farmer in the Rhône Valley. Shortly afterward, the plants in the farmer's vineyard began inexplicably to wither and die. The mysterious blight spread slowly to neighboring vineyards over the next few years, and once it gained momentum it steamrolled unabated through the grape growing regions of the entire continent. In two decades the phylloxera plague had decimated almost two-thirds of the vineyards in Europe. Grape growers were abandoning their lands and seeking jobs in the cities or fleeing to America, and the wine industry hovered on the brink of collapse.

Both the cause of the epidemic and the cure were slow to come to light. Upon examination the dead vines revealed blackened roots but nothing more, since the ravenous grape phylloxera had already moved on. Some blamed the wasting on the rain; some claimed it was an excessive iron buildup in the soil from the newly expanding locomotive industry, so miles of railroad track were summarily yanked out; still others declared it a scourge sent by God. Finally, researchers identified the true culprit as the tiny pest they named *Phylloxera vastatrix*, the dry-leaf devastator. It was known in common parlance as the grape root louse, albeit to the consternation of entomologists everywhere, who argued that the insect is not even a kissing cousin of the louse, but rather more closely akin to an aphid. Quibbling over the nomenclature continues to this day, with *Daktulosphaira vitifoliae* currently preferred.

Insecticides proved useless against the grape phylloxera, as did holy water from Lourdes, cow's urine, and toads buried in desperation at the base of each vine. When it became apparent that American grapes were spared from the plague, horticulturalists hit upon the idea of grafting the vinifera vine onto labrusca and other American grape rootstock. The practice was nothing new. Grafting is the age-old technique of attaching a scion of one plant to the root system of another so the two will fuse and grow as a single plant—the scion determines the flower and fruit the plant will bear, while the root provides the nourishment and is often chosen for its hardiness. Apples and roses, which don't breed true from seed, are commonly propagated by grafting. Europeans since Roman times had grafted grapes onto select vinifera rootstock to increase vigor, but to graft vinifera vines onto American rootstock was a bitter pill to swallow.

The exact means by which New World vines fended off the phylloxera was not yet known. The science of the day was just beginning to unravel the complexities of insect life stages and cycles, and Darwin's concepts of evolution and natural selection had only just been introduced to a skeptical public. So turning to American rootstock required no less a leap of faith than trusting in holy water. Besides, how could an infernal American grapevine be counted on to save Europe's vineyards when it had been responsible for bringing the plague in the first place? And what if the unbearable foxy taste should creep up from the roots and forever taint their precious *grand cru* grapes? Nonsense, came the reply, only the roots will be American, the grapes will still be vinifera through and through. With disaster imminent, the Europeans had no choice but to plug their noses and graft away.

It would take decades for the wine industry to recover, but recover it did. Vinifera grapes the world over are now grown on American rootstock to protect against phylloxera, although the battle has not yet ended. In recent years, previously unknown strains of phylloxera have emerged that can feed on rootstock once thought resistant. An outbreak in California during the 1980s had growers uprooting their vines and setting them afire in an effort to contain the devastation. Replanting on newly developed rootstock took place to the tune of over a billion dollars, and viticulturalists still struggle to keep a step ahead of the insect.

Although the occasional collector can dust off a bottle of Bordeaux from a pre-phylloxera vintage—1865 is said to have been a stellar year—and lament that European wines haven't been the same since the louse crossed the ocean, for the rest of us the point is moot. Without American vines there might well be no wine today at all, and European vintners remain forever indebted to them. Yet on the whole, winemakers tend to value our native species only from the ankles down.

What possible use, then, could Clara have in store for the trug of Concord grapes I'd just helped her to pilfer? Surely she didn't intend to press them into wine. So fearful are European vintners of sullying their reputations, it is illegal in most European countries to sell wines made from anything but vinifera grapes. But then, the Concord never aspired to be a winemaker's grape. Quite the contrary, it owes its popularity to Prohibition.

The Concord grape was developed by Ephraim Bull in 1849 after ten years of experimentation with some 22,000 labrusca seedlings on his farm in Concord, Massachusetts—not far from the homesteads of his contemporaries Emerson and Thoreau. Mr. Bull was searching for the ideal table grape: a flavorful grape that would flourish where European varieties had failed and ripen fully before the early New England frosts set in. When he finally found one to his liking, he named it the Concord in honor of his hometown, and in 1853 it won first prize at the Boston Horticultural Society Exhibition. Delightfully sweet with just a hint of tartness and the thick slip-skin characteristic of the labrusca, the Concord quickly became a favorite of farmers and home gardeners alike, although Mr. Bull never managed to profit much personally from sales of the vine.

It took a teetotaling dentist and his heirs to discover that the Concord's commercial potential lay in juice. Dr. Thomas Bramwell Welch was the communion steward at his church in Vineland, New Jersey. Concerned that wine in even sacramental amounts was potent enough to steer the congregation from the path of righteousness, Dr. Welch set about developing a nonalcoholic juice substitute to use at church services. In 1869, armed with forty pounds of Concord grapes and the basic tenets of pasteurization, Dr. Welch filled a dozen quart bottles with grape juice, sealed them with cork and wax, and boiled them on the top of his kitchen stove.

He waited several days, and just as he'd hoped, the bottles did not explode. They didn't explode because the wild yeasts in the grapes had been killed by the heat, so there was no fermentation and no buildup of gas within the bottles. He began producing Dr. Welch's Unfermented Wine as a communion beverage for his church. Due to a reluctance to break with tradition, sales to other local churches were never as brisk as the doctor hoped, so the business remained little more than a hobby, but today Thomas Welch is considered to have pioneered the processed fruit juice industry.

Near the end of the century his son Charles took over the company, changed the name to Welch's Grape Juice and redirected marketing to the general public. Sales soon increased dramatically, thanks to the growing temperance movement and a masterful advertising campaign. My favorite ad features a voluptuous blonde holding up a glass of grape juice, along with the caption, "The lips that touch Welch's are all that touch mine." But perhaps the company's ultimate publicity windfall came in 1913 when Secretary of State William Jennings Bryan, a staunch Prohibitionist, made headlines around the world by serving Welch's Grape Juice at a black-tie diplomatic function. Journalists took great delight in deriding the administration's "grape-juice diplomacy," but all the exposure was great for business.

After the repeal of Prohibition the Concord finally did gain a role in the American winemaking tradition when Jewish immigrants in New York launched the kosher wine industry. They turned to the Concord as a source since it was the grape most readily available to them, masking the musky flavor with loads of sugar. The wine's treacly nature has become a signature trait. Today the Concord vine covers arbors and fences in countless backyards across America, and more than 300,000 tons of Concord grapes are harvested commercially each year, primarily for use in processed juice, jams, jellies, and other preserves.

It was jam precisely that Clara had in mind for her grapes. *Marmellata di uva fragola*, she called it. Back in her kitchen at the end of the day she had me rinse the grapes and pull them from the stems. She weighed them, put them in an enameled cast-iron pot with half their weight in sugar, a ladle of water, and the juice of a lemon, and set the pot on the stovetop over a medium flame. The sugar dissolved after a few stirs and the grapes soon surrendered their juices, sending steam and an intense perfume billowing from the pot. After a few minutes the surface of the liquid roiled with bobbing pips, and Clara pulled the pot from the heat. Working in batches she passed the mixture through a food mill set over a large bowl to remove the seeds, then scraped the resulting puree back into her pot and returned it to the fire. She adjusted the flame to maintain a staccato blip, blip, blip, just low enough to keep the hot jam from spattering over the stove. Jam is best, she told me, when the boiling is vigorous and quick. From time to time she traced a wooden spoon through the bubbling jam, scraping the bottom of the pot to keep the pulp from sticking. In fifteen minutes or so the puree had grown dense and lustrous, its color deepened to an inky purple. Finally, Clara lifted her spoon and a jam droplet clung to the lip before sliding reluctantly back into the pot—the jam-maker's litmus test. "*È pronta!*" she said. All set.

My task, meanwhile, had been to bring an assortment of small clear jars to a boil in a large cauldron. I lined the hot jars up beside the stove and she used a wide-mouthed funnel to fill them with bubbling jam. We wiped the rims clean with a damp cloth, sealed the lids, and left them on the counter to cool. There was enough to fill six jars, with a bit left over, which she scraped into a majolica bowl. Just enough for dessert that evening, she said. You couldn't ask for a finer ending to a meal.

After our light supper of bruschetta with roasted peppers, a platter of prosciutto and fennel salame, and sautéed wax beans and cherry tomatoes with parsley, Clara gently reheated the marmellata and spooned it over dollops of fresh sheep's milk ricotta. She served it with a plate of almond cookies called *cantucci* from the village baker, and it was indeed a splendid evocation of the flavors of the season. Clara's jam was so far removed from commercial grape jelly as to seem derived from a different fruit entirely; intensely grapey, pleasantly sweet, and in combination with the creamy ricotta with its mild tang it achieved the understated elegance that is the hallmark of Tuscan cuisine.

In the years since, making Clara's marmellata di uva fragola has become an autumn tradition for me in New Hampshire, not far from the birthplace of the Concord grape. My neighbors have a vine, and they always have an overabundance they are willing to share. But a couple years ago I made a surprising discovery. My kids and I found a particularly productive wild grape vine clambering up a dead oak tree not far from our house. It bears scrawny little grapes, almost too seedy to eat, and the leaves are pockmarked with green bumps, the telltale signs of the labrusca's ability to coexist with the grape phylloxera. Still, we manage to find plenty of ripe clusters that the wild turkeys and cedar waxwings have overlooked, and when I cook the fruit down on the stove the resulting jam has tantalizing undertones that linger in the mouth, more sophisticated even than Clara's marmellata. And I'm always amused by the irony: For centuries winemakers have disdained the flavor of the labrusca grape when pressed into wine, but it was a vintner who showed me how to tap its true potential by simmering it into jam.

MARMELLATA DI UVA FRAGOLA

CONCORD GRAPE JAM

(Makes about 4 cups)

- 2 pounds Concord grapes
- 1 pound sugar
- ¼ cup water
- juice of a lemon

Combine grapes, sugar, water, and lemon juice in an enameled cast-iron or similar pot and heat over a medium flame. Stir to dissolve sugar and continue cooking until grapes give up their juices. Remove from heat. Working in batches, pass grape mixture through a food mill to remove seeds. Scrape the resulting grape puree back into the pot and return to a steady boil. Let puree reduce, stirring occasionally to keep it from sticking. To test for doneness, dip a spoon into the puree. If the jam is syrupy and runs off in a stream, continue boiling. When the jam forms a thick droplet that slowly plops from spoon, it is done.

Pack the jam into sterilized jars, seal, and process according to standard canning directions or refrigerate.

PART III

LE MARCHE

21

A PLACE OF LITTLE NOTE

Wedged between the Apennines and the Adriatic Sea, at about the calf of the boot of Italy, lies the region of Le Marche. With the exception of the sandspit ribbon extending along its coast some hundred miles, the region is mountainous but for where it is only hilly, its uplands dappled with medieval villages and rolling fields of grain, vineyards and olive groves, stands of sunflowers and fava beans. Thirteen rivers flowing from the spine of the Apennines have carved Le Marche into a series of deep, parallel valleys, arranged like so many accordion pleats opening to the sea and making travel difficult from north to south even today. Le Marche earned its name from its medieval role as a military march or borderland. It buffered the papal domain from enemies Byzantine, Holy Roman, and otherwise for almost a thousand years, its impenetrable interior rendering it a land of few residents and even fewer visitors. Guidebooks have called Le Marche a place of little note, hardly worth the effort to get to.

The region's image has changed somewhat in recent years. German and British sunbathers have discovered the Adriatic beach resorts of Le Marche and now descend in droves each August. Tourist promotion boards have begun touting the region as "the New Tuscany," at least if they have not been commissioned to confer that title on Umbria or Calabria or Puglia. Le Marche suffered heavy bombardment during World War II as the Allied forces worked their way up the coast. Vestiges of the trail of destruction still remain, and real estate agents have cropped up in villages big and small, eager to sell you an abandoned farmhouse or crumbling villa ripe for restoration.

I happened upon Le Marche while searching for language schools in Italy. After several visits to study Italian in the Maremma, I wanted to spend time in a part of the country I hadn't seen before. My experiences in Manciano had convinced me the best place to learn a language is in some forgotten pocket of the country, and by no coincidence, such places are also ideal for sampling authentic regional cuisine. Here a language student cannot lapse back into English because no one speaks it; here tourist menus don't exist because tourists seldom venture into town.

During my search I came across Centro Culturale Conero, a private language school in the village of Camerano just a few miles from the Adriatic port city of Ancona. With its 100,000 inhabitants, Ancona is the largest city in Le Marche as well as its capital. My edition of *Lonely Planet* called it a grimy, tattered town, though a good place to catch a ferry to Croatia. James Joyce said it was a filthy hole; like rotten cabbage, where he was swindled thrice. The school's website described Camerano as a small village away from mass tourism where you could easily find parking and no criminality. A village with no criminality near a grimy, tattered town that smelled of rotten cabbage in a region of little note. It was just the place for me.

The school was everything I'd hoped for—warm and intimate, with dedicated, enthusiastic teachers. It was especially quiet during my first visit in 1999, as NATO airstrikes on Kosovo directly across the sea had begun a week before my arrival. Other than a group of fourteen Swiss engineers whose company was paying for introductory language lessons while their employees worked a two-month stint in Ancona, the rest of the students had either canceled or rescheduled. The school's director, Marco Bravi, offered me a class to myself. During my lessons I could hear F-16 Falcons and Harriers flying overhead, and I expanded my vocabulary with new words like *appicare*, to set afire; *pulizia etnica*, ethnic cleansing; *profughi*, refugees; *sciacalli*—the jackals or hoodlums who come in afterward and loot the dead.

Marco met me at the train station in Ancona. He was about my age, maybe a few years older, with dark, closely cropped hair, a silver earring, and a broad smile. At well over six feet in height, he was tall, I thought, especially for an Italian. He spoke quickly as we drove the eight miles to Camerano, and I was tempted to ask him to slow down, to enunciate more clearly, but with concentration I could just manage to follow along, so I resisted, hoping he wouldn't discover I wasn't as fluent as he thought.

When we reached Camerano he gave me a brief tour through the village. Just as described, it was a sleepy medieval hill town of 6,000 residents. Its main piazza, Piazza Roma, provided the essentials, Marco said, pointing out a bakery, a fresh pasta shop, a family-run trattoria, a pizzeria selling pizza by the slice, a bar with bracing espresso, and an artisanal gelateria. If I needed anything, Wednesday was market day, and vendors arrived in trucks offering everything from lingerie and coffeepots to pruning shears and knockoff Gucci belts. Parking, though, would turn out to be limited. The one weekend I rented a car, I got a ticket for parking too close to a stop sign. Rules were rules, explained the traffic officer without sympathy. Next time I should just pull up onto the sidewalk like everyone else.

Marco concluded the tour with a stop at the school, then invited me to pranzo with his family. His wife, Ursula, greeted us when we pulled into the courtyard outside his home on the periphery of the village. She, too, was tall, with light brown hair in a boyish cut. She ushered me inside, asked about my train ride. I detected a bit of an accent, which Marco later told me revealed her German roots. They had met during their university years while working for a humanitarian aid group in Hungary after the dismantling of communism and the Soviet occupation of the country in the early 1990s.

Two sets of wide eyes peered out from the doorway, then withdrew as I entered the house. Annalisa, seven, had a face like her mother's and near-black hair held back in a wide headband, while Viola, four, had soft curls and an upturned nose. The two girls returned to their television program in the next room, while we chatted in the kitchen as Ursula finished cooking. She'd already dropped the pasta into boiling water. Her fishmonger had sold her some beautiful shrimp—they would cook up in just a few minutes and our pranzo would be ready.

Just as Ursula was bringing the meal to the table a squabble broke out between the two girls. Marco excused himself and stepped into the other room to mediate. The television went silent. Some stern words ensued, both girls marched to the table with pouty lips, and Marco returned, shaking his head and rolling his eyes.

Viola took a look at the bowl her mother had placed in front of her and burst into tears. She begged Ursula not to make her eat her pasta, almost choking on the words through her sobs. Then she saw the futility of negotiation and moved on to a blanket refusal. She wouldn't eat her pasta, she wouldn't!

Why not? Ursula asked. What's wrong with it?

There were shrimp in there, she yelled, as if the abomination should be obvious. Why, Mamma? Why, did you have to ruin everything and put shrimp in there?

Ursula sighed. Just eat around them, she said.

Viola began to moan. She shook her head and announced that she simply could not. She could not eat her spaghetti when the shrimp were touching them.

Marco reminded her that she liked shrimp.

Well, she explained, she didn't like shrimp today. She slumped and crossed her arms over her chest, emphatic. By then, Annalisa was crying, too. She wasn't hungry, she informed us, and wouldn't be eating her spaghetti, either.

Marco reached for Viola's bowl. Here's what we'll do. We'll just scoop all these shrimp away, he said, his voice taking on a soothing tone as he transferred the shrimp to his own bowl. She could eat her spaghetti without them, how was that?

This seemed to appease her, because after a couple suspicious stabs with her fork at the strands of pasta she began eating contentedly. In the meantime, Annalisa, who had managed in spite of her lack of appetite to finish all her spaghetti, held up her bowl to her mother for another helping.

Marco turned to me and shrugged. His friends who didn't have kids couldn't believe the chaos in his home. The outbursts, the fits, the injustices—and they always seemed to happen right when everyone sat down to the table to eat. Was it that way in America, too? I hesitated, searching for the words to say something erudite, or at least articulate. I was still a couple years away from having kids, so I couldn't speak from experience; still I supposed with children in the equation, you could expect a little pandemonium at mealtime the world over. But in the moment it took me to gather my thoughts, Viola started to shriek again and pointed to the bottom of her bowl. Her father had missed a shrimp.

SPAGHETTI CON GAMBERETTI E POMODORINI

SPAGHETTI WITH SHRIMP AND CHERRY TOMATOES

(Serves 4-6)

- 1 pound spaghetti
- 1 heaping tablespoon salt, plus additional, to taste
- ¼ cup extra virgin olive oil, plus additional 2 tablespoons for drizzling over cooked pasta
- 1 to 2 cloves garlic, minced
- pinch red pepper flakes
- 1 pint cherry tomatoes, halved
- 1 pound fresh rock shrimp, or other small, uncooked shrimp, shelled and cleaned
- zest of 1 lemon
- 1 large handful finely chopped Italian parsley, about 2 tablespoons

Bring a large pot of water to a boil over high heat. Once boiling, add a heaping tablespoon of salt, then add the spaghetti, stirring a few times to keep the strands from sticking together. Cook until al dente, 8 to 10 minutes, or according to package directions.

Meanwhile, heat ¼ cup olive oil and garlic over a medium-high flame in a large skillet. When the garlic starts to sizzle, add the red pepper flakes, salt, and cherry tomatoes. Let simmer about 1 minute, then add shrimp, stirring to coat. Continue simmering, turning shrimp once or twice, until they are pink on all sides and just cooked through, about 2 to 3 more minutes. Remove from heat while spaghetti finishes cooking.

Drain spaghetti once it is al dente, reserving a couple tablespoons of the cooking water. Add spaghetti and reserved cooking water to skillet, drizzle with remaining 2 tablespoons olive oil, lemon zest, and parsley, and return pan to a medium high flame. Cook for 2 to 3 more minutes, stirring to combine well. Transfer spaghetti to a large ceramic bowl and serve.

22

ROADSIDE MEAL

After pranzo, Marco brought me to meet my host family, a local couple in their late forties, Francesco and Cinzia, and their teenaged daughter, Angelica. Their son, Ennio, was away, in his first year at the University of Bologna, and they had converted his room to host students from the language school. Francesco happened to be an accomplished alpinist and mountain guide. He had published a guidebook to the Parco Pubblico del Conero and was putting the finishing touches on a revised edition when we met.

The regional park, named for the 2,000-foot Monte Conero at its center, stretches along the Adriatic coast south of Ancona and reaches inland to the outskirts of Camerano. It encompasses beach resorts, nature reserves and protected farmlands, limestone cliffs and caves, medieval fortresses and ruins, and archeological sites dating to pre-Roman times. It's threaded with trails for hiking, mountain bike and horseback riding, and calm harbors for sea kayaking, which is part of what drew me to the area in the first place.

During my stay I accompanied Francesco on several excursions along the rocky beaches and wooded trails within the park. It was mid-April, and across the countryside olive groves and apple orchards were coming into bloom, along with wild tulips in the fields and sprays of elderflower in the hedgerows. Scotch broom dappled the hillsides with swaths of yellow and took hold in every crevice in the limestone cliffs leading down to the sea. As we walked, Francesco would stop to jot down notes about washed-out or rerouted trail sections, wildlife sightings, and animal signs—a wheeling peregrine falcon, a nesting thrush, fresh martin scat.

On our way to and from the trailheads, we often spotted old women in faded housedresses and matronly shoes picking their way up steep stream banks and across grassy fields. Shoulders stooped, heads bowed, a woven basket slung over the crook of an elbow, sometimes a grandchild in tow, usually a paring knife in hand. They were out collecting *erbacce*, Francesco explained. In general the word means "weeds," but cooks in those parts used it to refer to the edible wild greens of the roadside. Once home, these ladies would give their gleanings a rinse under cool water and turn them into any number of springtime delicacies: soups, salads, filled pastas, savory tarts—the possibilities as numerous as the variety of greens collected. Now that there was a *supermercato* in town and people could buy vegetables year-round in cellophane packages imported from who knows where, there weren't as many old ladies out gathering weeds, but those who took the time were amply rewarded.

Dandelion greens, purslane, sow thistle, borage, nettles, mallow and chicory, wild garlic and onions. Francesco enumerated the plants that would end up in the foragers' baskets. Many of these erbacce were plants I regarded as annoying weeds. In my garden at home I yanked them indignantly from the soil, how dare they trespass in the plots I staked out for my spinach and Swiss chard and other proper greens?

I hustled to keep up as Francesco danced over boulder fields and floated up timeworn fishermen's trails. He had the lean, sinewy build of an alpinist, and thick, unruly hair, graying at the temples to match his salt-and-pepper beard. He took pains to point out any wildflowers and erbacce we came across, which is how I learned words like *ginestra*, *corbezzolo, ortiche,* the names for scotch broom and strawberry tree and stinging nettles, so much more lyrical in Italian than in English. Here, he slid down a precipitous washout on a sea-cliff to photograph sprigs of *finocchio marino*, which translates as marine fennel, though some English speakers call it samphire. There, he scrambled up an embankment to get a better shot of a clump of wild garlic shoots.

As we set out one afternoon Francesco drew my attention to a sea green vine twining up a *rosa canina*, a wild dog-rose bush. The vine's three-lobed leaves were deeply cut with fine serrations—like grape leaves, only smaller and less round. He plucked a tendril with a few leaves attached and handed it to me, its delicate-looking stem surprisingly fibrous and tacky, almost prickly between my thumb and forefinger. "*Il luppolo*," he said. As a child, he used to help his mother gather the young shoots of il luppolo in early spring to serve with pasta or in soup.

I often find my gardener's familiarity with botanical nomenclature serves me well in Italy, as many of the Italian words for plants are corruptions of their Latin names. The fuzzy-leaved, camphorous sage, *Salvia officinalis*, which grows within easy reach of almost every country kitchen door is *la salvia*. The nodding poppies along the train tracks, like those of Flanders Fields and the Land of Oz, *Papaver rhoeas* and *Papaver somniferum*, respectively, are *i papaveri*. And the linden tree, *Tilia tomentosa*, lending its shade to a chicken coop I had discovered along a rutted dirt road below Camerano is *il tiglio*. Its fragrant dried flowers are steeped to make a bedtime tea to treat insomnia.

Still, I did not make the etymological leap from il luppolo to *Humulus lupulus*. And in spite of the fact that seventy-five percent of the commercial American luppolo crop is cultivated in the Yakima Valley of Washington State where I grew up, I did not recognize the vine sprawling with such unbridled enthusiasm through the blooming canes of the rosebush. But the familiar often goes unrecognized when it appears in an unexpected setting, and Francesco's luppolo simply did not call to mind the endless rows of manicured vines planted with geometric precision in the *H. lupulus* fields outside Yakima.

When I finally looked the word up in my dictionary, I learned that Francesco's mother used to make him soup from hopvines, the twining plant whose flowers are used in making beer. The plant's botanical and common names suit it well, I found, thinking back on the half-smothered rosebush: *Humulus lupulus* derives from the Latin *humus*, the loamy soil that the vine prefers, and *lupus*, or "wolf," which alludes to the Roman naturalist Pliny, who wrote that the plant grows wild among willows like a wolf among sheep. Completing the etymological study, the English "hop" comes from the Anglo-Saxon "hoppan," meaning "to climb."

The chartreuse flowers of the hopvine, technically called strobiles but generally referred to as hops, have been added to beer for centuries as a preservative and for the pleasantly bitter flavor and aroma they impart. I would not have been surprised to learn that the shoots of the hopvine, also known as bines, were considered a delicacy in beer-making countries.

Wherever beer was made, hops, too, would have been cultivated, and wherever a plant is grown, it is only a matter of time before its culinary virtues are discovered, if it possesses any. In fact, the Belgians do serve *jets de houblon*, creamed hopshoots, for the two weeks each spring when the vine is first poking through the soil. In northern France you can dine for an equally brief stretch on lamb cutlets or veal sweetbreads or artichoke hearts *à l'anversoise*. The name refers to anything garnished with sautéed hopshoots. And in English country produce markets you can supposedly still find hopshoots tied in bundles and advertised as "poor man's asparagus," though these days their price probably exceeds the poor man's grocery budget.

But hops in Italy? The hopvine is actually native throughout Europe and western Asia, and it was grown in monastery and apothecary gardens throughout Italy from medieval times. Long before its flowers made their way into the ale vat the plant was prized as a medicinal for treating a host of ailments, from flatulence and toothaches to venereal disease and worms, though not always to proven effect. The most celebrated use of hops was as a sedative or cure for insomnia; their purported soporific qualities made them beneficial in cases where laudanum was contraindicated, which is probably how they ended up in the beer in the first place, acting in tandem with the alcohol to bring on drowsiness. The vine's leaves and flowers, said to stimulate milk production, were fed to dairy cows. This might explain the words of the army nurse who handed my grandmother a glass of beer in the maternity ward after my father was born at Fort Lewis in 1936: Drink this, it will help your milk come in.

Like many cultivated plants, hops readily escape the garden confines and flourish along the roadsides, which is how their tender shoots ended up in the baskets of the ladies gathering erbacce. Leafing through the cookbooks on my shelf after I returned to New Hampshire, I found mention of il luppolo in several places. The Italian expatriate Giacomo Castelvetro sang them high praise in his concisely titled *Brieve racconto di tutte le radici, di tutte l'herbe, ed di tutti i frutti, che crudi o cotti in Italia si mangiano*. (A lovely illustrated English edition, *The Fruits, Herbs, and Vegetables of Italy*, was translated by Gillian Riley but is now out of print.) Castelvetro was a 17th-century Modenese nobleman and Protestant sympathizer who fled his native country to escape persecution at the hands of the Roman Inquisition.

While exiled in London, he cringed at the heavy, meat-laden diet of his adopted countrymen and offered up a treatise on the garden delicacies of his beloved homeland. He recommended blanched hopshoots drizzled with olive oil and a few drops of vinegar, or else dusted in flour, fried, then seasoned with salt, pepper, and the juice of a bitter orange.

Throughout the region of the Veneto, wrote Anna Gosetti della Salda in her 1,200-page 1967 tome, *Le ricette regionali italiane*, hopshoots are simmered with Vialone Nano rice to make a classic risotto, while in the Piedmont they are sautéed and topped with fried eggs. In *La cucina romana*, Ada Boni's postwar tribute to the traditional cuisine of her native Rome, there are recipes for a luppolo frittata and a luppolo soup enriched with prosciutto, garlic, and beaten eggs. (It's a pity this book has not been translated into English; Signora Boni introduced countless cooks of my mother's generation to the vibrant and varied cuisines of Italy through her books *The Talisman of Happiness* and *Italian Regional Cooking*.)

All that remained was finding some hopshoots. I'd seen them growing wild in New Hampshire—the plant was introduced to New England by the early colonists for beer making and was cultivated commercially in the east until the 1920s when a downy mildew epidemic wiped out most of the crop and Prohibition wiped out most of the market. As in Italy, hops can still be found along the edges of fields and roadsides.

That summer I began making mental notes of the hopvines I encountered—beside an abandoned cellar hole, twining up my neighbor's crab apple tree, scaling the south-facing wall of a collapsing barn. I intended to return to these spots the following spring to harvest hopshoots, but then I stopped in at an organic farm across the river from me in Vermont and found that an adjoining field had been converted to a hopyard. It was smaller in scale than the Yakima Valley plantings I knew from my childhood, but unmistakable with its rows of towering wooden posts and intricate network of guy wires supporting the trailing vines.

The following May when the shoots under my neighbor's tree started pushing up through the soil, I returned to the hopyard, a brown paper bag tucked under my arm. I assumed the land belonged to the vegetable farmers; they were probably trying to capitalize on Vermont's burgeoning microbrew industry by selling organic hops. For optimal production, I reasoned, the young vines needed to be pruned back to a few strong stems, and by culling out only enough of the smaller shoots for dinner I was doing the farmers a favor. At least that is what I intended to say if I encountered anyone, although some corollary to the stolen watermelon theory—the melons are always sweeter when pilfered from the patch—must have been guiding me, as I was hoping to poach from the field unnoticed.

I walked past a row of greenhouses without seeing anyone, but as I started up the bank on the edge of the hopyard I suddenly felt my cheeks flush and the pulse drum in my temples. A woman in dusty jeans and a red flannel shirt opened one of the greenhouse doors, perhaps just stepping out for a cigarette. Or about to deliver a lecture on trespassing.

I turned midstride and retraced my steps, approaching her with my right arm extended to shake hands and introduce myself. I blathered about not seeing anyone around, about hops and pruning and salads and the Italians, talking too fast and stammering, hoping to convince her that even though I'd been carrying on like Peter Rabbit in Mr. McGregor's garden, I actually had innocent, even noble intentions.

She listened with a blank face, then finally broke in. "It's not ours."

"The field?" I asked. "It's not?" I pointed across the field to a stone farmhouse. "Does it belong to those folks? I'd like to get permission to harvest some hopshoots."

It was her turn to search for words. "Actually . . . the owner isn't living around here right now."

"Do you know his name? I could contact him by phone."

She shook her head. "Um . . . I don't think he has access . . . no, that probably wouldn't be possible." She glanced toward the hopyard, then back at me. "He's not going to be tending that field any time soon . . . um . . . he's in jail."

"Oh," I said, "I see." It occurred to me that my mysterious farmer might have been growing more than just hops in his field. The hopvine is a close cousin to the marijuana plant, *Cannabis sativa*. Both are members of the hemp family, and their leaves bear more than just a passing resemblance. This was before Vermont passed its Homegrown Cannabis Bill, so perhaps he'd landed himself in jail for trying to sneak a few pot plants in among his hops. "Then you don't suppose he'd mind if I picked a couple handfuls of his hopshoots?"

"Pick away," she said, waving a hand dismissively.

She turned and retreated into the greenhouse, and I crossed back to the field. It was studded with purplish-green shoots, thinner than pencils, poking through the soil like young asparagus spears. The more mature shoots had delicate green leaves, just beginning to unfurl, and they spiraled upward through the encroaching weeds, searching for something to scale. I crouched to the ground and started gathering, filling my bag in just five minutes, then slunk back to my car. I opened the passenger door to set the bag on the seat, and the woman appeared in the greenhouse doorway again. "Bon appétit," she called, and disappeared once again into her jungle of trellised tomato plants.

For the next three evenings my husband and I feasted on hopshoots. I tossed them with hand-cut tagliatelle, prosciutto, and flat-leaved parsley, and we raised a wineglass to Francesco and his mother. I served them blanched and dressed with olive oil (Marchigiani olive oil I had brought back in my suitcase from Camerano) and drops of red wine vinegar, with a nod to the expatriate Giacomo Castelvetro. And I stirred them into a steaming Venetian risotto *alla Signora Gosetti della Salda*. In texture and flavor the hopshoots were indeed reminiscent of asparagus, though with a pleasant bitterness that made us yearn for more. So I returned to the vegetable farm a week later, hoping to gather enough luppoli for Ada Boni's soup, but that had to wait until the following year because the field of delicate shoots had grown into a ganglion of fibrous vines and the fleeting luppolo season had passed.

For several years I returned to the hopyard, and a luppolo feast became an annual event. I never did discover the fate of the hop grower, though the farmers next door eventually purchased his field. They carted away his posts and tore out his plants and then reseeded the plot with grass. But a few intrepid vines still thrive on the edge of the field by the greenhouses, always sending up enough shoots for a meal or two. The vegetable lady has come to expect me each May. In the early years I arrived with my daughter clinging to my knees, then with my son, once he was born, and they'll sometimes come along with me even today. Like the women of Le Marche gathering erbacce, we usher in the bounty of the season with a meal made from a roadside weed.

ADA BONI'S ZUPPA DI LUPPOLI

ADA BONI'S HOPSHOOT SOUP

(Serves 4 to 6)

This recipe is inspired by the description in Ada Boni's *La Cucina Romana*, her 1929 love letter to the cuisine of her native city, Rome. I've never seen hopshoots in a store in the United States, and I've read they can cost upward of a thousand dollars a kilo in Europe, so unless you grow hops yourself, or know someone who does, you can substitute spinach.

- 2 ounces prosciutto or pancetta, finely diced
- 2 tablespoons olive oil
- 1 small onion, diced
- 1 clove garlic, minced
- 1 bunch hopshoots, rinsed and coarsely chopped, about 2 cups
- salt and freshly ground pepper
- 1 quart water or chicken stock
- 2 eggs
- 4 to 6 slices rustic country bread, toasted and brushed with olive oil

Render the diced prosciutto or pancetta with the olive oil in a heavy saucepan or soup pot over low heat, stirring frequently, about 5 minutes. Add the onion and garlic and cook until softened, 2 to 3 minutes, stirring to keep from scorching. Stir in the hopshoots, cook until wilted, then season with salt and pepper. Cover the vegetables with 1 quart water or chicken stock, and continue simmering until tender, about 20 minutes. Adjust seasoning by adding more salt if needed.

Break the eggs into a small bowl and whisk until smooth. Slowly drizzle eggs into simmering soup, stirring constantly.

To serve: Place a slice of toasted country bread in each bowl and ladle soup over the top.

23

WILD ASPARAGUS

lthough I was too late for hopshoots during that first trip to Le
Marche, my visit coincided with high asparagus season there.
Aristocrat among vegetables and quintessential sign of spring,
for a few short weeks the market stalls brimmed with neatly bundled
asparagus in its varied hues and sizes. Restaurants featured it on their
menus, remote villages held festivals in its honor. They served it *alla
Milanese*—blanched just until the tips drooped, then topped with a
fried egg and a dusting of finely grated Parmigiano cheese. Or steamed
and dipped in garlicky mayonnaise whisked by hand. You could find it
wrapped in prosciutto and roasted, drizzled with olive oil and grilled,
tossed with hand-cut pasta, or stirred into a risotto. Marchigiani cooks
rendered even the tough ends appetizing, steamed and pureed for a light
soup or a filling for ravioli.

And Cinzia featured asparagus in one of the most memorable meals
I was served in Le Marche, a late supper on a dreary evening a few days
after I arrived in Camerano. There had been rain most of the day and raw
gusts of wind. Francesco built a fire in the hearth when he returned from
work, and when the flames died down he placed a grate over the embers
to grill slices of firm, yellow polenta. We ate the polenta smothered in
ladles of Cinzia's slow-simmered *sugo di carne*, with steamed asparagus
anointed with olive oil and sea salt served alongside. It was a study in
contrasts in perfect keeping with the day—the rich meat sauce and hearty
polenta warming the body from the inside against a winter that had not
quite let go its grasp, while the delicate asparagus evoked all the vibrancy
and promise of spring ahead.

Cinzia insisted I accept a second helping of asparagus, it was all the more irresistible for being the first of the year. Francesco agreed, serving himself before passing the platter to me. Cinzia asked if I was familiar with the purple-tinged Violetto d'Albegna asparagus from Liguria, so tender it is often sliced paper-thin on the bias and served raw, or the celebrated white asparagus of Bassano. Plump and succulent, its pale moonbeam color comes from mounding soil over the spears as they emerge, thus preventing the light of day from turning them green. They were worth seeking out, if I ever had a chance.

But best of all, Francesco added, is *asparagi selvatici.* Wild asparagus.

I couldn't agree more. I knew well the pleasures of wild asparagus. In fact, I could tell Francesco a thing or two. Hunting wild asparagus with my mother, three sisters, and grandmother along the banks of the irrigation ditches and in vacant lots near my grandparents' farm in Washington State had been a ritual of spring. As a child growing up in the seventies it never occurred to me that people would buy asparagus in a store, or even grow it in a garden. It should have. The Yakima Valley has over 4,000 acres of land planted in asparagus, producing several million pounds of asparagus each year for commercial distribution across the country. But my family never bought any of it. Instead we gathered it, free for the taking, from the edges of orchards and fields.

Spears of asparagus are actually young shoots of *Asparagus officinalis,* an herbaceous perennial native to central Asia and the Mediterranean. The botanical name means "medicinal asparagus," referring to its traditional use in the pharmacopoeia as a diuretic and treatment for kidney stones. A member of the lily family, the mature plant stands over five feet high and has multibranched stalks covered with delicate, fernlike foliage. It produces tiny, pale green, bell-shaped flowers in summer, followed by red berries poisonous to humans. Mature sprigs of bolted asparagus strongly resemble their inedible relation, the asparagus fern, which often shows up as filler in florists' bouquets. The best way to hunt wild asparagus is to seek out the tall, feathery stalks gone to seed, because where there is a bolted spear there are sure to be others just pushing through the soil at the base of the plant. Asparagus plants die back to the roots in winter and send up new shoots in spring, so once you locate a plant you can return to collect from it each year.

My mother would load us all into her beige Volkswagen Squareback and set out on what she called her asparagus run, inching across dusty dirt roads between alfalfa fields and apple orchards from one secret patch to the next, stopping when we spotted the telltale sign of a bolted asparagus stalk. Harvesting the wild spears had all the festivity and exhilaration of a treasure hunt. Who spotted the first spear? Who found the biggest one? Who found the most?

They were joyous events, those outings, but they came at a price, for our unreasonable mother expected us to eat what we picked. For us, it was the thrill of the hunt that appealed, not the meal that followed. As a green member of the vegetable kingdom asparagus was ipso facto of dubious merit gastronomically, ranking right down there with lima beans and Brussels sprouts among things abhorrent. One spring we thought we had solved this dilemma, skipping ahead of my mother and grandmother to surreptitiously snap off the spears and toss them into the orchard rows. Looks like someone's beaten us to it, my mom kept saying, shaking her head as she examined one newly created asparagus stump after another in the ground. She soon wised up and put an end to the practice with threats of double servings for repeat offenders. At dinner my parents heaped their plates with fresh asparagus while we ate our spears dutifully—yes, Mamma, both of them; tips first and then the stalks. We ate them or no dessert for us. Early on, one sister decided she adored asparagus. She picked up the spears in her stubby fingers and ate them with theatrical relish. Obsequious sibling; the rest of us knew she was faking it, just doing it to make us look bad.

But tastes change, palates develop. Each of us discovered in turn our asparagus–loving sister had been right all along. With its subtly sweet herbal notes and delicate texture, asparagus captures the essence of spring, and wild asparagus above all. Its flavor has a vibrancy, an asparagus-ness that has inspired reminiscences and odes from Juvenal to Euell Gibbons. Once tasted, the commercial variety bound by rubber bands in the supermarket becomes forever diminished.

Technically though, roadside asparagus is not wild so much as feral. First brought to North America in colonial times, *A. officinalis* propagates readily from seed. Thanks to the birds that feast on the berries and disperse the seeds, it has naturalized throughout the country wherever it has been cultivated. The unparalleled flavor comes not from wildness but freshness. As with English peas and sweet corn, the flavor of asparagus begins to degrade immediately after harvest, taking on an unsavory edge that grows more pronounced with every tick of the clock. It also loses nutrients and tenderness with time. In the journey from field to grocery store, days can go by, even weeks, and supermarket asparagus inevitably shows its age through fibrous stems and withered tips beginning to unclench. It simply can't compare to asparagus brought in from the field and eaten straight away.

Yes, I could tell Francesco a thing or two, but I couldn't summon the vocabulary. My tongue and brain had gone numb from a day spent conjugating the remote past tense of irregular verbs, and I was too tired to find the words. All I said instead was, "I really like wild asparagus."

I caught my first sight of Francesco's wild asparagus a few days later when he brought me on another hike in the Parco del Conero. Our destination this time was one of the crown jewels of the park, a set of limestone rock formations known as Le Due Sorelle, "the Two Sisters," which rise up from the sea near an isolated sandy cove at the base of Monte Conero just south of Ancona. The cove is most easily accessed by sea kayak or boat—in summer you can take a ferry there. Or you can reach the beach on foot by means of a precipitous trail called Il Passo del Lupo, "the Wolf's Pass," which descends 1,200 feet to the sea from the town of Sirolo. In preparation for his updated guidebook Francesco wanted to review the condition of this onetime fishermen's trail. We set out, traversing a ridge, then threading our way past holm oak thickets and open slopes covered in flowering broom and spurge.

As we made our way through a series of white limestone cliffs the trail became steep and exposed, washed out in places. Even with all my experience as a hiker, I found myself with white knuckles more than once, clinging in the steepest sections to frayed cable handholds, their loose bolts secured to the rocks by rusty pins. Francesco the alpinist scampered effortlessly ahead of me, his wiry frame disappearing, then coming back into sight according to the twists and bends in the path. Watching me, he stopped to jot a few sentences in his notepad: FOR EXPERIENCED HIKERS ONLY. APPROPRIATE OUTDOOR FOOTWEAR RECOMMENDED. A few minutes later we passed an elderly couple. He in flip-flops, she in rhinestone-covered sandals; they were climbing back up from the beach, as nimble-footed as the wolf for which the trail was named.

Francesco put away his notepad and pointed to a lone slender stalk emerging from a crevice in the cliff at the edge of the trail. Just off the path, tantalizingly out of reach, he indicated a few more. *Asparagi.* There was no mistaking them for anything but asparagus, though they were spindlier than any asparagus I'd ever seen. The largest among them was no thicker than a knitting needle, the thinnest, the diameter of a crochet hook. In color they were a deep pine green, their tips tinged purple with a bronze patina. Their coloring and slender silhouette made them remarkably difficult to spot amid the trailside vegetation. I could stare straight at a spear without seeing it, then have it materialize before my eyes just by shifting my gaze. Farther down the path we came upon a few mature stalks gone to seed, and I knew it was not garden asparagus we'd found, but a different species entirely. Unlike *A. officinalis* with its dainty, feathery fronds, the spent stalks were coarse and prickly, with stems snaking skyward, twining several feet through the thick underbrush. It was, I would learn, aptly named *Asparagus acutifolius*, or "prickly-leaved asparagus." A native of the Mediterranean Basin, it grows in dry soils along woodland edges, with a preference for limestone. Throughout its range it is a prized delicacy of spring. Gathering it within the confines of the park was forbidden, Francesco told me. He brought my attention to a cleanly snapped stalk, then another; perhaps our sandal-clad friends couldn't resist breaking the rules.

Wild asparagus grew all around these parts, Francesco informed me, even on the back roads below Camerano. I couldn't wait to take a look around, I said. Perhaps I would find enough for dinner some night.

Francesco clicked his tongue, shook his head. I would be lucky to find so much as *un asparago* anywhere near town. There was too much competition from *le anziane*. The little old ladies. Turns out in addition to erbacce, they also gathered wild asparagus. They scoured the roadsides each spring with a predatory zeal and snatched up all the asparagus the instant it poked far enough through the earth. But Francesco knew of a place. It was a spot in the mountains not far away where wild asparagus grew in abundance. We could easily gather enough for a feast. He and Cinzia would take me there on the weekend.

During the days that followed I found Francesco had not been exaggerating about le anziane. In the afternoons after my lessons I started taking walks alone, exploring the narrow dirt roads and trails of the Conero Park system below Camerano. As I passed through pastures, olive groves, and vineyards, I frequently spotted twisting, prickly branched stalks of mature asparagus on the overgrown banks of the roads, and invariably there were two or three cleanly snapped stalks at their bases, evidence that an anziana had passed through before me.

That Sunday Francesco and Cinzia loaded their two cocker spaniels into the car and we headed to the mountains for a day hike. Their daughter, Angelica, had dance practice and a school essay to write, so she opted to stay home. We caravanned with another couple from Camerano and their two young sons. Our destination: Monte Revellone, a 2,700-foot peak in the foothills of the Apennines. Francesco had promised asparagus in abundance, and as we neared the trailhead I saw people traipsing through pastures gathering it, their cars parked haphazardly alongside the road. Poor fools, said Francesco, wasting their time on such slim gleanings. Just you wait.

Early morning clouds had given way to a strong, bright sun that hovered above the mountain peak. The lovelorn trill of songbirds emanated from the thickets and a soft breeze carried the scent of violets and wild roses across the meadow as we started up the rocky path. Sure enough, the trail was peppered with asparagus plants, but we managed to find only a few overlooked spears. Farther along the switchbacks we occasionally caught sight of a young couple who were snapping up the better part of the harvest just moments ahead of us.

Not to worry, Francesco reassured me. No one ever went to his spot. The trail led us past an abandoned limestone quarry and the remains of the Eremo di Grottafucile, a 13th-century monastery carved into the side of the mountain. A crucifix erected on a stone edifice marked the summit. The asparagus couple lay at its base, legs intertwined, enjoying the solitude and the communion with nature. Francesco the rock climber began scaling the tower as we waited for the others. One of the dogs had rolled in something dead and stunk from fifty paces. With their romantic, mountaintop atmosphere apparently diminished, the couple quickly rose, gathered the remains of their picnic, and made for the trail back down, carrying with them all the asparagus I'd hoped to harvest.

We waited for the rest of our party to join us. The boys tried their luck at climbing the base of the crucifix, and then we retraced our steps along the ridge for several minutes. Francesco stopped, looked around to make sure we weren't being watched, then ushered us off the trail to an overlook above a steep, narrow talus slope. Down there, he said, that's where our asparagus is. I assumed that Francesco the gentleman-mountaineer would scramble down through the rock debris, harvest the asparagus, and then climb back out of the abyss while we waited for him in the safety of the overlook. I had no intention of going down there myself, and I didn't think any of the others would do it either. But no. Follow me, he said to the boys. It's a game, a contest. Whoever touches down on the seat of his pants is disqualified. Leaping onto both feet at a time, he began to zigzag like a jackrabbit down the chute. The boys took a few tentative sliding steps, soon got the hang of it, and bounded after him, squealing with delight. Not to be left behind, down I followed in their tracks, the scree sliding along with me. To my surprise I found it easy to keep my balance as long as I kept moving and kept my eyes focused well ahead of me on the slope, and soon I was laughing giddily, too. Cinzia and the others followed, and we all made it to the bottom without so much as a splinter or scraped knee.

At the base of the talus field, the chute opened onto a meadow. It was dotted with asparagus plants, too many to count, their feathery stalks covered in dew and glistening in the sunlight as if cloaked in a veil of spun sugar. A veritable virgin asparagus forest; Francesco had not led us astray after all. We canvassed the meadow and surrounding woodland edges and gathered several pounds between us, smug in our largesse. No one had been there before us and no one would have the temerity to follow. The boys refused to surrender their asparagus to the canvas bags Cinzia had brought along, insisting instead on clenching their harvested spears in tight fists, which soon sagged and flopped like wilted bouquets of dandelions.

We followed a meandering game path until it intersected with the hiking trail, which took us back to the trailhead and then home. For several meals we dined like kings on *asparagi selvatici*. For a late dinner that night, Cinzia sautéed the spears and stirred them into *uova strappazate*, which is a delightful way to say scrambled eggs. The next day we ate asparagus tossed with Cinzia's tagliatelle, pancetta, and fruity olive oil, and that evening Francesco grilled them on the hearth and layered them with prosciutto and provolone on *piedine*, the tortilla-like unleavened flatbread of Emilia-Romagna. That Apennine mountain asparagus surpassed even the freshest garden asparagus, its pure flavor so pronounced as to be asparagus redoubled, with the earthiness so often characteristic of foraged edibles. It was like nothing I've tasted before or since and the memory of it lingers still.

I haven't yet managed to get back to Le Marche during wild asparagus season. But one of my first tasks, with my husband's help, was to put in an asparagus bed (*A. officinalis*) in the vegetable garden after we bought our house. It took three years before the plants were robust enough to harvest. Now we pick asparagus with abandon each spring. A few wild plants have cropped up along the fence-line separating our neighbor's field from ours. We harvest those, too. I've watched my two children caper ahead of me through the field from one plant to the next, in a race to find the most spears, and specters from my childhood run with them. I like to make *tagliatelle agli asparagi* at least once during the brief season. And risotto, and scrambled eggs, and roasted asparagus spears wrapped in prosciutto. If I rush the asparagus straight from the garden to the stovetop I detect in its fresh taste a trace of that wild Apennine flavor. And if there is a moment of quiet during dinner, I can close my eyes and envision those prickly, twining stalks reaching skyward. I can almost feel the rocks sliding beneath my feet as I leap down that talus slope.

UOVA STRAPAZZATE CON ASPARAGI

SCRAMBLED EGGS WITH ASPARAGUS

(Serves 4)

Eggs and asparagus are a classic combination, a simple way to celebrate the flavors of spring. Cinzia paired this dish with a salad of butter lettuce, cherry tomatoes, and shaved Parmigiano.

- 8 ounces asparagus, trimmed
- 1 tablespoon olive oil
- 1 tablespoon butter
- kosher salt and freshly ground pepper, to taste
- 8 large eggs
- 1 tablespoon fresh chives, thinly sliced

Slice asparagus lengthwise, unless stalks are very slender, then cut into 1-inch pieces.

Heat olive oil and butter in a large, well-seasoned or nonstick skillet until the butter sizzles, then add asparagus. Season with salt and pepper and sauté until tender, about 5 minutes, depending on size of asparagus. Remove from heat.

Break eggs into a bowl and beat well with a fork or whisk. Return skillet to low heat, pour eggs over the asparagus, sprinkle with chives, and allow to cook for about 20 seconds. Drag a wooden spoon or heatproof spatula through the egg and asparagus mixture a few times, just until eggs are cooked through but still creamy. Serve.

24

AFTEREFFECTS

E at as much asparagus as we did and the subject is bound to come up. Someone will mention the curious effect that asparagus has on one's pee. Francesco put it most succinctly, pushing back from the table and blotting his mouth with his napkin after finishing his tagliatelle. "*Quanto puzza!*" How it stinks. Though not normally a topic deemed appropriate for polite conversation, the singular peculiarity of asparagus-scented pee seems to forgive any breach of etiquette, for doctors and statesmen, men of letters and gastronomes have long seen fit to comment on it.

One of the earliest recorded mentions of the odor came in 1704 with the publication of *A Treatise of Foods* by Louis Lémery, physician to Louis XV of France. "Asparagus cause a filthy and disagreeable smell in the urine, as every Body knows." Across the channel in London in 1735, Queen Anne's physician John Arbuthnot wrote similarly in *An Essay Concerning the Nature of Aliments*, "Asparagus affects the urine with a Fetid Smell." In spite of the odor, both doctors prescribed asparagus as a diuretic and as an aid in passing kidney stones. Eaten to excess, cautioned Dr. Léméry, asparagus sharpened the Humours and heated the body, so persons of a bilious constitution ought to use it in moderation. Personally, I prefer to eat asparagus immoderately or not at all.

Benjamin Franklin not only remarked on the distinctive smell, he offered an antidote. "A few stems of Asparagus eaten shall give our Urine a disagreeable Odor, and a Pill of Turpentine no bigger than a pea shall bestow on it the pleasing Smell of Violets." Franklin actually had only a tangential interest in urine. His primary focus was flatulence, in particular the offensive scent thereof.

In 1781, while serving as ambassador to France, Franklin composed a letter to the Royal Academy of Brussels in response to a call for scientific papers. Provoked by what he considered the increasingly pretentious and frivolous endeavors of Europe's various academic societies, he offered a proposal for an arguably more pragmatic line of inquiry. "To discover some Drug wholesome and not Disagreeable, to be mixed with our common food, or Sauces, that shall render the natural Discharge of Wind from our Bodies not only inoffensive but agreeable as perfume." Presumably, he reasoned, if turpentine could counter the odoriferous effects of asparagus on pee, then surely something could be done for discharges of a related sort. "Why should it be thought more impossible in Nature to find Means of making a perfume of our Wind than of our Water?"

Perhaps the risk of renal failure associated with ingesting turpentine kept 19th-century cookbook author Pellegrino Artusi from following Franklin's advice. In *La scienza in cucina e l'arte di mangiar bene* (published in English as *The Art of Eating Well*), he recommended a few drops of turpentine for the chamber pot instead. The foul odor filling the air would thus be transformed into the sweet smell of violets.

Because of its suggestive, shaft-like shape, asparagus has enjoyed a reputation as an aphrodisiac since Roman times. In 19th-century France, bridegrooms were often served asparagus at their wedding feast to increase their stamina in the boudoir. But in his 1853 monograph *Phisiologie des substances alimentaire*, the Parisian pharmacist Stanislas Martin counseled husbands with a wandering eye to forego asparagus altogether, "for it has the drawback of giving an unpleasant odor, which has more than once betrayed an illicit dinner."

Not everyone considers the odor off-putting. Those with a pastoral or otherwise romantic sensibility might even find it has a certain appeal. Take Proust, famous conjurer of scented memories. With 3,500 pages of reminiscences to fill, he naturally devoted a few lines to *l'eau d'asperges*. All night long following a dinner party, he recounted in *Swann's Way*, "they played, in farces as crude and poetic as a play by Shakespeare, at changing my chamber pot into a jar of perfume." They were no madeleines, but they had a similar evocative power.

Gabriel García Márquez created the decidedly unromantic Dr. Juvenal Urbino in *Love in the Time of Cholera*. Fastidious and urbane, the doctor had his cooks serve him asparagus, out of season and regardless of cost, for "he enjoyed the immediate pleasure of smelling a secret garden in his urine that had been perfumed by lukewarm asparagus." Which suggests a primordial appreciation for earthy aromas even among the tightly buttoned.

Francesco and Cinzia were surprised to learn I was familiar with the phenomenon. They thought asparagus had this effect only on Italians. Perhaps I could smell it because I was half Italian, I said, having read somewhere that genetics play a role.

Which begged a question, said Cinzia, removing her tortoiseshell glasses and setting them on the table. She had dark, straight hair in a blunt cut just below her chin and she tucked a wayward strand behind her ear. She spoke in lilting tones that were even more musical when she was amused. Did that mean my odds of inheriting the trait were half, or did my pee smell half as bad? No one knew. But we had a good laugh, and the conversation drifted on to other subjects, taking one random turn after the next as lively after-dinner talk so often does.

I asked about the imposing brick building, with its graffitied walls and arched windows full of broken panes on the hill in the historic center of Camerano. I'd noticed it that afternoon while heading for a walk through the Bosco Mancinforte, the public park on the flank of the hill leading into Camerano. Francesco said the building was the old Farfisa accordion factory of Scandalli. Home to the finest accordions in the world, other instruments, too. In the 1960s, Francesco said, the company came out with the Farfisa electric organ, with its incomparable sound. Percy Sledge featured the tender, yearning tones of a Farfisa organ on the track of *When a Man Loves a Woman*, Elton John used one to pound out the catchy, carousel notes of *Crocodile Rock*. Farfisa lends a distinctive melancholy to the early albums of Pink Floyd, and Sly Stone played a Farfisa at Woodstock. The plant had been shuttered for decades, doomed by the advent of the synthesizer, but in its glory days it employed 700 workers. When Francesco was a child he used to wait outside the locked factory gates for his grandfather, who worked there. He could hear plinking and whirring and tapping from inside, and then a whistle would blow. The men would put down their tools and a moment of silence would ensue, followed by a rhythmic beat of footsteps as the gates opened and a stream of workers filed from the building, on their way home for the midday meal. In his mind he could still conjure up that sound, still feel the ghosts of those marching men.

Speaking of ghosts, said Cinzia, had I found the *funtanina* yet? The funtanina? What was that? The funtanina was an old, spring-fed stone fountain on the edge of Camerano, not far from the language school; I should check it out on my way to class. In the days before Camerano had running water, villagers would go to the fountain to draw water for their homes. Beside it was a bank of stone troughs where the ladies used to do their laundry. Cinzia grinned and said I should be careful not to go there too late in the evening, because I might encounter Gianna, the fountain's resident spirit. No one knew exactly her origins; some said she was a witch, others a fairy, still others that she was the ghost of a woman killed there long ago by a jealous husband. But legend had it she roamed the fountain at twilight—she'd been spotted there numerous times. Beware of Gianna, parents used to say, hoping to ensure their children remained inside after dusk instead of stirring up trouble into the wee hours of the night.

As I prepared myself for bed that evening, sure enough, I encountered that unmistakable aroma. Turns out, genetics do indeed have a part in creating asparagus-scented pee, an odor variously described as that of overcooked cabbage, mild skunk spray, or in a more Proustian vein, vegetable soup. Those who have no idea what I'm talking about have either never eaten asparagus or are among the roughly ten percent of individuals whose noses are oblivious to the scent. The source of the odor has been traced to a complex of sulfur-containing chemicals, including one unique to asparagus, aptly named asparagusic acid, but researchers still can't agree definitively on the culprit.

For a long time it was thought everyone produced the scent, but not all of us could smell it. Recent DNA studies have drawn a more complicated picture. Differences in the genetic code do affect the olfactory (smell) receptors in the nasal cavity and determine our ability to detect the scent. But genetics also determine whether the body breaks down asparagus to create the sulfurous metabolites in the first place, although a genetic marker hasn't yet been found. Additionally, our DNA appears to control the concentration at which these compounds are produced, so indeed one person's pee can smell half as bad as another's. The traits are genetically inherited, but not genetically linked.

If this seems like so much fuss over nothing it might help to know geneticists aren't all that interested in asparagus scented pee per se. More intriguing is what it might reveal about genetic variability in general. Unusual odors in the urine arising from genetic differences in metabolism are often a symptom of disease. That does not seem to be the case with asparagus, but the inability to produce the odor could be related to other as yet unidentified disorders or more important metabolic traits. In addition, the phenomenon is one of only a few examples showing genetic differences among humans in our sense of smell. Armed with enough asparagus, researchers hope to further unravel the mysteries of olfaction, the most primitive and least understood of all our senses.

My family's favorite way to eat asparagus—oven roasted—is so simple you hardly need a recipe. Take a pound of the freshest possible asparagus, trim the ends, and cut any especially fat spears in half lengthwise so they will cook at the same rate as the thinner ones. Place the asparagus in a single layer in a roasting pan, drizzle with olive oil, kosher salt, and freshly cracked pepper. Roll the spears back and forth a few times to coat them evenly with oil, and roast in a 400°F oven until the pan sizzles, the tips have darkened slightly, and the spears are pleasantly tender, ten to fifteen minutes, depending on the size and freshness of the asparagus. Serves four as a side dish. You can roll up a few roasted spears in a thin slice of prosciutto to make bundles. Place these bundles on a tray and pop them back into the oven for a few more minutes to serve as an appetizer. Or you can lay the roasted spears across four pieces of toasted and buttered country bread, top with a fried egg and some freshly grated Parmigiano cheese for a satisfying spring supper, served with a bottle of Sauvignon Blanc or Pinot Grigio.

If you catch yourself reflecting on a certain postprandial asparagus scent in the hours that follow, know that you are in the good company of court physicians, literary laureates, and postdoctoral fellows, who have long considered the aroma more than just a passing curiosity.

INVOLTINI DI PROSCIUTTO E ASPARAGI AL FORNO

OVEN-ROASTED ASPARAGUS WRAPPED IN PROSCIUTTO

(Serves 4 to 6)

- 1 pound fresh asparagus
- extra virgin olive oil
- kosher salt and freshly ground pepper
- 6 thin slices prosciutto
- balsamic vinegar, optional, for drizzling over asparagus bundles

Preheat the oven to 400°F.

Trim the ends of the asparagus and slice any particularly large spears in half lengthwise to promote even cooking. Arrange the spears in a single layer in a roasting pan, drizzle liberally with olive oil, and season with salt and pepper. Roll the spears back and forth a few times to coat them with oil.

Roast in the oven until the asparagus sizzles, the tips have darkened slightly, and the spears are pleasantly tender when tested, about 10 to 15 minutes, depending on the size and freshness of the asparagus.

When cool enough to handle, wrap slices of prosciutto around bundles of 4 to 5 asparagus spears, leaving tips and ends exposed. Return bundles to the roasting pan and place in oven for 5 minutes, or until just heated through. If desired, serve drizzled with good quality balsamic vinegar.

Note: You can skip the prosciutto and serve the roasted asparagus spears on their own for an elegant yet easy side dish.

25

STOCCAFISSO:
A LOVE STORY

During my visits to Le Marche I took a liking to the city of Ancona. I often accompanied Cinzia there when she had errands to do. We made the twenty-minute drive from Camerano, and I would roam about on my own while she tended to her business. Those who would call Ancona grimy and tattered, I decided, had perhaps not taken the time to appreciate its charm. A working city with a lively port and a panoramic view of the Adriatic, its historic center has broad boutique-lined streets closed to traffic and spacious piazzas where matronly shoppers alternate park benches with pierced and tattooed university students. It has Roman ruins, including the Arch of Trajan, a marble arch built on the harbor to honor the Emperor Trajan in the 1st century, and it has art, with works by Lorenzo Lotto and Titian in its art gallery, the Pinacoteca Comunale.

I went out a few times for seafood in Ancona with students from the language school. With its broad, placid harbor the city hosts one of the largest fishing fleets in the Adriatic, and its cooks are renowned for their light touch and ingenuity with fish. At La Vecchia Osteria in the heart of the city I sampled the region's famed *brodetto*, a hearty fish stew classically featuring thirteen types of fish—one for each person present at the Lord's Last Supper. I had pasta with baby clams and mussels at the venerable trattoria La Moretta. On another occasion, I pored over a restaurant menu, torn between too many options. Stuffed calamari grilled over an open fire. Mackerel braised with white wine and wild fennel. Roasted mullet wrapped in prosciutto. A soup of chickpeas, hand-cut pasta squares, and the tiniest of shrimp.

Perhaps the signora would enjoy the *stoccafisso all'anconetana*, the waiter suggested. This was dried cod, served Ancona-style, he explained, an iconic specialty not to be missed. But I wasn't persuaded. Why order dried fish from a restaurant overlooking one of the finest fishing harbors in Italy? I opted instead for *branzino al forno* with lemon, catmint, and cherry tomatoes. Roast striped bass, pulled from the waters that morning, which turned out to be an excellent choice.

I didn't think to ask why the restaurant featured dried cod on the menu, didn't know enough to wonder what the fish was doing in Ancona in the first place. So it didn't occur to me as strange that Ancona, with a trove of seafood at its front door, would choose as its signature dish not some casseroled native bream or sole, not a steamed indigenous mollusk or bivalve, but exotic *stoccafisso*. But when I learned of Ancona's storied connection to stoccafisso, I realized the opportunity I'd missed.

Stoccafisso, or stockfish, is cod—*Gadus morhua*—pulled not from the Mediterranean Sea but from Arctic waters a thousand miles away off the coast of Norway. The cod are then preserved by drying them hard as kindling in the open air, using just the sun and wind in a process that dates back more than a millennium. The word derives from *stokvis*, or "stake-fish," referring by most estimates to the wooden racks upon which the cod is dried. An uninitiated diner might confuse stoccafisso with salt cod, called *baccalà* in Italian, but that is *G. morhua* in another form, dried and preserved with salt. The different means of preservation yield distinctly different results. Baccalà is flaky, with a notable salty component, while stoccafisso has a meatier texture and more concentrated cod flavor.

Just the mention of stoccafisso to Anconans of a certain age is enough to bring tears to the eyes. A steaming platter served by Mamma, family gathered around the table, morsels of fish melting in the mouth. Such taste memories, such nostalgia, though as children the dish may have brought them tears aplenty of a different kind. Fits and protestations, too, sitting in front of a tepid plate of stoccafisso, Mamma brandishing a wooden spoon and saying eat your dinner, ungrateful child, or I'll serve it to you cold for breakfast. Their eyes watered and stung from the odor, the downright stench emanating from the basin in the kitchen where the stoccafisso soaked for days until it was finally rendered soft enough to chew. Studying Dante in school, these children were certain the unnamed muck upon which the Gluttons subsisted in the Third Circle of Hell must surely have been stoccafisso. They resigned themselves collectively to stoccafisso as the penance conferred by God upon their countrymen to atone for the gluttony of Caligula and Casanova, for the excesses of the Medici popes, the villainy of Rodrigo Borgia and Mussolini. But that did not make them like it any better.

They had not yet got past the odor. Because the extended soaking not only reconstitutes the cod, it draws out the smell. A distinct reek of rotting fish at low tide wafts up from the stoccafisso as it lies in its fresh-water bath. It permeates the kitchen, the house; some say even the clothing and hair. As for the fish itself, once it is simmered patiently until tender it retains only a whiff of the sea—a pronounced note, arguably with little appeal among the nursery set, but a flavor you come to appreciate as the palate develops. It is an acquired taste then, akin to a penchant for aged Stilton or caviar or bitter almonds, and when stoccafisso is introduced during the formative years, it somehow insinuates itself into your very being.

I learned all this thanks to Francesco. A few years had passed since my first trip to Le Marche, my attention diverted in the interim as my husband and I acquired a fixer-upper, a mortgage, two children, a cat, a dog, and a flock of chickens. I had written to Francesco and Cinzia to announce my upcoming arrival, and I mentioned stoccafisso. *Che fortuna*, Francesco responded, what luck. His friend just happened to be the president of the Accademia dello Stoccafisso, an organization in Ancona created in honor of the dish. Francesco would see we were introduced. The man's name was Bruno Bravetti; he could tell me everything I wanted to know about stoccafisso and then some. The world was small indeed, was it not?

The idea that a fish could be so important as to have its own academy fueled my curiosity all the more. Francesco set up an appointment for me with Signor Bravetti a few weeks later. In his sixties, bald, and with a closely trimmed white beard and thick glasses, Signor Bravetti greeted me outside the Palazzo Comunale just off Ancona's Piazza Cavour and escorted me to his third-floor office. It was the eve of his retirement from his day job as director of public relations for the municipality of Ancona. His career dovetailed nicely with his avocation, since the Accademia, which was headquartered at Ancona's Hotel Fortino Napoleonico in Via Portonovo, was formed to champion the city's most emblematic dish. A journalist by training, he is the author of *Stoccafissando*, a charming monograph detailing the cultural history of stoccafisso, its significance to Ancona, and the endeavors of the Accademia to promote its story. Francesco had directed me well.

I posed my questions and Signor Bravetti leaned back in his chair. He clasped his hands at the edge of his desk and drew in a deep breath. Why stoccafisso? Why Ancona? How could a fish be so important as to have its own academy? Because of the Council of Trent.

For those who have not brushed up on their catechism, the Council of Trent was the convention of bishops and theologians who met to codify the doctrines of Roman Catholicism after Martin Luther nailed his Ninety-five Theses to the door of Castle Church in Wittenberg and sparked the Protestant Reformation in the 16th century. Among the decrees laid out during the Council were the laws on fasting and abstinence as forms of penance, including the ban on the consumption of meat on Fridays (a modest gesture of suffering in remembrance of Christ, who died on the cross on a Friday) and other designated days throughout the year. According to the notions of the day, fish, being cold-blooded, was not considered meat, and "fish on Fridays" became an integral part of Catholic culture. In those days before refrigeration, fresh fish was only available near its source and it was a costly delicacy unaffordable for most of the population. Stoccafisso, on the other hand, was cheap, and it offered the Vatican a plentiful, non-perishable fish commodity to satisfy the needs of its widespread flock. As the primary port of entry to the Papal States from northern waters, Ancona soon found itself at the hub of a longstanding and lucrative union delivering stockfish to the inland faithful.

Stoccafisso had made its debut on the Italian table some hundred years earlier, courtesy of the Venetian merchant seaman Pietro Querini. En route to Flanders in 1431, his ship was blown off course during a storm and drifted north on the Gulf Stream. Querini and his crew washed up on an islet in the Lofoten archipelago of Norway above the Arctic Circle.

There they discovered row upon row of gutted fish, strung from poles and drying along the beach in the wind. The local inhabitants took the stranded men in and nursed them back to health on kindness and air-dried cod. The mariners overwintered on the island while restoring their ship, then set sail in the spring, carrying away a cargo-hold of stockfish and leaving behind, according to the Accademia, a few sown seeds, which might account for the presence of a dark-complected gene among the Lofoten population.

Wealthy Venetians looked askance at the stoccafisso stacked like cordwood when it first appeared at the fishmonger's stall, preferring the products of their own lagoon. Likewise the well-to-do inland dined on trout, carp, and eel taken from their private streams. But stoccafisso had found a steady customer in the poor, and it soon appeared in the holds of ships bound not just for Venice, but for Livorno, Genoa, Ancona, and beyond, until it had become a staple throughout the papal domain.

In exchange, merchant vessels returned to Lofoten carrying bolts of silk and wool, casks of wine and spices, lumber for shipbuilding. They also brought salt, a precious substance in those northern reaches where the sun's rays weren't strong enough to make salt through the evaporation of seawater. With salt, cod could be preserved in places too humid or warm or otherwise ill-suited for the air-drying method of the Lofoten archipelago, and by the 17th century maritime nations throughout the fish's range—from Norway, Iceland, and Greenland, to Canada and New England—had entered the international market with their salt cod. But Ancona remained true to stoccafisso.

No, Signor Bravetti did not like stoccafisso as a child, but the taste grew on him. He reminisced of the ever-present stoccafisso at Lenten meals, Christmas Eve feasts, and grape harvest celebrations. He described smoke-filled trattorie where fishermen with leathery complexions and chapped hands played cards, and women in drab housedresses and sauce-spattered aprons served up bowls of stoccafisso. To accompany it they poured carafes of Verdicchio wine, the same wine in which the fish was cooked. Verdicchio, a white wine made from the grape of the same name, has been cultivated in Le Marche since the 14th century. The name comes from *verde*, referring to the yellow-green skin of the grape, which gives the wine a subtle green hue. Crisp and dry, with a characteristic nutty flavor, the most prized come from the wine growing district of Ancona known as Castelli di Jesi.

Down at the docks, stevedores unloading shipments from Lofoten staged mock duels using stockfish for swords, then snuck their weapons under their overcoats and took them home for dinner. After the Fascist years and the political upheaval of the war, the city's eateries hosted groups of democrats and republicans, communists and anarchists, who convened to talk politics into the night after so many years of silence. Invariably their discussions ended in front of a meal of stoccafisso; eventually "to meet for stoccafisso" became synonymous with gathering to debate the politics of the day.

Until well into the 20th century, when Marchigiani sharecroppers raised a pig over the summer for slaughter in autumn, they often sold off the prime cuts—the hams and roasts and salami. With the proceeds they bought enough stoccafisso to feed their families for the entire year. Among the offal and lesser porcine tidbits that they kept for themselves—a few jars of lard, the trotters, tail, and jowls—the snout in particular often ended up simmered with the stoccafisso.

Italy imports over 3,000 tons of stockfish annually—eighty percent of the Lofoten Islands' harvest, leading one Lofoten mayor to proclaim, "God bless Italian housewives and their kitchens!" Still, that number represents a significant drop from past decades. What was once a poor man's staple has become a rare extravagance. A cook today can't be expected to find the time for the days of soaking, the hours of simmering. Then there is the price. The depletion of the North American cod population from overfishing has driven up the price of Lofoten cod considerably since the 1990s, often rendering stoccafisso the most expensive item on the menu or at the fish market.

Which is why the Accademia dello Stoccafisso stepped in. Fearing the demise of part of the city's historical identity a group of fervent Anconans united to create the Accademia in 1997. Its original purpose was to preserve the traditions both culinary and cultural of stoccafisso all'anconetana. The group began organizing annual dinners, cook-offs, and other events to celebrate the dish, and they recognized local restaurants that offered it as a specialty. Over the years the organization has expanded its scope, establishing cultural exchanges with Lofoten, along with neighboring Mediterranean cities where stoccafisso has played an important historical role. Concern for the status of the global supply of Atlantic cod has added an element of environmental stewardship.

Like most dishes born of poverty, stoccafisso all'anconetana has numerous variations. Housewives paired stockfish with whatever ingredients they found at hand in hopes of cobbling together a meal that would both please and nourish their families, since hunger is a sorry bedfellow. When stoccafisso made the leap to the city's trattorie and osterie, it became a more piquant, saltier dish, with the likes of olives or capers added to stimulate thirst and induce customers to order more wine. With so many interpretations, each as venerable as the next, the Accademia knew better than to proclaim an official recipe. Instead it cast a broader net and issued a code of parameters to define the genuine article:

1. Only Norwegian stockfish of the finest quality (designated as *Ragno*) may be used.
2. Brined or salt-cured cod (baccalà) may not be substituted.
3. The stockfish must be soaked in several changes of fresh water over the course of multiple days to rehydrate it and yield a mild flavor.
4. Bamboo skewers placed on the bottom of the pan are advised to keep the fish from sticking. (Native canes from Adriatic waters were used originally.)
5. The cooking oil must be extra virgin olive oil. Traditionally, this would have been the only oil available to Ancona's cooks, and its flavor contributes substantially to the finished product.
6. Yellow-fleshed potatoes are advised. Their mealy texture makes them singularly adept at absorbing the pan juices created while cooking.
7. The cooking wine must be a full-bodied white, by convention Verdicchio from Castelli di Jesi or Matelica.
8. Garlic, onion, celery, carrots, parsley, oregano, marjoram, rosemary, thyme, pepper, and sea salt are permitted as aromatics.

9. Other ingredients may be added according to local tradition, such as milk, olives, and fresh or preserved tomatoes.

Ancona establishments whose version adheres to the Code are awarded
a placard indicating the Accademia's nod of approval. Signor Bravetti
refrained from singling out a particular restaurant but assured me I would
be pleased with my meal at any establishment bearing the Accademia's seal.

I invited Francesco and Cinzia to join me for a stoccafisso dinner, but
Francesco declined, saying memories of the smell still haunted him. Their
daughter Angelica was eager to come; she wanted to see the expression on
my face when I tasted it. She liked the flavor of stoccafisso but couldn't
imagine an American would. On Cinzia's recommendation we made
reservations at La Cantineta, a venerable Ancona institution located in
Via Antonio Gramsci, near the port and the Ancona Theater, Teatro delle
Muse. The trattoria has specialized in stoccafisso and a few other traditional dishes since it opened in 1957. The décor hasn't changed much in
fifty years, either, with checkered tablecloths, woven rush chairs, knotty
pine paneling, and walls covered with old photographs and watercolor
paintings depicting local sea and townscapes.

Our waiter opened a bottle of wine, brought bread and a plate of
fried sardines with lemon. Finally came the stoccafisso. It was cooked *in
umido*, stewed in olive oil (extra virgin) and white wine (Verdicchio) with
thick slices of potato, finely diced tomato and a hint of rosemary. I took
a tentative whiff, anticipating at least a hint of the dreaded stoccafisso
stench rising from the bowl, but found no trace. It must have wafted out
the kitchen window overnight. The flavor was mild, pleasantly briny but
without the salty note of baccalà, the texture slightly firm in contrast
to the melting potatoes. Cinzia and Angelica looked at me expectantly,
waiting for a pronouncement.

One forkful was enough to justify the mission of the Accademia, to
explain better than words why stoccafisso was a tradition worth preserving.
G. morhua may be a product of North Atlantic waters, but stoccafisso has
been bounty from the port of Ancona for centuries, caught in a net cast
three hundred leagues away. I raised my glass and said, "*Viva lo stoccafisso!*"

STOCCAFISSO ALL'ANCONETANA

STOCKFISH, ANCONA-STYLE

(Serves 4 to 6)

The biggest challenge for American cooks is finding the stockfish for this recipe. Look in Italian or Scandinavian food shops or pick some up when you go to Italy. Last I checked, travelers are allowed to bring stockfish for personal consumption through customs.

- 1 pound high-quality, dried stockfish (preferably designated Ragno)
- ½ cup extra virgin olive oil, plus additional for coating the baking dish
- 1 stalk celery, including leaves, thinly sliced
- 1 small onion, finely diced
- 1 carrot, peeled and diced
- 2 cloves garlic, minced
- 1 small fresh hot red chili pepper, minced (or 1 pinch dried red chili flakes)
- 1 large sprig fresh rosemary, coarsely chopped
- 1 large sprig fresh Italian parsley, coarsely chopped
- sea salt and freshly ground pepper, to taste
- 1 pound medium-sized yellow potatoes, such as Yukon Gold, peeled and cut lengthwise into half-inch wedges
- 4 plum tomatoes, halved lengthwise, each half cut lengthwise into 2 to 3 wedges
- 1 tablespoon salted capers, rinsed
- 2 cups white wine (Verdicchio, if available)

To prepare dried stockfish, soak for two to three days in fresh water, changing the water at least twice daily. Trim away any bones or fins and cut softened flesh into 2-inch pieces. Place fish in a large bowl, cover with cold water, and set aside while preparing the rest of the ingredients.

Preheat the oven to 300°F. Coat a 9 x 13 ovenproof baking dish with 2 tablespoons of olive oil, then arrange the drained fish pieces in a single layer in the dish, skin-side down.

Combine celery, onion, carrot, garlic, chili pepper, rosemary, and parsley in a bowl. Spread half of mixture evenly over fish. Season with salt and freshly ground pepper.

Place potatoes over fish in a single layer, distribute the remaining vegetable mixture over the potatoes, then layer on the tomatoes. Scatter capers over the fish, and season again with salt and pepper. Drizzle remaining olive oil over fish, followed by the wine. Bake uncovered for about 2 hours, until potatoes are tender when pierced with a knife.

To serve, lift out the fish and vegetables with a slotted spatula, and garnish with spoonfuls of the cooking liquid. Leftover olive oil/wine mixture can be saved for another meal to toss with pasta or drizzle on roasted vegetables.

26

LA SFOGLINA

Cinzia told me she made pasta once a week, sometimes more. During my sessions at the language school I would return from my morning lessons to find her at her kitchen table, rolling out dough with a three-foot dowel, her *mattarello*. On a few occasions I came home in time to help her fill and shape or cut the pasta. We made *farfalle*, little butterflies, and *cappelletti*—tiny pillows stuffed with minced chicken and mortadella. One time we made them with a filling of pureed artichokes, parsley, and cheese, and we cut the scraps into *quadretti*, little squares left to dry on a flour-dusted plate and saved for soup.

It was from Cinzia that I learned of the region's proud pasta-making history. The women of Le Marche, she told me, take their pasta making seriously. She conceded her neighbors to the north in Emilia-Romagna were the acknowledged masters of the craft. They listed among their accomplishments the invention of tortellini—the meat-stuffed, pleated coils of pasta inspired by the folds of Venus' belly button. And they gave the world tagliatelle, the long thin strands of golden egg pasta created in honor of Lucrezia Borgia's blond tresses on her wedding day. But the Marchigiane pasta-makers were no less impassioned.

Farmlands and fields of wheat blanket the hillsides of Le Marche as it stretches from the Apennines to the Adriatic coast, and so it is with soft white flour from their own grain and fresh eggs from country hens that the ladies of Le Marche make their pasta *fatt' a mano*. Pasta rolled by hand. There are those who worry it is a dying art, incompatible with the fast pace of modernity, but Cinzia is not so sure. Dwindling are the groups of old women who convene around a neighbor's kitchen table to sip espresso, exchange gossip, and roll out pasta in the mornings, yet still they gather. Tagliatelle, pappardelle, lasagne, cappelletti, quadretti, maltagliati. They cut and stuff and shape according to the day's whim, then return home to drop their shares into pots of boiling water for the midday meal. And even small villages can still support a *pastificio* in the main piazza—a pasta store where elderly women in starched aprons and hairnets sell *pasta fresca*, fresh egg pasta made on the premises, gone by noon each day.

My grandma Teresa made her pasta this way, but I was too young to pay close attention. When my mother assumed the task for family gatherings she purchased a hand-cranked machine, a classic Atlas stainless steel pasta maker. It is the machine I first made pasta with, as a young girl under her tutelage. My mom still uses it today, dusty now with the flour of fifty years of pasta making, and we use it together each December when I return to my childhood home in Washington for the holidays. We roll out dough, then stuff, seal, and cut ravioli for upward of thirty people when our extended family convenes for Christmas dinner. That Atlas machine makes fabulous pasta. I have one of my own and use it often in my New Hampshire kitchen. But in Le Marche purists deem pasta made by hand with a rolling pin to be in a class unto itself. The dough is not so much rolled as stretched, creating a dimpled, porous surface with tiny pockets and hummocks to trap and absorb the sauce and give the pasta an inimitable springiness.

On a follow-up stay with Cinzia years later, I asked her for a lesson with the mattarello, but she demurred. Far better, she said, for me to see a true master at work, someone who had been making pasta every day for decades, and she knew just the person. The next day there was a note tacked to my door: PASTA LESSON. WEDNESDAY 3:00. TRATTORIA STROLOGO.

For more than seventy years the Strologo family has run a modest trattoria in a triangular-shaped building opening onto the lower end of Piazza Roma in Camerano. Cinzia had made arrangements with the *padrona*, Matilde Strologo, for me to observe a pasta-making session. Matilde does all the cooking, but she depends on a *sfoglina* for the pasta. *La sfoglina* is the woman employed by a restaurant or private household for the sole purpose of rolling out the day's pasta. She is a venerated and beloved figure in the culinary tradition of northern Italy, but her trade is on the verge of disappearing. The term means "pasta maker" and comes from the dialect of nearby Emilia-Romagna, for the woman who rolls out *la sfoglia*, or sheet of dough. I've also heard this woman called *la pastaia*, a word that also refers to the machine that has all but replaced her.

At the appointed time Matilde ushered me into the trattoria kitchen through the back door. She offered me an espresso and introduced me to Bianca, her sfoglina of innumerable years. Bianca offered a shy smile, then lowered her eyes as she shook my hand, her fingers dusted with flour. In her seventies with thinning hair dyed jet black, she had dark, lively eyes and a sturdy build, her shoulders slightly stooped from years leaning over a worktable. She wore a silver cross around her neck, a white apron over her black cotton sweater and knee-length skirt, and a pair of purple-sequined slippers.

Bianca had just finished mixing a batch of bright yellow dough made from a bag of flour and forty eggs. She upturned the mixing bowl, scraped the formidable mound onto the counter, and divided it into ten balls, each the size of a grapefruit. After dusting one ball with flour, she flattened it into a disk and reached for her mattarello. She used a process unique to pasta making, rolling the dough back on itself around her mattarello, then running her hands along the pin from the center to the edges and back again, her palms slightly cupped, fingers together as she coaxed the dough outward. Her hands flitted back and forth across the pasta, simultaneously stretching and rolling it up until she had wrapped the entire sheet around her dowel. Then she unfurled it, rotated it ninety degrees, and started rolling and extending it once again across her pin. She braced herself with her legs and back as she worked in smooth, deliberate strokes, an almost hypnotic repetition of motion as the dough round grew ever larger. Within five minutes, less time than I can roll out an equal amount of pasta with my machine, she had produced a sheet so thin she could see the veins on the back of her hand through it.

It is a technique that takes almost longer to describe than to execute. In fact, it demands a quick tempo, for the pasta becomes brittle and uncooperative as it dries. Like any art, success comes only with practice. Mastery comes only after countless batches of dough. Bianca started making pasta when she was twelve years old. She learned from her aunt, who stood behind her and covered her hands with her own, guiding Bianca's hands until she developed a feel for the work. Matilde recently took on another sfoglina to assist Bianca, a young woman from Moldova named Elena. When Elena applied for the position, Matilde sent her home with a sack of flour and a matarello. When you've used up all twenty kilos, Matilde told her, come back for an interview and we'll see what kind of pasta you make.

Bianca had cut back at work, only making pasta three days a week for the trattoria. What did she do the other days? Make pasta for her husband, for her grown sons and their young families. And what would they do when she was gone? When there was no one to roll out pasta for them anymore? Suffer. They wouldn't starve, said Bianca, but they would suffer, for while you can get full on packaged pasta, you can never be sated.

I returned to the States with my own mattarello, purchased from a street vendor in Camerano on market day. I don't yet rate as a Marchigiana housewife—I'm not fluid enough, and my sheets of pasta aren't as consistently translucent as I would like—but I can appreciate the appeal of the pasta maker's task. The dough itself is supple and forgiving, a gift for the fingers as it responds to their touch and stretches to incredible lengths under their command. The repetition of sound and movement lulls the mind, with the soft knock of the mattarello and sweep of the palms, the hands falling into a rhythm and the rest of the body following. The process is its own reward, which is perhaps why the craft endures, even if it isn't valued as highly as it used to be.

To be an accomplished pasta maker, Cinzia told me, was once a badge of honor in Le Marche; in many cases a prerequisite. Girls learned at their mothers' skirts, and among families of a certain station—those wealthy enough to afford a steady supply of flour for the daily pasta, but not so affluent as to employ a staff of servants to prepare it—a young lady of eligible age could not hope to marry unless her pasta met with the approval of her prospective mother-in-law. The lore, Cinzia said, abounds with cautionary tales.

One story tells of a girl whose betrothal was in negotiation to a young man in a neighboring village. The dowry had been settled with a handshake, to include among other essentials a matrimonial bed, sheets of fine linen and hemp, a spinning wheel and loom. In her trousseau the girl had packed an heirloom pastry board and rolling pin. In the balance lay only the verdict from the mother of the groom, for she had yet to taste the girl's pasta. Her son was a hearty but discriminating eater, and she would not have him go ill-fed. Did love enter into the equation? Probably not. Arranged marriages were common in Italy until the years following the Second World War, though with time the couple could grow to love one another, could they not?

The parents of the hopeful bride invited the groom's parents to share a meal. For convenience I'll call them the Neri and the Rossi families—the Black and the Red—though they could perhaps have been any reconciled Guelph and Ghibbeline, Montague and Capulet. On the morning of the appointed day Signora Rossi and her widowed mother appeared at the Neri family doorstep. Signora Rossi had errands to run in town. Her mother's feet were weary from the walk. Could she not rest here with Signora Neri and her daughter?

Of course she could. The old woman stood dressed in mourning black, a bag of needlework hanging from the crook of her elbow. After an exchange of glances Signora Neri knew there wasn't a thing wrong with the old lady's feet. Her real assignment was to keep an eye on the young girl. Signora Neri ushered Nonna Rossi into the kitchen and settled her into a chair by the hearth. Signora Rossi would return with her husband promptly at one o'clock for the midday meal. So there would be six of them dining, including Signora Rossi's mother. The Rossis' son had remained at home to spare the girl any embarrassment should her efforts not be well received.

Under scrutiny that day was only the girl's pasta. She would make tagliatelle, the classic pasta ribbons of Bologna, beloved also in Le Marche. The name derives from the verb *tagliare*, to cut, as they are traditionally cut by hand with a long, sharp knife. By arrangement the girl's mother was allowed to help with the rest of the meal. If the signorina proved worthy, her mother-in-law would welcome her into the fold and share the Rossi family recipes; the girl could master them in good time. For her part, Signora Neri had been twirling about the kitchen since dawn, preparing her finest sugo for the pasta, enriched with minced beef and chicken giblets, redolent of tomatoes, marjoram, and thyme. She had kneaded the dough for a loaf of bread and whisked the batter for her *ciambella*, a delicate pound cake studded with muscat raisins and aniseed. With her sugo bubbling languidly on the stove she packed her risen bread dough and her round of cake batter in a basket, wrapped her shawl around her shoulders, and set out for the main piazza to bake her goods in the village oven.

She left her daughter to her own devices, a basket of eggs and a canister of flour on the table and the old woman absorbed in her knitting in the corner. The girl tied an apron around her waist, pulled out a rolling pin and pasta board. She noticed her hands shaking, felt a knot in her stomach. Maybe a cup of tea would calm her nerves. She made a tisane of fresh sage leaves and chestnut honey, filled two porcelain cups and offered one to Nonna Rossi, who lay down her needlework to clutch her cup with both hands, letting the warmth soothe her stiff fingers.

Nonna Rossi observed the girl, admiring her almond eyes and smooth complexion. Her arms were a bit thin, her feet too small to suggest the sturdy constitution a farmer might want in a wife, but her demeanor was pleasant enough.

The girl scooped flour into a mound on the wooden pasta board, made a well in the center and broke half a dozen eggs—large ones, straight from the family henhouse, with thick sturdy shells and deep orange yolks—into the hollow. The classic formula for fresh egg pasta is 100 grams flour per egg per generous serving. This translates to 3.512 ounces flour (or three-quarters cup plus two-and-a half teaspoons) per egg, a quantity both cumbersome and difficult to remember. That the divine proportion of pasta making should be so simple and mathematically elegant when presented in grams ought to be reason enough to convince the National Bureau of Standards to quit its petulant foot-dragging and convert to the metric system at once.

Experienced pasta makers, relying on touch and intuition and generally working without the luxury of a scale, still speak in terms of "an egg and the flour it will hold" to yield an ample portion, acknowledging that even the golden ratio is an approximation, dependent on the weather, the type of flour, and the availability and size of the eggs. My grandma Teresa, who cooked through the Depression and two World Wars, used one cup flour, one egg, and a half eggshell of water as her standard formula, simultaneously stretching an egg to serve two people and creating a softer dough that sealed readily when encasing her Christmas ravioli.

The girl pierced the yolks with the tines of a fork and began beating them with a sure hand. At least she hoped it looked that way. She had helped her mother make the daily pasta for as long as she could remember. But without her mother's watchful eye, even this simple act seemed awkward and filled her with uncertainty. She continued stirring with a circular motion, gradually incorporating flour from the inner wall of the well. With her other hand she swept flour up from the outer base of the well to keep the eggs from breaking through and spilling onto the counter.

She worked quickly and quietly, one hand stirring, the other drawing flour into the eggs. Once the dough formed, she set down her fork and started kneading, her torso swaying, her forearms and shoulders relaxing as the ball of pasta grew pliant and smooth in her hands. From the corner came the spit and cackle of the woodstove and the clicking of Nonna's knitting needles as she fixed her gaze on her handiwork. She allowed herself a glance upward without missing a stitch, then hurriedly lowered her eyes, a suggestion of a smile lingering on her face.

After a full ten minutes of kneading, a worrisome thought crept into the poor girl's mind and took hold. What if she hadn't made enough? How could she hope to convey an impression of abundance and largesse with a measly six-egg ball of dough? She'd used up all her eggs, so she flattened the pasta into a disk, dimpled it deeply with her fingers, drizzled water over the surface and sprinkled it with flour. An unorthodox maneuver, surely she'd never seen it done before, but it seemed her only recourse.

It was a grave mistake. It is virtually impossible to incorporate additional flour and liquid into a satiny ball of well-kneaded dough. She rolled the dough up like a jellyroll and water gushed out the ends. As she kneaded, a slippery paste developed on the surface. She dusted the ball with flour and more flour until there was none left to add, but the more she kneaded the dough, the stickier it grew. The girl exhaled sharply, blowing a stray wisp of hair from over her face. She hung her head, then looked up into the eyes of Nonna Rossi. The old lady had dropped her knitting in her lap and sat staring, openmouthed.

The girl covered the lump of pasta with an overturned bowl. She washed her hands, removed her apron and draped it over the back of a chair. The dough just needed to rest, she informed Nonna Rossi. In an hour it would be relaxed and ready to roll out, she just knew it; meanwhile she needed a dose of fresh air. Nonna Rossi watched the girl leave through the kitchen door, then went back to her knitting.

Pasta dough certainly benefits from a rest of thirty minutes to an hour at room temperature. The flour continues to absorb liquid and the dough relaxes, making it easier to roll out. But Signorina Neri's sticky ball of dough seemed beyond hope. In tears, she strode down the cobblestone road to the village, to the church in the piazza. She entered the vestibule, slid into a pew at the back of the dark, empty nave, and started to pray. She prayed to the Virgin Mary, then called upon such saints as might be particularly sympathetic to her plight: to Saint Martha, patron saint of cooks and homemakers, to Saint Agnes of Rome, patron saint of engaged couples, and for good measure she put a word in to Saint Jude, patron saint of desperate cases and lost causes.

An hour had passed by the time she returned home. Nonna Rossi was snoring softly, asleep in her chair, her skein of yarn tumbled to the floor. She awoke with a start as the girl entered through the kitchen door and the two stared at the overturned bowl on the counter. The girl crossed the room, placed a hand on the bowl and paused as she closed her eyes. With a brisk sweep she lifted the bowl and opened her eyes to reveal a satiny, taut round of pasta dough waiting underneath. She gasped and Nonna Rossi made the sign of the cross.

So that forlorn mound of dough of hers had only needed a bit of time. Time and maybe a miracle. Regardless, it had transformed itself to become a pliable, beautiful, eminently workable thing. The girl divided it in half to make rounds of a manageable size. With her three-foot mattarello and a newfound confidence she rolled and stretched, rolled and stretched each one to a gossamer sheet, so thin she could see her hand through it, could envision the band of gold that would soon grace her finger.

Her mother returned just as she was cutting the last sheet of dough into long thin strips of tagliatelle. The guests arrived shortly thereafter, and Signora Neri showed them to the dining room, where the table was set with her best lace tablecloth and linen napkins, her hand-painted majolica dishware and pewter cutlery. The girl brought a pot of water to a rapid boil and added a handful of coarse sea salt. She knew by the silky feel of the tagliatelle as they slipped through her fingers into the pot, by the gentle resistance of the single strand that she bit into, testing it for doneness, that here was pasta to satisfy even the most discerning palate.

Once drained, she tossed the steaming tagliatelle delicately with her mother's sugo, added a shower of grated Pecorino cheese, and brought it to the table. After the pasta was apportioned, all eyes fell on Signora Rossi as she raised a forkful to her lips. She chewed it slowly, contemplatively, then lifted her wineglass to the girl. "*Complimenti*," she said.

When the meal was over, after the ciambella and fruit, the espresso and sambuca, after the songs sung to the accompaniment of Signor Neri on his *fisarmonica*, the parents of the promised couple made plans to register the dowry with the parish priest. The Rossi family gathered their belongings, said their goodbyes, and departed, Nonna Rossi clutching Signora Rossi's arm in one hand and her knitting bag in the other.

The old woman's bag felt lighter, less bulky without the half dozen eggs and sack of flour she had tucked in with her needlework. She cast a look over her shoulder to the livestock in the open stalls below the courtyard. The hens had all but pecked away the sticky lump of dough she had tossed into their coop. Such a nice young girl, she could be taught to make pasta.

🌱

TAGLIATELLE ALL'UOVO

FRESH EGG TAGLIATELLE

(Serves 4 to 6)

The classic formula for fresh egg pasta is 100 grams flour per large egg per generous serving. This comes out to be about ¾ cup flour, gently scooped and not tamped, per egg. Still, this is just a starting point; the exact proportions can vary depending on the flour, the size of the eggs, and the humidity. Add more flour if the dough seems too sticky, or a couple tablespoons of beaten egg if the dough is too stiff.

FOR THE PASTA:
- 4 large eggs, plus additional beaten egg, if needed
- 400 grams (about 3 cups) all-purpose flour, plus additional, if needed
- semolina flour, for dusting

Scoop the flour onto a dry cutting board or into a large bowl. Make a well in the center of the flour, crack in the eggs, and stir with a fork until you can no longer whisk. Use your hands and a dough scraper to incorporate the rest of the flour, knead 8 to 10 minutes, until smooth, adding flour a spoonful at a time if the dough seems too sticky, or a spoonful of beaten egg if the dough seems too stiff. Set ball of dough aside for about 30 minutes or up to 2 hours, covered with an upturned bowl or wrapped in plastic.

Divide the dough into four pieces, working with one piece at a time and keeping the rest covered. Roll each piece out with a mattarello (a wooden dowel-style rolling pin) into a translucent sheet, dusting it lightly as you work, to keep the dough from sticking. Alternately, roll the dough pieces into strips with a pasta machine, working down to the thinnest setting, or perhaps the next to last setting, depending on your machine. The pasta should be thin enough to see your hand through, but not so thin it tears when you work with it.

Cover a table or counter with dry, clean cloth towels or a tablecloth and lay the sheets out flat to dry for about 20 minutes, or until slightly leathery and not tacky to the touch. Flip them over a couple times to help them dry evenly.

Before cutting the pasta into tagliatelle, dust each sheet of pasta with semolina. Roll each sheet up halfway, jelly roll fashion, then roll up from the opposite end until the two rolls meet in the center. With a large chef's knife, cut the rolled pasta crosswise into ribbons. To unfurl, slide the point of your knife lengthwise underneath a few inches of the cut pasta. Have the dull edge of the blade align with the gap where the pasta rolls meet, then tip the dull edge up as you lift the knife. Place your free hand on top of the tagliatelle and give it a gentle shake to help the tagliatelle unfold. Lay the pasta out across a large tray covered with a clean towel, making sure the strands are well separated. If you're not using the tagliatelle right away, cover them with another towel and refrigerate, up to several hours. You can make the tagliatelle in the morning, then refrigerate them until dinner time.

TO COOK AND SERVE:

Bring a large pot of water to a boil and add a heaping tablespoon of kosher salt. When the water returns to a fierce boil, drop in the pasta all at once and stir immediately to keep it from sticking. Continue boiling, stirring frequently, until cooked, which for fresh pasta can take anywhere from 30 seconds to 2 minutes. Test a strand occasionally, until al dente, slightly firm to the bite, then drain in a colander. Shake the colander a few times to rid the pasta of excess liquid, and then blend it immediately with the sauce of your choice.

27

SQUASH BLOSSOMS FOR SALE

An open-air produce market popped up most mornings in Camerano, just off Piazza Roma in the Mercato Comunale. Farmers from around the region set up stands with heaping baskets and geometric stacks of vegetables brought in from their fields. The place was noisy and crowded, with customers elbowing past each other to get the best selection and have their shopping done before work. When I had time before class, I liked to go there with Cinzia and enjoy the bustle as she selected fruits and vegetables for the day's meals.

Cinzia's favorite purveyor had a stall in a back corner. One morning she greeted us from behind her rickety table laden with the day's harvest—purple artichoke buds no bigger than a hen's egg, slender carrots with soil still clinging to their roots, lettuce in loose, chartreuse heads and wine-red rosettes, plump shell peas and fava beans. On the ground she had a wooden crate filled with neat rows of what the Italians call *zucchine* and we refer to collectively as summer squash: dark green zucchini, bright yellow crooknecks, light green squash with dark green stripes known as cocozelles. They were tiny little things, no bigger than a quarter in diameter and scarcely longer than a hand's breadth in length. And some still had the flowers attached to one end.

It was a modern-day market scene. Her cornucopia of vegetables, especially the summer squash, reminded me of an oil painting entitled *La Fruttivendola* that hangs in the Brera Art Gallery of Milan. Painted in 1580 by Vincenzo Campi of Cremona, the work depicts a young produce vendor seated with her wares in the countryside. She is a comely maiden, with a porcelain complexion and rosy cheeks. The low-cut bodice of her beribboned dress reveals an ample bosom, and she gazes at the viewer with a coy tilt of the head. Equally inviting is the produce she offers—a clump of grapes in her upraised hand, a load of ripe peaches gathered in her apron on her lap, assorted bowls, platters, and baskets of red cherries, dark figs, and fava beans strewn with pink roses.

Known in English as *The Fruit Seller*, the canvas is one of the earliest examples of Italian still-life painting, influenced by the market scenes of the Dutch mannerist painter Pieter Aertsen and his pupil Joachim Beuckelaer, and an inspiration in turn for the detailed still-lifes of the great Caravaggio. For centuries, religious scholars and art historians have debated the symbolic meaning of the painting's fruits and vegetables, from the biblical to the salacious. Economists have cited the work as evidence for the commercialization of agriculture, anthropologists have studied it for developments in ceramic technique and woven basketry, costume designers have turned to it to re-create Renaissance period dress. But horticultural researchers look at *La Fruttivendola* and notice the squash.

The many varieties of winter and summer squash familiar to us today, from acorn to crookneck, pumpkin to zucchini, are members of the species *Cucurbita pepo*, an American plant native to Mexico and the southeastern United States that was first domesticated some ten thousand years ago. Our word "squash" comes from the Narragansett *askutasquash*, meaning an uncooked or unripe fruit. In pre-Columbian times, Europeans knew only gourds, most of which were too bitter and tough to eat. They still had their place in the kitchen though, hollowed out and dried for use as serving vessels and utensils, and some were palatable if eaten when very young and fresh.

You often read that Columbus brought squash seeds back to Spain with him, but the contemporary account of his voyages, a series of letters by Peter Martyr D'Anghiera, the Italian teacher at the court of Ferdinand and Isabella, mentions only "seeds of all kinds," making the assertion perhaps yet another example of Columbus receiving more credit than he actually deserved. All that can be claimed for certain is that various squash seeds made their way back to European ports during the Age of Exploration. Varieties that had been isolated in parts of America commingled and cross-pollinated in the gardens of herbalists, monks, noblemen, and botanists, resulting in innumerable new cultivars. Some of these were larger, or better tasting, or otherwise more desirable than others, and they have either endured or given rise to the varieties we know today.

Researchers have found the written record frustratingly muddled and lacking in details regarding the dissemination and development of plants from the New World to the Old—chroniclers of the day often lacked the botanical background to describe what they were seeing, and they tended to be more interested in massacres and plagues, jewels and precious metals anyway. But historians have found an unexpected trove of information in the works of Renaissance artists. The first known image of New World squash in Europe, for example, was found in the prayer book of Anne de Bretagne, illustrated by Jean Bourdichon between 1503 and 1508. The frescoes of Giovanni da Udine in the Villa Farnesina in Rome, completed about a decade later, contain several images of American winter squash and pumpkins.

And Vincenzo Campi's *La Fruttivendola* speaks volumes. Scholars point out the large, ribbed pumpkin (*Curcurbita pepo*, subspecies *pepo*, Pumpkin Group) resting underneath a platter of apricots at the vendor's feet. They debate whether the wicker basket holds Old World warty melons (*Cucumis melo*) or winter squash (*Cucurbita maxima*) of New World descent. Of particular note is a wooden box on the right margin of the canvas containing dainty red pears and a stack of slender green squash of some sort. They aren't zucchini; all evidence indicates that vegetable wouldn't show up until much later. More likely they are related to a cocozelle (*Cucurbita pepo*, subsp. *pepo*, Cocozelle Group). Still popular today, you can buy seed in the United States from companies that specialize in heirloom vegetables. What's more, these young squash have the blossoms still attached, making them perhaps among the earliest proof of squash flowers for culinary use in Italy. All those centuries ago, the Italians already knew how to make the most of their vegetables.

Cinzia referred proprietarily to her fruttivendola as *la mia contadina*, "my farmer." With her scuffed shoes and threadbare scarf tied over thinning gray hair, she came from plainer stock than Campi's Junoesque young woman. She was in her sixties, and prematurely stooped. She had black lines under her fingernails and callused hands, burnished skin and deeply incised crow's feet from years spent working the earth under a hot sun.

Cinzia motioned to the crate of summer squash. Their blossoms bright orange as an egg yolk, they could have come straight from Vincenzo Campi's brush. Squash blossoms wither soon after picking, Cinzia explained. They curl closed like a taffy wrapper and the flavor fades out of them. These were fleshy and fresh, an indication they had been harvested that morning. The squash themselves would be tender, the flowers sweet. She told her contadina she'd take an assorted dozen.

Cinzia made fresh tagliatelle while I was at my morning class, and when I returned for the midday meal she already had a pot of water on the stove to boil. After trimming the ends from the summer squash she sliced them into thin coins. To my surprise she didn't discard the blossoms, but removed the pistil from inside each one and cut the petals into thin strips. She heated a couple tablespoons of good olive oil with a minced clove of garlic and a pinch of red pepper flakes. When the garlic grew fragrant and sizzled, she added the squash, tossed them in the oil, then left the rounds undisturbed for a couple minutes on each side to brown lightly. Into the pan went a sprinkle of salt and a few grinds of pepper, along with the squash blossoms and a handful of fresh basil leaves that had been torn into pieces. She stirred the squash for another minute until the blossoms wilted, then removed the skillet from the heat.

Cinzia added a spoonful of sea salt to the boiling water and dropped in her fresh pasta just as Angelica appeared from the corner bus stop, home from school. Francesco followed a moment later, and he beamed when he saw the bright rounds of squash in the skillet, *che deliziosa*.

When I told him about the visit to Cinzia's contadina that morning he raised an eyebrow and said there was more to Cinzia's contadina than met the eye. You'd never think it to look at her, he said, but that peasant attire of hers was just for show. She and her husband had a villa tucked away in the country somewhere, with a fancy sports car parked out front. Come autumn they would disappear for a few weeks on vacation, no one knew where, but they'd been spotted heading south. She was wearing gold bracelets and a long mink stole.

Cinzia interjected. "*Basta!*" she said, enough teasing. She drained the pasta and added it to the skillet with the cooked vegetables, tossing it with a liberal dose of olive oil. She upended the skillet into a serving dish and brought it steaming to the table with a grating of Parmigiano.

The summer squash had a sweet, almost buttery flavor from browning in the oil, and a toothsome tenderness to complement Cinzia's hand-rolled pasta. The blossoms added a festive touch—bright strips of confetti scattered throughout. Barely wilted from the heat, they contributed a subtle squash essence of their own.

I'd eaten the blossoms of *C. pepo* before, dipped in a light batter and fried until crisp. It's a classic preparation, with origins that reach back centuries, though try as I might, I couldn't find a recipe dating to Campi's day. Vincenzo Corrado—monk, astronomer, man of letters, and chef at the noble court of Naples—did, however, include a recipe in his 1773 cookbook *Il cuoco galante*. This gallant cook mentioned the blossoms took readily to stuffing before frying, which is the first way I tried them. In venerable Roman trattorie I had sampled them filled with a cube of moz-zarella and a piece of anchovy, as well as with ricotta and bits of prosciutto or fresh herbs. I'd even harvested the flowers from my own garden and prepared them myself, inspired by a recipe from Lorenza de Medici's *Italy: The Beautiful Cookbook*. (This is a beloved book of mine, with recipes too useful, pages too dog-eared and stained to decorate a coffee table as the publisher intended.)

Signora de Medici recommended the male blossoms, given their larger size, as being more suitable for stuffing. A botanist will tell you that squash plants are monoecious, which means they produce separate male and female blossoms on the same plant. Bees and other insects attracted to the flowers in search of nectar transfer pollen from the stamen inside male flowers to the stigma of female flowers. You can easily tell the difference between the two because the male blossoms are slightly larger and have a long, slender stem, while the female blossoms have a short stem and a swelling at their base that resembles a miniature squash but is actually an ovary. Once fertilized the ovary develops into what is technically a fruit, though most of us call it a vegetable. Blossoms on a squash plant are a bit like chickens in a coop. You only need one rooster to service several hens; likewise, one male flower can admirably pollinate a harem of females. And just as the superfluous cockerels end up in the frying pan or on the rotisserie spit, an enterprising cook can put the male flowers to exceptional use in the kitchen.

Crisp and delicate, *fiori di zucca fritti* are a celebration of the season. But I'm not always up for the heat of deep-fat frying in the height of summer in my unair-conditioned kitchen when squash blossoms are at their peak. To toss them into pasta opened a new door for me. To use the female flowers was a novelty as well. Some connoisseurs, I've since learned, insist the female flower has better flavor, though my palate doesn't seem discriminating enough to tell the difference.

During the course of my travels throughout central Italy I went on to find the flowers in unexpected places. Filled with ricotta and braised in tomato sauce. Stirred into a risotto and a frittata. As a topping for pizza, a garnish for soup, tossed raw into green salads. After each visit I returned to New Hampshire eager to try more new dishes at home. But one summer my garden threatened to stymie my plans. A cool, wet spring and a marauding woodchuck had left me with but one spindly squash plant. I held out hope for its eventual recovery, but if I wanted to cook with young summer squash and squash blossoms any time soon, I would have to buy them.

Now, it is hard on a New England gardener to buy zucchini in high summer. We are loath to stoop so low. Serious gardeners know how to train tomatoes up a trellis and pinch off the suckers for enhanced fruit production. We know how to hill up potatoes and how to vernalize artichoke seedlings for northern climes. But anyone can grow a zucchini. They are practically effortless to cultivate—the ideal vegetable for children and novices, just poke the seeds in the ground and watch them grow. And they are famously prolific, two seeds can produce enough zucchini to feed a family of four all summer long. To buy zucchini in August marks a gardener as either a failure or a pretender.

One afternoon, with dinner for eight planned for the following night, I set aside my ego for the good of the menu and stopped off at a vegetable stand. The place had developed into quite the operation over the years, with pick-your-own strawberries and blueberries, heirloom tomato and sweet corn tastings, landscaped picnic grounds. The owners employed a bevy of coeds, home for the summer, to help in the fields and at the register. Lissome, pony-tailed young women trotted around in flip-flops, cut-offs, and spaghetti-strap tank tops, earning the stand the patronage of a statistically significant number of eligible bachelors and mildly lecherous middle-aged men. Not to mention the place sold beautiful produce.

I felt I needed a trench coat and dark glasses lest someone should spot me buying zucchini. Alongside bins of eggplants and heirloom tomatoes was a wooden trug heaped full of them. They were young by American standards, though larger than what I'd encountered in Le Marche, and their blossoms had already wilted and sloughed off. Still, I couldn't hope to find better without access to a garden. (The tired, little fingerlings in plastic clamshells, shipped thousands of miles and sold as "baby zucchini" in gourmet stores don't count; they've lost all their charm.) Pan-seared with herbs, these zucchini would make the perfect accompaniment to the lamb leg I intended to roast on a spit. Too bad there weren't any squash blossoms; it would have been nice to serve them stuffed with ricotta and braised in a sauce made from my own tomatoes for the first course.

As I reached into my wallet it occurred to me to ask the coed at the counter if she could muster some squash blossoms up. She gave me a blank look, then conferred with another counter girl. She'd never had this request before, she'd have to check in with the Boss. She pulled a walkie-talkie from her hip pocket and radioed for reinforcements.

A few minutes later a large woman with loose, leathery skin entered through a side door and I repeated my request. I'd noticed the long rows of zucchini plants behind the stand, I told her. I just wanted a few male blossoms—they wouldn't bear fruit. I'd be happy to walk out there and harvest them myself.

Her eyes widened, taken aback. She looked at me as though I'd asked to yank her plants out by the roots and set fire to her field. She was sorry, she said crisply, unauthorized visitors were not allowed in the vegetable rows.

I persisted, explaining that I was a gardener myself, I would be very careful. I started to tell her about the botanical intimacies of the zucchini plant, about male and female flowers, roosters and hen houses. Such presumption. She had no time for simile and metaphor—she needed all her squash blossoms, couldn't spare a one. She had the coed ring up my produce and excused herself, she had broccoli to trim.

I tried another farm stand and received a similar response, so I headed home, blossomless and perplexed. Come August in my corner of New England it is not safe to leave your car window rolled down in a public parking lot for fear someone will put a torpedo-sized zucchini in the passenger seat. I once saw a picnic table piled high with oversized zucchini in front of a farmhouse. A hand-lettered sign in front of it read ZUCCHINI FOR SALE, TEN CENTS A CORD. Yet I couldn't find someone to sell me a single flower and help stem the glut in the bargain.

Funny, just a few short years later and squash blossoms have become suddenly chic, a favorite of upscale restaurant chefs even here in New Hampshire. These very produce vendors now display lush bouquets of squash blossoms in handcrafted vases that would have Vincenzo Campi setting up his easel. They command prices I'm not willing to pay, but fortunately I haven't had a crop failure in years.

As for the stuffed blossoms that fateful summer, on the morning of my dinner party I thought to try the Pumpkin Man just north of town. He was a retired dairyman who helped my octogenarian neighbor bring in her hay every summer. He had started growing pumpkins early in his career as a means of pocket money for his five children. His wife had long since passed away, his children were grown, and he'd sold off his Holsteins, but he still put in a pumpkin patch each year out of habit.

Pumpkins and zucchini, like all subspecies of *Cucurbita pepo*, are more the same than different. Gardeners intending to save seeds from one year to the next must space these two squash plants far enough apart to keep them from cross-pollinating, otherwise the following year's plants won't produce vegetables true to form. Anyone who has had a mystery squash turn up in the compost pile has witnessed the strange results of such inadvertent unions. Similarly, zucchini and pumpkin blossoms, while genetically diverse, are culinarily indistinguishable.

I found the Pumpkin Man in his barn, tinkering with his tractor. When I asked about the flowers in his pumpkin patch he looked up and waved his wrench toward the field. "They're out back," he said. "Help yourself, just don't step on the vines." He apologized for not accompanying me, but he was right in the middle of changing his timing belt.

I walked out to the field and plucked sixteen bright blossoms, their trumpets just beginning to open. I had to give a couple of them a tap at the base to evict the bumblebees, which rose up slowly and zigzagged off, heavy with pollen.

The Pumpkin Man was still at work on his engine when I returned. "You get what you needed?" he said without looking up.

I thanked him and asked how much I owed him.

He wiped his hands with a rag and brushed the question off with a grunt. "Not a thing," he said, and explained that flowers this late in the summer wouldn't mature into pumpkins anyway, they'd get nipped first by a frost.

I mentioned the reaction I'd received from the other farmers, their unwillingness to part with even a few flowers. He shrugged his shoulders and pondered for a minute. Maybe they just hadn't been growing vegetables long enough yet to understand how things worked. After all his years as a dairyman he'd come to realize that raising pumpkins was a lot like raising cows. He swept his hand across the expanse of the patch. Even with a whole field of heifers out there, he said, you still only need a few bulls.

TAGLIATELLE ALL'UOVO CON ZUCCHINE, BASILICO, E FIORI DI ZUCCA

TAGLIATELLE WITH SUMMER SQUASH, BASIL, AND SQUASH BLOSSOMS

(Serves 4)

An assortment of tiny summer squash in varied colors makes this a beautiful dish, and it becomes sublime when fresh, handmade egg pasta is used. If you grow squash in your own garden, harvest when they are no bigger than a quarter in diameter. If you don't have time to make your own pasta, you can substitute dried egg-fettuccine with excellent results. An 8-ounce package of De Cecco brand will serve four people.

- 6 to 8 very small, assorted summer squash (about the size of a quarter in diameter), blossoms still attached, if possible
- 3 tablespoons good quality olive oil, plus additional for drizzling over pasta
- 1 clove garlic, minced
- 1 pinch red pepper flakes
- salt and freshly ground pepper, to taste
- 8 to 10 fresh basil leaves, torn loosely into pieces
- 1 pound fresh tagliatelle
- ½ cup grated Parmigiano cheese

Put a large pot of water on to boil while preparing the vegetables.

Rinse and trim ends from summer squash, reserving blossom ends. Slice squash into thin rounds. Remove pistil from center of each blossom and slice petals into thin strips.

Heat olive oil, garlic, and red pepper flakes in a large sauté pan over high heat until the garlic becomes fragrant and sizzles, about 30 seconds. Add the squash rounds, toss to coat evenly in the oil, and season with salt and pepper. Leave undisturbed for 1 to 2 minutes, until squash starts to brown. Flip squash and continue cooking another 1 to 2 minutes, to brown the other side. Stir in squash blossoms and basil leaves. Remove from burner and allow blossoms to wilt from residual heat.

Meanwhile, add a heaping tablespoon of salt to boiling water in large pot. Add tagliatelle and stir to keep from sticking together. Let water return to a boil and cook 3 to 4 minutes, stirring occasionally, until pasta is al dente. (The exact timing will vary, depending on the thickness of the pasta, how recently it was made, and the type of flour, so test a few strands for doneness.)

Drain tagliatelle in a colander, then add to the sauté pan with the cooked squash along with another generous drizzle of olive oil. Toss to coat well, transfer to a serving dish, and garnish with freshly grated Parmigiano cheese.

28

THIS LITTLE PIG

Much as I learned from Cinzia and Francesco about the piatti tipici of Le Marche, I discovered *porchetta* on my own. Porchetta is an ancient dish, an archetypal dish. It is a whole pig stuffed with herbs and garlic, then spit-roasted over a wood-burning fire until the exterior glistens the color of a Stradivarius and the meat is meltingly tender. Found throughout central Italy, the residents of Tuscany, Umbria, Abruzzo, and Lazio also consider it a regional specialty—Ariccia, in the Alban Hills near Rome, is particularly famous for its porchetta, and particularly outspoken in claiming its paternity. The town of Norcia in Umbria asserts with equal fervor that it was the one to sire the dish. Actually, porchetta's origins reach back even further, stemming from the ancient Etruscans who first inhabited the area and were great grillers and roasters.

So while you could go elsewhere to find porchetta as good as what is made in Le Marche, no where will you find it made any better. And if you are looking for the heart and soul of Marchigiani cooking you are sure to find it in porchetta. You can sample it at country fairs and festivals, at weddings and reunions, at market stalls and roadside stands. My first taste came from the back of a truck in the town of Loreto.

Loreto is a hill town just inland from the Adriatic in the province of Ancona, about half an hour's bus ride from Camerano. Thousands of people each year for centuries have journeyed there to see the Sanctuary of the Holy House of Mary. Though now perhaps eclipsed in fame by the shrines devoted to Our Ladies of Lourdes, Fatima, or Guadalupe, Loreto was once among the most important places of pilgrimage in Europe. Though not much interested in pilgrimaging myself, when I learned of the town's proximity I decided to pay the place a visit.

The Holy House (*La Santa Casa*) is said to be the childhood home of the Virgin Mary, wafted stone by stone from Nazareth on the wings of angels to protect it from marauding Saracens at the end of the Crusades. The town of Loreto, taking its name from the laurel grove near where the house appeared, soon sprang up to support the stream of visitors. Christopher Columbus made the journey to offer gratitude for his safe return from the New World. Galileo Galilei came, as did Montaigne, Stendahl, Napoleon, and Casanova. Mozart played the organ there. In 1920 Pope Benedict XV declared Our Lady of Loreto the patron saint of aviators. Charles Lindbergh is said to have tucked an image of Our Lady in his haversack on his solo journey across the Atlantic, though I'm dubious. A Lady of Loreto medallion accompanied Umberto Nobile and Roald Amundsen on their 1926 flight over the North Pole in a dirigible, and the astronaut James McDivitt brought one in his luggage on the Apollo 9 mission.

Despite an assortment of Papal bulls and edicts over the years to verify the authenticity of the Holy House, Catholics are not required to believe the aeronautical account of its appearance in Loreto. An alternate theory proposes the stones may have been brought by fleeing crusaders—whether from Nazareth or not remains unclear. Recently unearthed Vatican papers suggest a Byzantine family by the name of Angelos or De Angelis paid to have the stones transported to safe haven in Italy. This does little to dampen the enthusiasm of true devotees, who see no reason to let a few archival documents get in the way of a good miracle.

The primitive dwelling stands today encased in an intricate marble reliquary designed by Bramante, its threshold worn with grooves from centuries of pilgrims passing over it on their knees. A lavish basilica encloses the reliquary, containing works by several masters of late Renaissance architecture and painting, and the adjacent museum and art gallery houses several canvases by Lorenzo Lotto. The shrine is also famous for the small wooden statue of a Black Madonna above the altar, a replica of a 13th-century statue lost to a fire in 1920. If you ask the right person you will be told she has granted many miracles.

With so many visitors arriving each day, it's no surprise that the boulevard leading up to the Holy House has something of a carnival midway feel. Souvenir shops sell ampules of holy water and Black Madonna statuettes, and street vendors hawk tourist brochures and fake Rolex watches. Eateries of every sort open out onto the piazza, since all those travelers have to be fed, and that is where the porchetta truck came in.

It was parked just off the piazza, a long window running across one side to reveal a mobile kitchen with stainless countertops and butcher block cutting boards. A hand-lettered sign read SPECIALITÀ: PORCHETTA COTTA A LEGNA—roast pork cooked over a woodfire. The display case featured the top half of a roasted pig, its head still attached, complete with ears and snout, should there be any doubt about the menu. There had been a line of customers trailing down the street when I'd arrived in the early afternoon, but at that hour, almost five o'clock, business had slowed in the quiet void between the midday and evening meals. I hadn't planned to eat yet, but the scent of herbs and roasted meat wafting across the street had drawn me in. A stout man with his back to the window busied himself behind the counter sharpening knives. He turned toward me upon my approach and asked if I wanted a panino.

Porchetta is sometimes served as a second course, cut in thick slices and drizzled with a spoonful of the roasting juices collected from a tray underneath the spit. More often it is sold in a panino, piled high between two slices of bread and wrapped in brown paper to become street food extraordinaire, and that is what the *porchettaro* was offering.

Lean or fatty, he asked, and did I want a bit of *la crosta* or *la concia*? These last turned out to be pieces of crackling rind and the herb-mix rubbed into the pork. Unschooled in proper porchetta eating etiquette, I said I'd like *un po' di tutto*.

Brava, he replied. Good girl, as if he were talking to the family dog. Most women these days were afraid of fat and would only eat the leanest cuts, he said. But a little fat was good for you, and porchetta wasn't the same without it. He sliced open a crusty bread roll, switched knives to carve off thick slices from the roast, and assembled my panino. After wrapping it in parchment he passed it to me through the window and motioned to a stack of napkins. Not seeing an empty bench nearby, I decided to eat standing up at the counter. Each bite brought a full array of flavors and textures. Silky, succulent meat, salt and crunch from the rind, heady garlic and an herbal sweetness from fennel and rosemary, all encased in chewy bread that had sopped up the juices. I closed my eyes, lost in my panino, and when I looked up I noticed the porchetta man was watching me.

"*È buono!*" I told him.

Yes, he nodded. Of course. He wore a threadbare butcher coat underneath a white apron. He had a thick head of dark hair and an unruly cowlick that spilled onto his forehead. A salt-and-pepper moustache made a similar arc over his upper lip.

Inquisitive by nature and feeling especially emboldened—perhaps it was the presence of Our Lady in such close range, but more likely because my grammar lesson that morning had been spent practicing the subjunctive in hypothetical situations—I embarked on a conversation with him. If I were to try to make porchetta at home, I began—

He interrupted. One could never hope to make porchetta like this at home. It would be *assolutamente impossibile!* For starters, one would need a whole pig.

And if I were to find a whole pig at home?

Not just any pig, he told me. Not some factory pig raised in a crate. I'd have to find an old-fashioned pig. A pig that had spent its days in a pasture, a pig that had wallowed in mud and taken naps in the grass under the sun.

I was in luck then, I told him, I happened to know where I could find such a pig back home in New Hampshire. Then I had to explain to him where New Hampshire was.

It has to be a sow, he said. Sows are more tender than boars.

I figured I could arrange for that, I said.

He leaned over the counter to peer at me more closely. And how would this sow be fattened, he wanted to know. Marchigiani farmers raised their hogs on sheep's milk whey, on beet pulp and apple cores. The hogs foraged at their leisure on fallen chestnuts and acorns.

My New Hampshire hog farmer, I conceded, wasn't actually a farmer, he was a grade-school teacher who raised a few pigs on the side. He ran a summer ice-cream stand and his pigs dined on melted ice cream, Halloween pumpkins, and kitchen scraps.

The porchettaro pondered this for a moment. He gave a dismissive grunt, but allowed as how one might be able to impart flavor to a pig with such a diet.

Still, I admitted, I lacked both a wood-fired oven and a rotisserie spit large enough to accommodate a whole pig.

He smacked his hand down on the counter, triumphant. Then it was just as he'd declared at the outset. Impossible to make a true porchetta.

Surely, I protested, even Marchigiani cooks must occasionally find it impractical to roast an entire pig. They didn't cook for fifty every night, did they?

The porchettaro pressed his lips together in a straight line. He ran the back of his hand across his forehead and took in a couple deep breaths. True, porchetta was meant to serve a crowd. However, there did exist a method if one had smaller numbers in mind. If done right, he supposed it captured the requisite cross-section of flavors. He'd never tried it himself, but he could tell me how it was done: I could take a whole pork loin, butterfly it lengthwise, slather it with garlic, herbs, and some minced pork liver, wrap it in a pork belly, and tie the whole thing up with kitchen twine. After a long stint in a slow oven I would have something I could rightly call porchetta to serve sixteen souls.

And if I had a smaller group in mind? Was there not a single cut that would serve say, six people? I spoke tentatively; I could see his patience was wearing thin.

He put his hands together as if in prayer and wagged them my way. Then I would not have porchetta! he said, almost spitting the words. Even Our Lady could not curtail his exasperation. He closed his eyes, paused, and tried again. I would not *have* porchetta, he repeated slowly. I would have something served *in porchetta* instead. As if that clarified everything.

The term *in porchetta*, he explained, refers to other meats, cooked in the style of a whole roast pig. It makes up a proud but separate tradition in the cooking of Le Marche. There is rabbit *in porchetta*, also lamb and duck. This last, he told me, takes particularly well to the treatment, as the fatty skin bastes the meat as it cooks and crisps up almost as nicely as a crackling pork rind. In Ancona, mussels and sea snails are served *in porchetta*, and I could find recipes for freshwater carp *in porchetta*, even eggplant. Naturally, the porchettaro assured me, I could use a smallish

cut of pork. He recommended a shoulder roast for its flavor and tenderness. A five- to six-pound bone-in roast would do, preferably with the
skin still attached. Remove the bone, or have the butcher do it for you,
and score the skin with a sharp knife in a crosshatch pattern at half-inch
intervals, slicing into the fat but not the flesh.

Make a paste of two tablespoons olive oil, two teaspoons salt, two
teaspoons pepper, four cloves minced garlic, a pinch of red pepper flakes,
three generous sprigs chopped rosemary, and a small bouquet of fresh
wild fennel fronds, finely chopped. Wild fennel, *Foeniculum vulgare*, is an
herb with a licorice-like flavor and feathery leaves that resemble dill and
Queen Anne's lace, to which it is related. Native to the Mediterranean,
immigrants brought the herb with them to the United States, where it has
naturalized in coastal areas, growing in vacant lots and weedy hillsides.
The cultivated variety, sometimes called Florence fennel, has a swollen,
bulblike base and a delicate flavor much beloved by Italians, eaten raw
in salads or cooked. Its dried seeds are used in baking and in sauces, and
as a seasoning for sausages and salami. But wild fennel has a distinctive
pungency that its domesticated cousin lacks. It is a key ingredient in porchetta, and a Marchigiani cook wouldn't prepare something *in porchetta*
without it. I've gathered wild fennel in the hills above Santa Barbara in
Southern California, where it is considered an invasive weed, but you
can substitute a tablespoon of fennel seeds, lightly toasted in a skillet and
finely ground, for a close approximation if you can't find it growing wild.

Make a deep cut in the flesh so the roast opens up like a book and
rub in the chopped herb mixture. Massage the roast thoroughly on all
sides, working the herbs into every crevice, he instructed, the meat wants
care and tender caresses from your fingers, not haphazard smacks and
pats. If I happened to have a slice of pork liver on hand, now would be
the time to use it.

I planned to, I said. I could detect the earthy hint of liver in my sandwich, adding its undertones rather like the anchovies in a good Caesar
salad dressing.

Mince the liver and spread it over the flesh side of the roast, he continued, then roll it up, brush it with olive oil and any remaining herb
mixture, a sprinkle of salt and more ground pepper, then tie it securely
with kitchen twine and refrigerate it overnight, uncovered, so the flavors

marry. The next day, let the rolled shoulder come to room temperature on the counter for an hour, then set it on a rack lined with a few celery stalks in a roasting pan, fat-side up. Cook for two hours at 250°F, then pour a glass of white wine over the roast and continue cooking, basting occasionally with the pan juices, for another two to two-and-a-half hours or so, until the meat is fork tender. If I were to roast a few potatoes alongside the pork and braise a pot of greens, say escarole or kale, I would have myself a meal to remember, he said, kissing his fingertips and raising them into the air.

I caught a piece of pork in my fingers as it slipped from my panino, and he reached for another napkin, passing it to me through the window. He was glad to have cleared up the confusion. He knew I hadn't tried to be difficult, he simply hadn't explained himself clearly, the problem not one of translation but semantics. The pig, he wanted me to know, had been a protagonist in the lives of the Marchigiani people for centuries. A farmer who raised a pig could keep his family from going hungry all year, and in his line of business he felt a certain obligation to ensure the animal received its due respect. Which included cooking it properly.

He noticed I'd finished my sandwich. Enjoy your shoulder roast in New Hampshire, he said.

"*Grazie*," I said, and thanked him for the panino and the recipe.

And since no customers had come to wait in line he offered up a parting gift, a story his grandfather used to tell. His grandfather grew up in poverty under the oppressive *mezzadria*, the sharecropping system in place in most of central Italy before World War II. One morning with the first hard frost of early winter a fellow villager and his grown son prepared to slaughter the family pig. The men shot and dressed the animal, doused it in boiling water, and scraped the hide. They tied the pig by its feet and hung it from the rafters in the barn. The father sharpened his cleaver and split the pig down the middle into two equal halves, distinguishable only by the presence of the tail on one side. Half would remain with the family and half would go to the landowner by way of the *fattore*, the corrupt overseer who kept the farm's books. Only this year the family had killed not one, but two pigs. Since spring they had been fattening one of the sow's piglets in secret, with plans to sell it on the black market to help make ends meet.

As the pork sides hung in the barn to age for a few days before butchering, who should come up the lane but the dreaded fattore? The farmer and his son rushed to the barn to hide the illicit hog just as the fattore knocked on the door. He was brought to inspect the hanging pig and lavished the farmer with praise. What a great size the beast had attained, what fleshy thighs, what thick layers of fat. Even more stunning, the fattore said as he made notes in his ledger, indeed something he'd never seen before in all his days, was that the pig had two tails, one on the right side and another on the left.

SPALLA DI MAIALE IN PORCHETTA

ROAST PORK SHOULDER, PORCHETTA-STYLE

(Serves 6–8)

For intimate dinners of six to eight people (my favorite number), when a whole roast pig seems a bit over the top, this slowly roasted pork shoulder captures the flavors, silky texture, and crackling bits of porchetta. Look for a cut called the Boston butt, which contrary to its name does not come from the rump of the pig, but from the upper end of the shoulder, or else a picnic roast. If you can find one with the skin or layer of fat still attached, all the better.

- one 5- to 6-pound bone-in pork shoulder roast, preferably with skin still attached
- 2 tablespoons olive oil, plus an additional tablespoon for coating outside of rolled roast
- 2 teaspoons kosher salt
- 2 teaspoons black peppercorns, coarsely ground in a spice grinder
- 4 cloves garlic, minced
- 2 sprigs fresh rosemary, chopped, about 2 tablespoons
- 2 fresh wild fennel fronds, chopped (or substitute a tablespoon dried fennel seed, lightly toasted in a skillet)
- 3 to 4 ounces pork liver, minced (or substitute chicken livers, or omit entirely)
- 1 glass white wine
- 3 to 4 stalks of celery, to serve as a rack for roasting

Remove the bone from the shoulder roast or ask your butcher to do it for you. Score the outer layer of skin or fat in a crosshatch pattern at half-inch intervals, slicing into the fat but not the flesh. Make a deep, lengthwise cut through the flesh side of the roast so it opens like a book.

Make a paste with the olive oil, herbs, and seasonings. Rub the herb mixture into the roast, taking care to coat the meat thoroughly. Spread the optional minced liver over the herb mixture. (I know most people don't like liver, but I promise the flavor dissipates like the anchovies in Caesar dressing, leaving an evocative background note.) Roll up the roast and tie securely with kitchen twine. Rub the outside with any remaining herb paste, salt, and pepper, then drizzle with another tablespoon of olive oil. Place in the refrigerator overnight, uncovered.

The next day, pull roast from the refrigerator, and let it come to room temperature for an hour or so. Preheat the oven to 250°F. Put a rack in a large roasting pan, place stalks of celery crosswise over the rack to create a bed for the roast, then put the roast, skin-side up, in the pan.

Cook for 2 hours, uncovered, then pour a glass of white wine over the meat. Continue cooking, basting from time to time with the pan juices, for another 2 to 2½ hours, until the meat is fork tender and the inside temperature is 180°F. Let the roast rest at room temperature for 10 to 20 minutes before slicing.

Slice thinly, drizzle with the pan juices, and serve with roasted potatoes and braised greens, or place on crusty rolls moistened with the cooking juices and serve as sandwiches.

AFTERWORD

The Italians have a saying, *A tavola non si invecchia mai*. At the table you never grow old. It's a sentiment that captures the essence of an Italian meal. With its multiple courses and flowing wine, with the quality yet simplicity of its ingredients, with the aromas and flavors, the conversation and companionship, the pleasures of a good meal are so great as to suspend time. I experienced a similar enchantment of time as I fleshed out my journals to write the pages and chapters that would become *A Blissful Feast*. The hours I spent writing were hours spent in the company of the people on the page, so time came to a halt at my writing desk as well. That my kitchen table serves double duty as my work desk suggests maybe there was a parallel force at play.

Still the days passed, turned into months and years. Having two children slowed my writing pace; personal projects tend to end up on the back burner when kids come along, though I didn't expect it to take me over fifteen years. Even so, my daughter, Margot, and son, Joseph, gave me perspective I wouldn't otherwise have had. I knew from the start that Italian cooking was home cooking at its heart, but I did not appreciate the simultaneous effort and satisfaction of putting dinner on the table every night until I had a family of my own. Having kids also meant my trips to Italy grew fewer and farther between. Briefer, too. The family budget and limited time off from work meant we spent our vacations visiting grandparents and cousins in Washington and California instead of heading off to Italy.

While I could not return to Italy as often as I'd hoped, I managed to bring an Italian *gioia di vivere* to the table. My husband Bert played an integral part in passing along this joy in living, for he is a buona forchetta of the first order. I've watched him show Margot and Joseph how to eat peas straight from the pod and wrap a slice of prosciutto around a wedge of melon. He has taught them the fine art of *fare la scarpetta*, the Italian practice of using a hunk of bread to sop up the remaining sauce in the pasta bowl or the last of the pan drippings from the plate. The phrase means "make little shoes," as you'd do when wiping your feet on the mat before entering the house. Fare la scarpetta is considered impolite, but everyone does it anyway. In a similar breach of etiquette Bert has also made sure our kids know the pleasures of rolling a steaming ear of corn across a stick of butter.

Over the years I've carved out a week here, a week there, to return to Rocca Canavese or Manciano or Camerano, and the passage of time has brought with it the bittersweet cycling of life. In Rocca Canavese, Felice passed away a while back at the age of 88, followed just a few months later by Giuseppina, at 84. Catterina and Augusto are grandparents now. They hope to sell the bakery one day soon and retire. Catterina looks forward to spending time with her grandchildren and Augusto bought some beehives. He constructed an apiary building behind the house and plans to keep busy tending his hives and selling wildflower and chestnut honey. Giacomo and Marina now have two teenaged sons. Giacomo recently started cultivating a small vineyard and making wine with a friend. Each year the operation seems to grow a bit, so who knows where that will lead. In Manciano, Alessandra is married and has a son in high school. The three of them live two floors above Franca and Eraldo in the family palazzo on the edge of town. The language school did not survive *la crisi*, the economic crisis of 2008. In the wake of the school's closing, Alessandra turned a passion for flowers and design into a profession, and now owns a florist shop in Via Marsala. Clara and Manlio stopped making wine at La Stellata after thirty years, and consider themselves semiretired. Clara still dabbles in interior design projects, and she helps out in the kitchen at a friend's agriturismo. In Camerano, Cinzia and Francesco recently welcomed their first grandchild. Cinzia still makes pasta once a week, and Francesco continues to write works on mountaineering and guidebooks to the Conero area when he's not out traversing the trails and scaling the rock cliffs in the hills.

My most recent trip to Italy came just last summer. I brought Margot with me on an abbreviated Grand Tour, a high school graduation present before she headed off to college. We landed at Fiumicino Airport in Rome and bought train tickets for Orbetello. With our train scheduled to leave within the hour, all I had time to show Margot of the Eternal City was the Mercato Centrale, the new food emporium at Stazione Termini. The Colosseum, the Sistine Chapel, the Trevi Fountain, the Pantheon, the Spanish Steps—these and the rest of the star attractions would have to wait for another day.

We wandered under the market's vaulted brick ceilings, surrounded by the din of arriving trains and rolling luggage and chatter in innumerable languages from travelers passing through the station in the Capital of the World. I basked in Margot's sense of wonder as we watched artisans shape pasta and load pizza into wood-fired ovens, vendors cutting slices from haunches of prosciutto and scooping out towering cones of gelato. We sought out provisions for the two-hour train ride—two crusty rolls from a bakery, a couple servings of roasted summer vegetables steeped in herbs and oil, and marinated olives from a food stall. We set off to find a cheese-seller for a wedge of Pecorino, then checked the time and saw we were about to miss our train, so we elbowed our way back through the crowd and across the underpass, reaching our platform just as the train pulled up.

Alessandra met us at the station, her son Damiano accompanying her. On the drive to Manciano I learned we'd just missed Franca and Eraldo, they were up in the mountains near Monte Amiata for a few days' vacation. *Che peccato!* What a shame, the last time they were in Margot's company, I was carrying her in my belly.

While the main purpose of our visit was to see friends and family after too long an absence, our trip soon acquired a culinary thread. We had to buy another suitcase to accommodate all the delicacies we wanted to bring back to the States—aged wedges of Pecorino Toscano, three kinds of jam, gianduiotti chocolates, soft amaretti cookies, a bag of the ancient grain called *farro*, three bottles of wine, a black Tuscan truffle. And we started keeping a list of the dishes we wanted to prepare for Bert and Joseph once we returned home—the roasted vegetable dish from the train station, wide pasta ribbons with a slow-simmered sauce of duck and tomato, a salad of romanesco summer squash sliced into coins and tossed with lemon and arugula, vitello tonnato, stuffed peaches, tiramisu, and semolina dolce. This last I assured her I'd made before, she just didn't remember, and she said it was time I made it again.

And we arrived just in time for late-summer figs. In Italy figs reach their peak from the end of August into September. The trees bear a smaller, lesser pulse of fruit in early summer, but the late crop is more luscious and abundant. That first evening in Manciano I took Margot on a walk up Via Marsala to explore the warren of cobbled roads in the town's historic center. I showed her the library that once housed the language school, my favorite bakery and the Bar Centrale, the clock tower that we'd heard ringing the hour when we arrived. We watched the sunset across the Tyrrhenian Sea from an overlook near the Aldobrandeschi Fortress, and on our way back down the hill I pointed out a fig tree laden with fruit just beginning to turn color. I picked a couple ripe figs and handed one to Margot.

Figs don't grow in New Hampshire. Fresh figs in our stores come in plastic clamshell containers from California and they've lost any flavor they've ever had, so I only buy dried figs at home. But fresh figs! They were as much a revelation for Margot as they'd been for me on my first trip to Manciano all those years ago. We hunted through the branches for purple fruit, found a few more, and ate them as we finished our walk. Over the next few days, in between outings with Alessandra and her family to the hot springs of Saturnia, to the Synagogue in Pitigliano, to the beach at Capalbio, Margot and I went on treks through the back roads, retracing my old routes in search of fig trees I remembered—a wild one on the bank of the dirt road to Montemerano, another one on the edge of an olive grove in Via delle Fonti, a sweet, green-fruited tree at a hairpin bend in a gravel road with no name.

According to D. H. Lawrence, the proper way to eat a fig, in society, is to quarter it lengthwise and open it, so that it is a glittering, rosy, moist, honeyed, four-petaled flower. Then you scrape the flesh off—with a knife, if you have impeccable manners, or with your teeth, if you are not so prim in your habits—and you throw the skin away. But we plucked our figs from overhanging branches up and down the countryside and ate them skin and all.

After Manciano, we took the train up the coast to Torino and spent the first night with Giacomo, Marina, and their sons. Marina brought out a platter of figs at the end of dinner, and Giacomo told us they came from a tree he'd recently planted. His old tree, the one whose figs I'd once harvested for Giuseppina to cook into jam, that tree was suffering from some incurable malady. Giacomo pointed it out in the courtyard the next morning, its limbs half-dead, its few fruit rotting and covered with wasps. He'd soon be pulling it out and planting something else in its place. That afternoon, after the welcoming hugs and kisses and the recounting of our adventures, Catterina said she, too, often harvested figs from untended trees. At the next meal she brought a bowl of mottled yellow ones to the table, and for the rest of our stay, relatives kept bringing us figs, by the bowl, by the bag, by the box.

Still there is something about eating figs straight from the tree. One morning before our departure, Margot and I set out early for a run, hoping to avoid the horseflies that had pursued us in the noontime heat the previous day. With the sun already gaining strength and a chorus of cicadas calling from the treetops as we passed, we came upon an ancient, sprawling fig tree in the corner of an orchard, a few contorted limbs extending over the stone wall that encircled the property. The figs on the lower branches were hard and green, growing in the shade of the upper limbs, but higher up, a branch better positioned to catch the light bore a cluster of plump, purple figs.

I sighed and shook my head. Such a pity they were out of reach. But Margot waded through the Queen Anne's lace and chicory on the edge of the road and scrambled up the crumbling wall, foothold by handhold by toehold. She groped with her left foot, found purchase on a protruding rock waist high, and craned her head back to peer up through the leaves. She paused for a moment to contemplate her next move, her long braid dangling like a plumb line, and then she lunged upward, one hand grabbing the branch, the other one reaching for the fruit. With a rustle of leaves the limb bent earthward as her fingers grasped two figs, and it bobbed back into place as she jumped to the ground. She handed a fig to me, soft and warm from the morning sun, and together we savored the sweet flesh. We walked for a bit in silence, absorbed in a moment so perfect time ceased to exist.

ACKNOWLEDGMENTS

T o push up your sleeves and prepare a meal for others is an unparalleled labor of the heart. Small wonder then, that good home cooks tend to be giving by nature. Without the generosity of the cooks who welcomed me into their kitchens to share their stories and recipes, I wouldn't have had anything to write about. To Joe and Mary Picatti, Giuseppina Chiadò Puli, Catterina Chiadò Pulì, Augusto Bertinetti, Giacomo Chiadò Puli, Marina Gilli, Margherita Aimone, Alessandra Sbrilli, Franca Giusti, Clara Divizia, Francesco Burattini, Cinzia Martinelli, Marco Bravi, Ursula Bergmann, and all the other cooks I encountered during my travels in Italy I extend a heartfelt thanks, *grazie di cuore*.

As for the writing itself, I don't have words enough to thank Nicola Smith, Barbara Kreiger, and Anna Minardi for their friendship, encouragement, and comments on early drafts. Much appreciation goes out to my literary agent, Regina Ryan, for her perseverance and belief I had another revision in me, and to Jessica Case at Pegasus Books, for her willingness to take this project on. Thanks, too, to the tremendous team at Pegasus, who took the manuscript and transformed it into such a lovely book, to David Carlson, for graciously considering my input on the jacket cover, to Susan Picatti Mclean, for help with the website, and to David Picatti, for sharing his photos and reminiscences.

Finally, I'm infinitely grateful to my family. *Grazie infinite* to Bert, Margot, and Joseph, for taking pictures and sharing so many meals, to my mom, Darlene, who instilled a love of cooking in all four of her daughters, and to my dad, Jim, who will forever have a seat at the head of the table.

ABOUT THE AUTHOR

Teresa Lust is the author of *Pass the Polenta: And Other Writings from the Kitchen*. She is a graduate of Washington State University and holds a master's degree from Dartmouth College. Lust currently teaches Italian for the Rassias Center for World Languages at Dartmouth and teaches cooking classes. She lives in New Hampshire.